curry leaf

cloves

garlic

cardamom

nutmeg

coriander

cinnamon

bay leaf

saffron

cumin

pepper

ginger

GW00455665

Jiggs Kalra's

DAAWAT

The television series

Jiggs Kalra's

DAAWAT

The television series

with

PUSHPESH PANT

Foreword by
Sahibzada Syed Habib-ur-Rehman

Illustrated by
Andrea D'Costa Pereira

ALLIED PUBLISHERS LIMITED

ALLIED PUBLISHERS LIMITED

Regd. Off. : 15 J.N. Heredia Marg, Ballard Estate, Mumbai 400038
Prarthna Flats (2nd Floor), Navrangpura, Ahmedabad 380009
3-2-844/6 & 7 Kachiguda Station Road, Hyderabad 500027
16-A Ashok Marg, Patiala House, Lucknow 226001
5th Main Road, Gandhinagar, Bangalore 560009
1/13-14 Asaf Ali Road, New Delhi 110002
81 Hill Road, Ramnagar, Nagpur 440010
17 Chittaranjan Avenue, Kolkata 700072
751 Anna Salai, Chennai 600002

© JIGGS KALRA
First published, 2001
ISBN 81-7764-149-2

Published by Sunil Sachdev and printed by Ravi Sachdev at Allied Publishers Limited, Printing Division,
A-104 Mayapuri, Phase-II, New Delhi - 110 064

To the memory of my
Beloved Mother,
the source of all my inspiration, whom I miss terribly.
There's solace in knowing that she's watching out for me from Up There,
letting me know that the umbilical cord, especially the culinary one,
is intact, and that she expects more
in the future.

Foreword

Sahibzada Syed Habib-ur-Rehman
Chairman, Welcomgroup

Food is one of my great interests and I am often accused of 'living to eat'. Over the years, I have particularly enjoyed experimenting with food from all over India. These experiments have thanks to God's mercy, also given me plenty of 'food for thought'. Sharing my passion for food is Jiggs Kalra, who I consider a great 'Ambassador for Indian cuisine.' It gives me immense pleasure to be able to add this foreword to a book on Indian cuisine that he and Pushpesh Pant have put together. With their painstaking research, trials, sampling and enthusiastic communication through multimedia, these are two people who have jointly helped in making Indian food important all over the world.

India is an ancient civilization where our forefathers were fortunately blessed with the abundance of nature – sunshine, water, different types of soil and rich flora and fauna – and through this God-given bounty developed cuisine that is different from east to west and north to south. This is also a land where the cuisine of each area reflects the influence of those who visited and set up bases, assimilating and creating a fusion of rare dishes that have thereafter become household names for future generations.

The Iranians, Turks and Arabs, the Dutch, French, Portuguese and British, who travelled to India by land and sea, came essentially for silk, spices, and other condiments. Their visits resulted in books extolling the riches of India and adding to the perception that this was a land of untold wealth. Some came for trade, others came as invaders, while a third moved in to settle and mingle with the locals. All of them left their indelible stamp on the culture of the region, helping in making India's food richer and more varied.

One of the greatest strengths of our country has been its geographical location. Different races and nationalities who have come and settled amongst us, whilst mingling with the local population, have yet managed to retain their distinctiveness. This is 'unity in diversity' of a special kind, for despite its incredible differences there is an underlying connection and Indian cuisine cannot be mistaken for food from any other part of the world. Consider the 'Roghan Josh' of Kashmir

'Chettinad Chicken' of Tamil Nadu, the 'Dhokla' from Gujarat and 'Smoked Hilsa' from West Bengal, 'Tengra Fish' from Assam and Goan 'Sorpotel', or for that matter, 'Khad Khargosh' of Rajasthan and 'Apams' from Kerala. Each dish is different and distinct in taste, style and presentation – but most importantly each one is equally delicious and part of the treasure-house that comprises Indian cuisine.

WELCOMGROUP has from its inception been concerned and involved in bringing these special dishes into the limelight. Much time and effort has been given to research and training, so that these rare recipes become known first in India and thereafter internationally. Jiggs was involved in a number of our ventures, and we are happy to showcase many of the recipes in his regular newspaper column and TV serials. A certain degree of success has been achieved in this by our chain, and I am gratified to note that Indian cuisine is now in the forefront all over the world.

The combined efforts of Jiggs Kalra and Pushpesh Pant have resulted in a book, where Indian cuisine finds a new ladder to rise to even greater heights. *Daawat* will give all food lovers worldwide, many hours of pleasure in trying out India's known and lesser-known recipes. The duo have created a book through which gourmands can add to their knowledge of the treasures of Indian cuisine.

Contents

xii

Making of Daawat
An Introduction

Pushpesh Pant

Daawat–the word itself is enough to make one drool. Translation is hardly necessary – an invitation to a feast or a banquet, a very special meal – in Hindi, Urdu, Arabic, the sound is unmistakable and irresistible. In our case, a few years back, there was an added temptation. We were invited to produce a pioneering food show on Indian television by the then Director-General of the Doordarshan Delhi, Sashi Kapur and Jaya Chandiram of the Central Production Centre – lovingly referred to as the CPC by inmates and guests. The proof of the pudding they say is in the eating, and another adage cautions that too many cooks spoil the broth. Accepting the challenge meant defying conventional wisdom. We in turn began by inviting dozens of chefs – young and old – accomplished masters and promising talent, men and women from the four corners of our vast and varied land – to showcase the fabulous culinary heritage of India. The fare was for once not for eating – at least, not by the salivating audience!

For Jiggs this was the natural sequel to his magnum opus *Prashad* that in print had arranged a wonderful encounter with Indian Cooking masters for thousands of readers at home and abroad. The *haldi* stained cookbook has by now attained an exalted status in countless kitchens, has been translated in Hindi, and enjoyed an unprecedented print run. For Pushpesh, familiar with the *mise en scène* of film making, it was an exciting initiation into the world of *mise en place*. Both of us were well aware of the complexity of the task. Our work would have to pass the test of two disciplines – video infotainment and gastronomy.

The crew assigned to us had to grapple with problems of its own. They were veterans of many a creative battle – tested and tried in recording ballets, talk shows, quizzes and live OB's (outdoor broadcasts), plays, serials and national programmes of music, but were strangers to the world of golden hued sautéd onions and aromatically crackling cumin seeds. They voiced their apprehensions candidly – on this show food was the star. The cameras had to be positioned accordingly. Ditto for mikes to catch the fleeting sizzle and bubbling boil. How to balance this with the sparkle in the eyes of the peppy anchor and the magic fingers of the dexterous craftsmen? The chefs, wonderful cooks they may be, could not all be interestingly articulate. Not used to working in the glare of spotlights they may become frozen faced. How were we going to cope with this? Others had more prosaic, but crucial for the show, queries – like where would the water from the sink drain out on the set?

What all of us shared was a heady exhilaration – we were jointly the hosts and determined to serve the most fantastic fare for millions of our invisible guests. Jiggs, never the one to be happy unless the labour undertaken is prodigious, suggested – and his suggestions have the tendency to end up as dictates! – we may give the viewers something new and in addition to what was expected. Why not research the *ayurvedic* basis of Indian cuisine and incorporate interesting useful information about the ingredients being used? What started as a lark has by now become an obsessive quest for both of us but that is a different story.

Suffice it to be noted here that in the context of *Daawat* this meant engaging in most fascinating interdisciplinary research. The two of us travelled across the length and breadth of the land interacting with *vaidya* and *hakim*, scholars of history and nutritionists. The preparatory research work was greatly facilitated by friends and family. The exertion was back breaking – and never was the cliché about burning the midnight oil more apt. More than one secretary retired hurt or ego-bruised in this campaign. Jiggs suffered a heart attack but resumed the command after bypass surgery in the USA. Pushpesh tottered on the verge of nervous breakdown for months – not that any one noticed anything abnormal!

And, of course, between the two of us we drove everyone else crazy. Banshi Kaul, the producer in charge, was often seen humming Kashmiri folk songs to get in the right mood to sit at the panel after waiting God knows how many minutes between changing shifts, lunch or tea breaks or stage setting. Once he got in step he forgot about his first love, the drama productions and the pressing housing problem. The floor managers all very soon became expert tasters and did a wonderful job of putting the guest stars at their ease. Cameramen responded to the challenge superbly – Jagdish, Paddy, Shiva, Partho, Debu, Anil – and embarked on this expedition with a lively competitive spirit. They bantered with each other and kept the camera control unit in good humour. Niraj, the cheerful production assistant, kept stirring things up.

By the time we went on floor or entered this most unusual kitchen to shoot the second schedule – Jaya had been transferred and soft spoken Vasavraj had taken over. He was equally interested in the quality of the food programme and did not let our enthusiasm flag. There was never a dull moment. The programme was being shot on what is politely referred as a shoestring budget. Obviously, the mandarins at Mandi House had not till then heard of Milton Freidman's wise words – 'There is no free lunch'. Jiggs had not only to be at his creative best but also his most persuasive self to ensure that the show went on despite constraints. Guest appearances had to be gratis. The props for the set, a refrigerator, microwave, food processor etc., had to be acquired on long term loan. The prevailing code on DD does not allow display of signage and this made scouting for anonymous sponsors doubly difficult. Jiggs somehow managed to pull all the required rabbits from under his numerous colourful turbans.

Finally, the set was put up, the props were in place, the burners on the side to speed up the shooting were organized, the backroom boys and girls on our (culinary) side were put through their paces, and the CPC team got its technical act together and we were raring to go. Jiggs donned his designer *kurta-pyjama* lovingly crafted by Ritu Beri, draped himself protectively with a colourful thematic *mirchy* adorned apron and trooped on stage to welcome his viewers.

No one shouted 'Action' but the feel was just like the launch of a blockbuster. Months of preparation were finally coming to fruition. As the chef's understudies – the helpers – chopped chillies, myriad memories flashed back. Our minds went back to the odd exercises we had gone through to avoid gliches.

An overtly self-assured chef had handed over a recipe that mentioned 200 gms – no less – of red chillies. He took offense when requested to cross-check. We were treated to choicest abuse and read a sermon about the sanctity of kitchen lore. His jaw dropped visibly when the prescribed amount of the spice was measured out and shown to him. Not too great a sport, this gentleman continued to hum and haw, refused to thaw, but the recipe for the show was rectified.

This taught us a valuable lesson. Professionals however glorified, senior or talented, could not be taken at their face value (pun intended). Jiggs immediately began setting up his own reliable weights and measures department. Notes were compared with housewives, other chefs – some traditional and unlettered, but no less gifted or experienced than their qualified colleagues and scientists. Then followed the conversions. It felt as if one had returned to junior school. Teaspoons into grams and ounces into litres, pounds into kilos – in brief the works. Then there was the translation chore. Not only English to Hindi or vice versa, but in keeping with the true spirit of unity in diversity, a handful of regional language terms as well. Cooking jargon and kitchen slang spiced up our life. The satisfaction lay in striving for perfection and easy communication. This is the place to add though, that the quest for the best is an unending one. Many of the recipes have been perfected – refined further and fine tuned – after the show. What you are presented with in this book is the distilled essence of our labours.

From the beginning everyone had agreed that the show should be a fast paced one. We began with recording four recipes per show. It was a blend of a 100 metres sprint and a marathon with the hurdles thrown in between. We would begin early morning, almost with the crack of dawn, to buy the freshest ingredients and give our – not always welcome – 'rise and shine' call to our colleagues. Then, the scripts for the day had to be organized – typed, xeroxed, collated and distributed to chefs, assistants, producers and their assistants. This left just enough time for a shower and change before checking in at the CPC studio. We were working both shifts and did not have the luxury of taking breaks. A make-shift camp kitchen was set up by the side of the set and scrumptious nutrition was provided for the unit by Team Daawat. This lent the work a bit of the flavour of the outdoor shoot and a family picnic.

Like all forays outdoor, at times there were unforeseen emergencies requiring swift administration of first aid. An Executive Chef, then presiding over the operations of a Five Star kitchen, had quite obviously become more used to shouting out commands from the armchair in the aircon office than to operating equipment. Puréeing something hot he forgot to put the lid on the blender before switching it on. The spouting geyser sprayed his starched uniform, reminding us of Holi frolics, and scalded the poor man. What hurt more was not the burn but the barely suppressed laughter. He was somewhat relieved when reassured that the NG shot will not be used.

Used to unquestioning obedience from their kitchen brigade, quite a few chefs, we realized, had become a bit like the doctors: 'I am always right, how dare you dispute my dispensations?' At the same time the shooting made us aware of our own not always charming foibles. The journalist in Jiggs was forever stealing a march over them and leaving them speechless with scoops – discovery of a forgotten grandmaster in the by-lanes of some obscure town, source of a rare ingredient, a lost recipe, scientific corroboration of his intuition. And the teacher in Pushpesh could not be left behind – the temptation was there all the time to correct mistakes, lecture long – burdening all and sundry with scholarly footnotes and cross references.

There were times when nerves were frayed and tempers ran high. Sometimes the lights were out because of an unforeseen power cut. We sweltered and worried – not only about the uncooked food spoiling but also about falling behind schedule. At other times, the dedicated team of cameramen and floor manager used to us was not there and the substitutes did not disguise their lack of interest in the proceedings. We tried to keep the chin up, diverting attention and amusing each other with jokes, Urdu couplets and old film songs. Those working for TV were better used to the *Rukavat ke liye khed hai* (sorry for the interruption) caption and could bear with life's slings and arrows much more stoically. The popular couplet consoled us on the dog days – *Umr jalwaon mein basar ho ye zaroori to nahin, nind dard ke bistar pe bhi aa hi jati hai!*

But to compensate for the odd day of stress and distress there were dozens full of joyous cooperation, talented youngsters taking to the studio kitchen like fish to water, and even those diminutive in size performing like large-hearted seals. A little encouragement went a long way with them. **Praveen Anand** from Chennai proud of his inheritance – rich and ancient Tamil tradition. He was always keen to educate us about the subtler points of the Southern cuisine. The mind boggling varieties of *sambhar* and *rasam* were soon left behind. *Pulassus* and *kozhambus* were compared with the North Indian delicacies. He was reluctant to concede supremacy to any edible originating north of the Vindhyas but had an open mind and dexterous hands. His ready smile was infectious and working with him was unalloyed joy. **Vikrant Kapoor** was his antithesis – trendy and fidgety, talkative and toe-tapping. But no less skilled and curious. He had a showman's flair and showed signs of love at first sight with the camera. He was willing to be groomed for the more unorthodox jobs – *gosht ki parandi* evolved with him in mind to execute an exquisite conception.

Daawat – like the real life Daawat – provided a unique opportunity to organize a reunion with old friends. **Sudhir Sibbal** chipped in to do the *Panir ka chilla* besides other meaty mouth watering offerings and took on a lot of leg pulling about the public sector in good humour. His modest demeanour disguises exceptional achievements. He is a member of the Chef of Chefs – an exclusive club with membership restricted to those chefs who have cooked for Heads of States.

xviii

Then there was **Davinder Bungla** whose is the classic story of the rustic village lad from the hills having made good in the big city. He descended in Delhi, Jiggs reminisced, an uncut diamond with just the basics of baking picked up from his father, a cook with some Anglo-Indian sahib in Nainital. Quick to learn, he made great use of the opportunity dame luck sent his way. He kept referring to Jiggs as Guruji on the sets and recalled with unabashed gratitude the help rendered in the past. With the passage of years he has blossomed as one of the best patisierres in the country. He has worked with the likes of the legendary Schuetzenberger. He was not shy of experiments that pushed him to the edge – he has the aptitude and the temperament of the diamond cutter – eager to dazzle the lovers of his craft with delicate artistry. The finished product does not have a trace of the hard work, and the risk of spoiling it all with a single false stroke. Jiggs treats him like a favourite pupil and Devinder responds with filial affection, respect and a hint of naughtiness. Some of the most exciting presentations in this collection resulted from this synergistic partnership – the *Shrikhand Strudel, Malpua Omelette, Anjeer Akhrot Rabarhi Mille Feuille.*

Pratap and **Bharat** were the Reddy brothers who kept the flag flying for the Andhra-coastal and hinterland. We made them refresh their respective memories about home cooking after the years spent cooking in different styles – they laboured ungrudgingly to prepare *Coondapur Masala* peppered chicken, and for the vegetarians an unusual *Chenaikandae Masala Barthathu.*

Raminder Malhotra may have appeared only in a couple of episodes of the show but he was always there. Milton tells us of those who also serve who stand and wait. Raminder stood but never stood still. He did a hundred things to make life easier for those performing. He oversaw the *mise en place*, corrected the mistakes of helpers, manned the side stove, switched pans – identical like the Siamese twins – to hasten the proceedings when the recipe script read – 'fry till golden brown' or 'boil simmering constantly till a thick sauce is obtained'. He cooked an absolutely out of this world *Pista ka Saalan* for the carnivorous viewers and balanced his platter with an equally exquisite *Bhein Chaman Gushtaba.*

There were some chefs who act like the *lakir ke fakir* – straitjacketed conformists – competent they may be, creative they never can be. If one lets them be, food will soon be fossilized. Fortunately, early in our screening tests we learnt to spot this species and could avoid casting them in stellar roles. The sign of genuine artistes we feel is spontaneity and originality. They enrich their repertoire with classics but are never afraid to innovate and experiment. Be it a musician, dancer or a painter, they are keen to mark the performance or the work of art with their distinctive stamp. To present something new is the irrepressible urge of genius. This awareness was what really fuelled the show. Every one knew that they – meaning 'we' – were being watched, assessed and compared by millions of viewers. The mother of all competitions was on.

Making of *Daawat* was a fascinating experience for all of us. We interacted with a great diversity of talent. Some legends, now past their prime, lions in winter, others eager beavers jostling for attention. Some of them masters of technique and kitchen craft but lacking in imagination and devoid of the creative spark, others walking in a trance-like state chasing culinary mirages oblivious of the imperative of soiling the hands. Many jealous of others like rival prima donnas.

The on-going human drama was just one facet of this programme. The menu planning for each episode had to be meticulous and we had to be of necessity even-handed to different regions of this culturally diverse country. At the same time the main idea was to convey the joy of cooking and fine dining to the viewers. DD being a public broadcaster could not risk being branded an elitist channel catering to the fancies of the privileged. The recipes had to be finalized keeping in mind various sensitivities.

Poor Jiggs has often had to take the flak for including 'expensive' ingredients like saffron or almonds, or for complicating life by detailed description of preparatory steps. The show provided an excellent opportunity to demystify the real food lovers about these things. Seeing *is* believing – they would now see that only a few threads of saffron or slivers of almonds were being used, that too optionally as garnish. They would also see that the step by step description made cooking almost effortless and saved wastage. Graphic cards provided some relief and were essential for recap or jotting down the recipe. The treatment of various ingredients is often no less important than the ingredients themselves. The display on screen made this point emphatically. We strove hard to communicate that all these were dishes that could be prepared at home – maybe some only at special celebratory occasions.

Many other interesting experiments were undertaken. We had an episode devoted to *One Dish Meals, Biryanis, Dhansak, Daal-Baati Churma*, another to *Pickles and Preserves*. When the *Prawn Balchao* was being prepared the vinegary fumes wafted through the air conducts and reached the panel far removed. Appetites were stoked and a break was preponed!

The phrase has it wrong – *ghar ki murgi daal barabar*. *Daal* is run down, so is the poor ghar ki murgi. We had not one but two episodes singing the paens of pulses and legumes. The *Daal Special* pitched strongly for national integration including *kulthi* from the Himalayan foothills, the incomparable *mah di daal* from Punjab west *te* east, and *cholar daal* from Sonar Bangla and *sambhar* from the land of Chola bronzes and *Kanjivaram* silks. *Daal Plus* something else, *Lao Chingri* added shrimps to *chana daal* to make it special, *kaddu* – in this case bottle gourd – was added to the pulse in true Hyderabadi tradition to rekindle memories of Nizam's *khas khana khwan*, while *keeraikootu* had a refreshing touch of greens to enliven the proceedings. The crowning glory of this episode was an inspired creation – an original for the show – *Soney Chandi ke moong*. The name befits a jeweller's shop and the marbles of reduced milk wrapped in silver and gold leaf truly do the 'coral' proud.

We tried our best to serve memorable meals on festive days. X'Mas was treated as the *barha din* with the traditional turkey served in the Indian garb of *musallam*. *Tandoori Jheenga Flan* kept it company. Savoury pancakes tempted the vegetarians and when the X'mas pudding was unveiled you could almost hear jingle bells, jingle bells, jingle all the way. For *Pongal* we were ready with *Venn Pongal* and *Chakkara Pongal* and the high of Holi was sustained with *Chura Mattar Banarasi* style.

Another time an entire episode was devoted to fishy enterprise. *Kekrah Peri Peri, Doi Maach, Meen Moiley and Bhaarla Saaranga* were finger licking, lip smacking each in its own right – the recipes representing almost the entire Indian coastline.

Fusion is a word quite in fashion now. It was familiar to few then. We dare say that the *Daawat* team was perhaps the first in the land to blaze a daring trail in uncharted territory. What we attempted was not hit or miss hodgepodge. There was a careful coupling of ingredients, cooking techniques, complimenting each other mutually, compatibly. *Uttar Dakshin Murghbandi* – echoing the musical *jugalbandi* of yore is just one example. On other occasions we defied Kipling to let the east and west meet. *Bataer Kofta* stuffed with tartare of prawns in pepper gravy belongs to this cosmopolitan global village genre.

For long we have felt that Indian cuisine lacks in eye appeal because practitioners of the culinary craft have not given due attention to presentation. We tried to rectify this while cooking a feast for the eyes. *Dahi mein subzion ka Guldasta* and *Khatte Baingan* are delicacies that were transformed stunningly a la Cinderella or the Ugly Duckling for this programme.

Nor were the perennial favourites neglected. *Samosa, Vada* were given their due and *murgh* and *paneer tikka* received salute with much fanfare.

We were proud to serve some exotic dishes, real blue-blooded classics in *Daawat* – *Shahjehani Qorma*, the dish devised by a hakim to nourish the last of the grand moguls enfeebled by long years of imprisonment. A veritable tonic for the body and mind. The legendary *Taar Qorma* intoxicatingly rich and said to have exceptionally revitalizing properties. And *Mushq-e-Tanjan*, the sweet, meat pulav long considered the ultimate test of an old world *riqabdaar*.

On the one hand we had simple pleasures of life like *Thaeer Saadam* – what can compare with its systemic cooling but dew drops kissed by equally white rays of the moon? On the other we had sinfully tantalizing *Bataer Bhara Murgh Pasanda* and *Bharwaan Zaafraani Murgh*. What mattered was not the name, but the confluence of aesthetic and therapeutic elements. This was the basis on which classics and contemporary creations were chosen. Jiggs was constantly raking his mind and straining the pre-pentium age computer to harmonize regional with the seasonal, topical with the universal, familiar with the exotic. But don't let this give you the idea that we were footloose and fancy free. We proposed, the chefs disposed. Tempering of the food included keeping their temperaments in mind.

There is no dearth of people who liked the stuffed stuff. We provided enough to please the vegetarian and well as the non-vegetarians. *Bharra Murgh* with *Khumbi ki Tari* vied with *Bharwaan Guchchi. Bharwaan Jheenga Zaafraan* shared the honours with *bharwaan karela tamatar ki tari*.

Then there came a time when we could not have enough of *kofta-phaldhari, lauki ka, aloobukhare ka, bharwaan mahi*.

Some of the sweetest memories relate to *Rabarhi* and *Khoya* making during the show. *Chhenna* making was learnt and taught side by side. *Gulaab Jaamun* and *Shrikhand* appeared in attractive and unusual manifestations.

We can't deny that there were some dishes that were for the enthusiast with endurance – calling for some practice and a little patience – *palak kaleji ka roulade* for instance, but others were simplicity itself without lacking in elegance – *Nalliwala* meat or *Lahori Aloo*. Many dishes needed a little lateral thinking to make them centre pieces – *Baghare Baingan ka Timbale* and *Jheenga Murgh Jugalbandi* – a stunning combo of fish and fowl!

Bhuna Chooza Saunf-Pudina, Ajwaini Macchi Jheenga illustrated how a single spice and a herb can give distinctive identity to a dish.

As we write these lines all this seems of another age. *Daawat* spawned a score of food and recipe shows. We ourselves followed it up with the trend setting *Zaike ka Safar* but we do have the feeling that everything continues to be compared with *Daawat*. The food and the hospitality. Yes! The *Daawat* recipes were twice blessed like the quality of mercy in *The Merchant of Venice*. They were savoured by celebrity guests who too were featured in the show – at least in the first series of episodes. Cricket stars to fashion designers, super speciality doctors to captains of industry, bureaucrats and authors, diplomats and editors, *Daawat* had the pleasure and the privilege of entertaining them. Such is the stuff memories are made of.

Daawat was telecast at prime time – Sunday afternoons. It was watched avidly by the whole family. This disproved that food shows are of limited interests for housewives only. The kids watched it to order their mothers what to cook for them next time and the grandmothers watched it to tell the youngsters 'Didn't I tell you this is done differently!' We are not claiming that it was the most watched show but it certainly became the talk of the town in many parts of India. We got used to being stopped on the road and accosted – pleasantly – with queries about the featured recipes, or 'What is cooking this time? Pushpesh had worked on *Humlog* and *Buniyaad* with Manohar Shyam Joshi and he recollects that the experience was akin to the addition of these long running soap operas. We were new to the game and did not know what TRP ratings were. But DD guys and dolls seem to be grinning with the results of their in-house audience research. It was a matter of great satisfaction to learn that *Daawat* was in demand abroad. Telecast rights were sold to some foreign countries early and to date, it remains one of the few sizeable commercial successes of the country's public broadcasting channel.

The popularity of Daawat cut across all classes. We can't forget the admonition we received from the food loving gatekeeper at the CPC 'Why don't you people make this programme in Hindi?' Suggestions and corrections came via mail, phone, word of mouth and threatened to sweep us along in a tidal wave.

Much as we enjoyed making *Daawat* for the small screen, the itch to do the book remained. However gripping the colourful image and the compelling sound bites, it is ephemeral, fleeting.

To savour the flavour you must have something more tangible than the pie in the – or to be precise from – the sky. The book allows you access to the recipes – they now truly belong to you. Peruse them and use them as and when you like. There is no rush to grab the pencil and search for the scrap of paper to jot down the recipes.

Robert Louis Stevenson it was who remarked that it is better to travel hopefully than to arrive. Making of *Daawat* made us realize that preparation for the feast is as enjoyable as imbibing the repast. It was not only the discovery of India with its many splendoured gastronomic riches, it was also an opportunity to explore oneself. The alluring aromas enveloped us on the sets making us ask ourselves repeatedly, 'Is anything more important in life than living tastefully?'

Daawat, the TV series, and now the book, invites you to join us on this voyage celebrating fine dining and good taste. Bon appetit!

How to Follow the Recipes

A few tips on how to follow the recipes. While everything has been done to ensure that the recipes are perfect, there is every chance of the timing—and timing alone—going awry. Consequently, minor adjustments in the quantity of liquid required to cook an ingredient may be necessary. Remember, these recipes have been perfected with ingredients from the city in which the recipes have been perfected.

To make cooking simple, the ingredients have been listed in the order in which they will be used, the exception being the main ingredient(s). For example, when cooking a mutton dish, the mutton itself would be used after many of the other ingredients have been cooked. However, since it is a mutton dish, it is listed as the first ingredient.

All weights are **nett**, not **gross.** If the recipe says 1Kg/2¼lb of mutton, weigh the ingredient after cleaning, if necessary, boning, and obtaining the right size. Similarly, if 12.5g/¼ cup of fresh coriander is required, it should be weighed after cleaning (removing the stalks), washing and chopping. In other words, complete the PREPARATION and then WEIGH THE INGREDIENT unless the preparation includes COOKING. In which case, weigh prior to cooking but after initial preparation.

Whenever PREPARATION TIME exceeds two hours, it is likely to cause consternation. Rest assured. Your individual attention is not always required. For example, you do not have to oversee meat under marination for 2, 4 or 6 hours, or even overnight as the case may be. Read the recipes at least twice before you start cooking. A split second's delay in hunting for the spice could ruin the dish. Almost every recipe calls for some paste or the other. It is best to make enough quantities in advance and refrigerate them.

THE REMAINING WEIGHTS AND MEASURES

Every column should carry both metric and American weights. So it will be with this one. The problem is that to most cooks a measuring teaspoon (tsp), tablespoon (Tbs) or cup means the cutlery and crockery they use in their homes. It might astonish you, but no teaspoons and tablespoons in a single cutlery sets. That's because they are either made from very old dies or handmade. The cups are even worse and the less said about them the better. In any event, cup and spoon and spoon measures come in special sets that are meant only for the kitchen and not to stir or pour your tea in.

The recipes in this column have been perfected in the metric as well as spoon and cup measures. The quantities will therefore be given in both metric and American (spoon and cup) measures. As it is difficult to exactly convert from one to the other, adjustments have been made ensuring that the taste would not vary in the slightest.

Fortunately, in Indian cooking, a few extra grams of onions or ginger or tomatoes will not make much of a difference. Nor would a few extra millilitres of water. Nevertheless, whenever the recipe demands exactness, it will be provided. For example, readers should expect to come across something like 3 cups + 4 tsp.

The following chart should help with the conversions:

1 gram	=	0.035 ounces
10 grams	=	0.35 ounces
100 grams	=	3.5 ounces
200 grams	=	7.0 ounces

To convert grams into ounces, multiply the grams by 0.035.

To give convenient working equivalents, the metric measures will be rounded off into units of 5 or 25 (see the following chart) :

OUNCES	GRAMS	Nearest Equivalent	Conversion
1	28.35	28	20/30
2	56.70	57	50/60
3	85.05	85	75/90
4	113.40	113	100/120
5	141.75	142	150
6	170.10	170	175
7	198.45	198	200
8	226.80	227	225
9	255.15	255	250
10 283.50	284	275/290	
11	311.85	312	300/325

OUNCES	GRAMS	Nearest Equivalent	Conversion
12	340.20	340	350
13	368.55	369	375
14	396.90	397	400
15	425.25	425	425
16 or 1 lb	453.60	454	450

For convenient conversions, the following chart will be useful :

1 tsp (teaspoon)	=	5g
2 tsp	=	10g
3 tsp	=	15g
1 Tbs (Tablespoon)	=	15g
1 Tbs	=	3 tsp or ½ oz
¼ cup	=	4 Tbs or 2 oz
$\frac{1}{3}$ cup	=	5 Tbs + 1 tsp
½ cup	=	8 Tbs or 4 oz
$\frac{2}{3}$ cup	=	10 Tbs + 2 tsp
¾ cup	=	12 Tbs or 6 oz
1 cup	=	16 Tbs or 8 oz
1 cup (liquid measure)	=	237 ml
1 oz (dry measure)	=	28.35g
16 oz (dry measure)	=	1 lb
16 oz (liquid measure)	=	2 cups or 1 pint
2 pints	=	4 cups or 1 quart

To convert the commonly used ingredients, clip the following chart. It is a convenient guide.

SUGAR & SPICE

Castor (Confectioner's) Sugar	1 cup	200g
	1 Tbs	14g
Granulated Sugar	1 cup	225g
	1 Tbs	15g
Carom (Ajwain)	1 tsp	2.5g
	1 Tbs	7.5g
Black Onion Seeds (Kalonji)	1 tsp	3g
	1 Tbs	9g
Black Peppercorns (Kali Mirch)	1 tsp	4g
	1 Tbs	12g
Coriander Seeds (Dhania)	1 tsp	2g
	1 Tbs	6g
Cumin Seeds (Jeera)	1 tsp	2g
	1 Tbs	6g
Black Cumin Seeds (Shahi Jeera)	1 tsp	2.5g
	1 Tbs	7.5g
Fennel Seeds (Saunf)	1 tsp	2.5g
	1 Tbs	7.5g
Fenugreek Seeds (Methidaana)	1 tsp	4.5g
	1 Tbs	13.5g
Kasoori Methi Leaves	1 tsp	0.5g
	1 Tbs	1.5g
Broiled and Powdered	1 tsp	1.5g
	1 Tbs	4.5g
Pomegranate Seeds (Anaardaana)	1 tsp	3.3g
	1 Tbs	10g
Black Mustard Seeds (Sarsondaana)	1 tsp	2.5g
	1 Tbs	7.5g
Poppy Seeds (Khus Khus)	1 tsp	3g
	1 Tbs	9g
Sesame Seeds (Til)	1 tsp	3.3g
	1 Tbs	10g

SUGAR & SPICE

Priyala Seeds (Chironji)	1 tsp	4g
	1 Tbs	12g
Cloves (Laung)	1 tsp	2.5g
	1 Tbs	7.5g
Red Chilli Powder (Lal Mirch)	1 tsp	3g
	1 Tbs	9g
Turmeric Powder (Haldi)	1 tsp	3g
	1 Tbs	9g
Cumin Powder (Jeera Powder)	1 tsp	3g
	1 Tbs	9g
Mace Powder (Jawrtri)	1 tsp	3g
	1 Tbs	9g
Green Cardamom Powder (Chotti Elichi)	1 tsp	3g
	1 Tbs	9g

PASTES

Cashew Nut Paste	1 Tbs	15g
Fried Onion Paste	1 Tbs	20g
Garlic Paste/Ginger Paste	1 ¾ tsp	10g
	2 ½ tsp	15g
	3 ¼ tsp	20g
	4 tsp	25g
	5 tsp	30g
	3 Tbs	50g

VEGETABLES

Coriander (chopped)	1 cup	50g
	1 Tbs	3.25g
Green peas (shelled)	1 cup	160g
Mint (chopped)	1 cup	35g
	1 Tbs	2g
Mushrooms		
Whole	1 cup	120g
Sliced	1 cup	95g
Onions		
Sliced	1 cup	110g
Chopped	1 cup	130g
Potatoes (diced, cubes)	1 cup	170g
Tomatoes		
Chopped	1 cup	175g
Concasse	1 cup	240g
Purée	1 cup	260g
Carrots		
Julienne	1 cup	55g
Cubes	1 cup	150g
Beans		
Dices	1 cup	120g
Diamonds	1 cup	110g

FLOUR

Whole wheat flour (Atta)	1 cup	145g
Cornflour	1 cup	100g
Gram flour (Besan)	1 cup	110g
Flour of roasted Channa	1 cup	115g
Flour (all purpose)	1 cup	140g
Bread Crumbs	1 cup	120g

DAIRY

Cheddar Cheese (grated)	1 cup	110g
Khoya	1 cup	200g
Cream	1 cup	240ml
Milk	1 cup	240ml
Yoghurt	1 cup	250g
Yoghurt Cheese	1 cup	260g

FATS AND OILS

Clarified Butter or *Desi Ghee*	1 cup	210g
	1 Tbs	13g
Vegetable Fat	1 cup	200g
	1 Tbs	12.5g
White Butter	1 cup	200g
	1 Tbs	12.5g
Groundnut Oil	1 cup	240ml
	1 Tbs	15ml
Mustard Oil	1 cup	240ml
	1 Tbs	15ml

DRIED FRUITS AND NUTS

Almonds		
With skin	1 cup	160g
Blanched and peeled	1 cup	140g
Cashew Nuts (peeled)	1 cup	140g
Peanuts (shelled and peeled)	1 cup	140g
Pistachio		
With skin	1 cup	150g
Blanched and peeled	1 cup	140g
Raisins	1 cup	170g
Walnuts (chopped)	1 cup	120g
Coconut (grated)	1 cup	110g

LENTILS

All Lentils	1 cup	200g
All Dry Beans	1 cup	200g
All Gram (White, Bengal, etc.)	1 cup	200g

CEREALS

Rice	1 cup	200g
Semolina	1 cup	200g

LIQUIDS

Lemon Juice	1 cup	240ml
Water	1 cup	240ml
Baking Powder	1 tsp	4g
Vegetable Soda	1 tsp	6g

EPISODE 001

with Chef Manjit Singh Gill,
WELCOMGROUP

Shahjehani Qorma is food as elixir at its best. Legend has it that the royal hakim created this to ensure nourishment for the depressed, anorexic emperor who was incarcerated by an ambitious son. It is believed to be wonderfully balanced combining the therapeutic with the aesthetic. In its conception and execution this *Qorma* matches the vision of the builder of the Tajmahal.

Shahjehani Qorma

Kid/Lamb in Apricot, Coconut, Pistachio and Almond Gravy

Ingredients

1 Kg/2 lb Leg of Kid/Lamb
75g/6 Tbs *Desi Ghee* (Clarified Butter)
250g/2 cups Onions

1g/2 tsp *Zaafraan*/Saffron
30ml/2 Tbs Milk

The *Shahjehani Paste*

15g/1½" piece Ginger
12 Dried Apricots
½ Coconut
12 Almonds
12 Pistachio
1.5g/½ tsp *Zeera*/Cumin Powder

900g/3½ cups *Chakka Dahi*/Yoghurt
  Cheese/Hung Yoghurt
1.5g/½ tsp *Haldee*/Turmeric Powder
1.5g/½ tsp Black Pepper (freshly
  roasted & coarsely ground)
Salt

The Dry Masala

10 *Lavang*/Cloves
10 *Chotti Elaichi*/Green Cardamom
6 sticks *Daalcheeni*/Cinnamon (1")
4 Whole Red Chillies

2 blades *Javitri*/Mace
¼ *Jaiphal*/Nutmeg
15g/4½ tsp *Khus-khus*/Poppy Seeds

Serves: 4
Preparation Time: 2:30 hours
Cooking Time: 50-55 minutes

Preparation

The Kid/Lamb : Clean, wash, bone and cut into 1½" cubes.

The Onions : Peel, wash and finely chop.

The *Shahjehani Paste* : Whisk yoghurt cheese in a large bowl. Scrape, wash and roughly chop ginger. Refresh apricots in lukewarm water, drain, remove pits and coarsely chop. Remove the brown skin, wash and coarsely chop coconut. Blanch almonds and pistachios separately for 2 minutes each, peel and keep aside. Put all these ingredients in a food processor/blender, add

120ml/½ cup of water and pulse to make a smooth paste. Put yoghurt cheese in a bowl, add cumin, turmeric, black pepper and salt, whisk until homogenous, add the paste and mix well.

The Marination : Put the meat cubes in the *Shahjehani Paste*, mix until every cube is evenly coated and reserve for 2 hours.

The Dry Masala : Sun-dry the spices, put in a mortar and pound with a pestle to make fine powder. Alternatively, put the spices in a grinder and, employing short pulses, grind to a fine powder. Sift and reserve.

The Saffron : Soak saffron in lukewarm milk and crush the threads with a pestle or the back of a spoon to make a paste.

Cooking

Melt *ghee* in a *handi*/pan, add onions and sauté over medium heat until light golden. Then add the marinated meat along with the *Shahjehani Paste* and cook over high heat until the liquor begins to boil. Add dry masala, stir, add water (approx 240ml/1 cup), bring to a boil, reduce to low heat, cover and simmer, stirring occasionally, until the meat is cooked. Now add saffron, stir, and continue to simmer until the gravy is of medium thin sauce consistency. Remove and adjust the seasoning.

Thaeer Saadam

Southern Curd Rice

Ingredients

250g/1¼ cups Basmati Rice
Salt
240ml/1 cup Milk

1 Kg/4 cups Yoghurt
5g/½ " piece Ginger
2 Green Chillies

The Tempering

20g/1½ Tbs Butter
22.5 ml/1½ Tbs Cooking Oil
1.25g/½ tsp *Rai*/Mustard Seeds

4 Whole Red Chillies
A pinch of *Heeng*/Asafoetida
16 *Kaari Patta*/Curry Leaf

The Garnish

100g/3 oz Grapes

Serves: 4
Preparation Time: 1:15 minutes

Preparation

The Rice : Pick, wash in running water, drain and reserve in water for 15 minutes. Drain.

The Milk : Bring to a boil, remove and cool.

The Yoghurt : Whisk in a bowl.

The Vegetables : Scrape, wash and cut ginger into fine juliennes. Wash green chillies, slit, seed, finely chop and discard the stems. Wash curry leaf.

The Tempering : Wipe red chillies clean with moist cloth. Soak asafoetida in 15ml/1 Tbs of water.

The Garnish : Wash grapes.

The *Thaeer Saadam* : Put the drained rice in a *handi*/pan, add salt and water (approx 600ml/2½ cups), bring to a boil, cover and simmer, stirring occasionally, until the water is absorbed. Then add milk, bring to a boil, reduce to low heat and cook until rice is mashed and of porridge consistency. Remove and cool. When cool, add ginger and green chillies, stir, add yoghurt, mix well and refrigerate for at least 30 minutes.

The Tempering : Heat oil in a frying pan, add mustard seeds and stir over medium heat until they begin to pop, add red chillies and asafoetida, stir, add curry leaf and stir until it stops spluttering. Remove the curd-rice from the refrigerator and pour on the tempering. Adjust the seasoning, garnish with grapes and serve chilled.

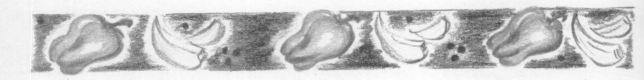

EPISODE 002

with Chef Manjit Singh Gill,
WELCOMGROUP

Kofta is what all meat balls aspire to. The range is truely fascinating — from melt-in-the-mouth variety to the packed-with-exotica specimen. The vegetarian versions match the non-vegetarian *kofta* at every step. We were delighted to offer our viewers selections from the entire gamut of *kofta*. The mince *kofta* was enhanced with saffron and *aloobukhara* while the *shaakahari kofta* displayed a unique 'fruition'— raw bananas providing the oyster casing for the pearls of oyster mushroom and the *lauki ka kofta. Lauki ka kofta* acquired an emerald drape of *Paalak ki Tarri.*

Lauki Ka Kofta Paalak Ki Tarri

Bottle Gourd Kofta stuffed with Dried Plums in Spinach Gravy

Ingredients

The Kofta

300g/11 oz *Lauki*/Bottle Gourd/Marrow
Salt
16 *Aloobukhara*/Dried Plums
16 Almonds
60g/½ cup *Besan*/Gramflour

1.5g/½ tsp Red Chilli Powder
1.5g/½ tsp *Amchoor*/Mango Powder
A pinch of Baking Powder
Cooking Oil to deep fry *kofta*

The Gravy

1 kg/2¼ lb Spinach
75ml/5 Tbs Cooking Oil
2 Onions (medium)
30g/5¼ tsp Garlic Paste (strain)
9g/1 Tbs *Dhania*/Coriander Powder
1.5g/½ tsp Red Chilli Powder

90ml/6 Tbs Tomato Purée (canned)
3g/1 tsp Black Pepper (freshly roasted &
    coarsely ground)
Salt
A generous pinch of crushed *Kasoori Methi*/
    Dried Fenugreek Leaves

Serves: 4
Preparation Time: 1:10 hours
Cooking Time: 30 minutes

Preparation

The Marrow/White Pumpkin : Peel, wash and grate. Sprinkle salt and reserve for 20 minutes. Then squeeze the grated marrow in a napkin to ensure it is completely devoid of moisture.

The Plums & Almonds : Slit from one side, carefully remove the pits, refresh in water for 5 minutes, drain and keep aside. Blanch almonds, cool and rub vigorously to remove the skin. Replace the pits with the blanched almonds.

The *Kofta* : Mix gramflour, red chilli, *amchoor* and baking powder and salt, with the dried marrow/white pumpkin, knead well, divide into 16 equal portions and make balls.

The Stuffing : Flatten each ball between the palms, place a stuffed plum in the middle, make balls again and refrigerate for 15 minutes.

9

The *Kofta* : Heat oil in a *kadhai*/wok and deep fry over medium heat until golden. Remove to absorbent paper to drain the excess fat.

The Gravy : Clean spinach, rinse in running water, drain, put in a *handi*/pan, add salt and boil until cooked (do not cover), drain, put in a blender and make a purée. Peel, wash and finely chop onions.

Cooking

Heat oil in a *handi*/pan, add onions, sauté over medium heat until translucent and glossy, add garlic paste, and *bhunno*/stir-fry until the onions are golden. Then add coriander and red chillies (dissolved in 30ml/2 Tbs of water), and stir until the moisture evaporates, add spinach, and *bhunno*/stir-fry until specks of fat appear on the surface. Now add tomato purée, *bhunno*/stir-fry until specks of fat appear on the surface, add water (approx 240ml/1 cup), bring to a boil, reduce to low heat and simmer for 7-8 minutes. Now carefully add the *kofta*, simmer for 2-3 minutes, add pepper and salt, and stir. Take *kasoori methi* on one palm, crush with the other, sprinkle on top, stir, remove and adjust the seasoning.

Aloobukhara Kofta

Kid/Lamb Kofta stuffed with Dried Plums in Spinach Gravy

Ingredients

The *Kofta*

800g/1 lb 13 oz *Kheema*/Kid/Lamb Mince
  (twice minced)
16 *Aloobukhara*/Dried Plums
16 Almonds
5g/½" piece Ginger

4 Green Chillies
1.5g/½ tsp *Anaardana*/Pomegranate
  Powder
Salt

The Gravy

75ml/5 Tbs Cooking Oil
5 *Lavang*/Cloves
5 *Chotti Elaichi*/Green Cardamom
1 stick *Daalcheeni*/Cinnamon (1")
4 Onions (medium)
30g/5¼ tsp Garlic Paste (strain)
20g/3½ tsp Ginger Paste (strain)
6g/2 tsp *Dhania*/Coriander Powder

3g/1 tsp Red Chilli Powder
200ml/7 oz Tomato Purée (canned)
Salt
3g/1 tsp *Chotti Elaichi*/Green
  Cardamom Powder
1.5g/½ tsp *Javitri*/Mace Powder

Serves: 4
Preparation Time: 1 hour
Cooking Time: 30 minutes

Preparation

The Plums & Almonds : Slit from one side, carefully remove the pits, refresh in water for 5 minutes, drain and keep aside. Blanch almonds, cool and rub vigorously to remove the skin. Replace the pits with the blanched almonds.

The *Kofta* : Scrape, wash and finely chop ginger. Wash green chillies, slit, seed, finely chop and discard the stems. Mix ginger, green chillies, *anaardana* and salt with the mince, knead well, divide into 16 equal portions and make balls.

The Stuffing : Flatten each ball between the palms, place a stuffed plum in the middle, make balls again and refrigerate to firm up the meat (approx 15 minutes).

The Gravy : Peel, wash and finely chop onions.

Cooking

Heat oil in a *handi*/pan, add cloves, green cardamom and cinnamon, stir over medium heat until the cardamom begins to change colour, add onions and sauté until translucent and glossy. Add garlic and ginger pastes, *bhunno*/stir-fry until the onions are golden, add coriander and red chillies (dissolved in 30ml/2 Tbs of water) and stir until the moisture evaporates. Then add the tomato purée, *bhunno*/stir-fry until specks of fat begin to appear on the surface, add water (approx 600ml/2½ cups) and bring to a boil. Reduce to low heat and then carefully (to ensure the meatballs do not break) add the *kofta*, cover and simmer until the meatballs are cooked (approx 7-8 minutes). Remove the *kofta* carefully to the serving dish and pass the gravy through a fine mesh soup strainer into a separate *handi*/pan. Return gravy to heat, bring to a boil, add *kofta*, green cardamom and mace, stir, remove and adjust the seasoning.

Zaafraani Kofta

Breast of Chicken Kofta in Saffron Gravy

Ingredients

8 Breasts of Chicken
15g/2½ tsp Ginger Paste (strain)

15g/2½ tsp Garlic Paste (strain)
Salt

The Filling

300g/11 oz Chicken Mince
30g/1 oz *Taaza Anaar*/Fresh Pomegranate
16 Pistachio
10g/1″ piece Ginger
4 Green Chillies
1.5g/½ tsp Black Pepper (freshly
    roasted & coarsely ground)

1.25g/½ tsp *Shahi Zeera*/Black Cumin
    Seeds
0.75g/¼tsp *Chotti Elaichi*/Green
    Cardamom Powder
0.25g/½ tsp *Zaafraan*/Saffron
Salt

The Gravy

50ml/¼ cup *Desi Ghee*/Clarified Butter
5 *Chotti Elaichi*/Green Cardamom
30g/5¼ tsp Garlic Paste (strain)
20g/3½ tsp Ginger Paste (strain)
8 Green Chillies
150g/5 oz Boiled Onion Paste
30g/1 oz Almond Paste (Melon Seed
    Paste in summer)
180ml/¾ cup Yoghurt

1 litre/4¼ cups Clear Chicken Stock
    (or water)
Salt
0.5g/½ tsp *Zaafraan*/Saffron
1.5g/½ tsp *Chotti Elaichi*/Green
    Cardamom Powder
30ml/2 Tbs Cream

Serves: 4
Preparation Time: 1:10 hours.
Cooking Time: 35-40 minutes.

Preparation

The Chicken : Remove the skin, bone but retain the winglet bones, wash and pat dry. Then place the breasts between two plastic sheets and flatten each individually with a bat without rupturing the meat.

The Marination : Mix the ginger and garlic pastes with salt, evenly rub the flattened breasts with this marinade and reserve for 15 minutes.

The Filling : Scrape, wash and finely chop ginger. Wash green chillies, slit, seed and finely chop. Put these and the remaining ingredients in a bowl, and mix well. Divide into 8 equal portions.

The Stuffing : Place the breasts on a flat surface, place a portion of the filling in the middle ends of the foil to prevent water from seeping in. Keep aside.

The Gravy : Wash green chillies, slit, seed and finely chop. Whisk yoghurt in a bowl.

Cooking

Heat water in a *handi*/pan, add the foil-wrapped chicken *kofta* and "poach" for 4-5 minutes. Remove and keep aside.

To prepare the melt *ghee* in a *handi*/pan, add cardamom and stir over medium heat until it begins to change colour, add garlic and ginger pastes, stir until the moisture has evaporated. Add green chillies, stir, add onion paste, *bhunno*/stir-fry until specks of fat begin to appear on the surface (ensuring that the *masala* does not get coloured), add almond paste, *bhunno*/stir-fry until specks of fat begin to appear on the surface (ensuring that the *masala* does not get coloured). Remove *handi*/pan from heat, stir-in yoghurt, return *handi*/pan to heat and *bhunno*/stir-fry until specks of fat begin to appear on the surface (ensuring that the *masala* does not get coloured). Then add stock (or water), bring to a boil, reduce to low heat, simmer until reduced by half. Remove *handi*/pan from heat, pass the gravy through a fine mesh soup strainer into a separate *handi*/pan, return *handi*/pan to heat, unwrap and add the "poached" *kofta* and salt, and bring to a boil. Reduce to low heat, add saffron, stir, add cardamom powder and stir-in cream. Remove and adjust the seasoning.

EPISODE 003

with Chef Manjit Singh Gill,
WELCOMGROUP

There is scarcely a carnivore in India who prefers his meat sans bones. There are those who prefer the shanks, and others who swear by the chops. Ginger enlivens this old favourite.

And for the vegetarians, the bouquetiere of vegetables donning a yoghurt cape proved irresistible.

Ginger Lamb Chops

Braised fat-free Kid/Lamb Chops

Ingredients

12 Kid/Lamb Chops (3-rib)
250g/1 cup Yoghurt
65g/½ cup Onions
15g/1½" piece Ginger
6 flakes Garlic
175g/1 cup Tomatoes
30g/5¼ tsp Raw Papaya Paste

1.5g/½ tsp Black Pepper (freshly roasted
  & coarsely ground)
Salt
2.25g/¼ tsp *Chotti Elaichi*/Green
  Cardamom
0.75g/¼ tsp *Javitri*/Mace
5ml/1 tsp Lemon Juice (from the garnish)

The Garnish

10g/1" piece Ginger

45ml/3 Tbs Lemon Juice

Serves: 4
Preparation Time: 2:15 hours
Cooking Time: 25-30 minutes

Preparation

The Kid/Lamb Chops : Remove the two side ribs, carefully scrape the third rib to expose the bone (which will make it look like marble), trim, wash and pat dry.

The Vegetables : Peel, wash and finely chop onions. Scrape, wash and finely chop ginger. Peel and finely chop garlic. Remove eyes, wash, quarter, remove the pulp and finely chop tomatoes.

The Marination : Whisk yoghurt in a large bowl, add the remaining ingredients, except cardamom, mace and lemon juice, and mix well. Evenly rub the chops with this marinade, arrange the chops in a non-stick skillet or frying pan, pour on the remaining marinade, cover and reserve for 2 hours.

The Garnish : Scrape, wash and cut ginger into juliennes. Reserve in the lemon juice.

Cooking

Uncover the non-stick skillet/frying pan with the marinated chops, place it on the stove, bring to a boil over medium heat, reduce to low heat, cover and simmer until the chops are tender. Remove the chops and keep warm. Reduce the gravy until of sauce consistency. Then sprinkle the green cardamom and mace, and stir. Remove, stir-in lemon juice and adjust the seasoning. Garnish with pickled ginger.

Dahi Mein Subzion Ka Guldasta

Bouquetiere of braised fat-free vegetables on bed of honey-glazed Aubergine Slices

Ingredients

175g/6 oz Carrots
150g/5 oz Potatoes
110g/¼ lb Cauliflower or Broccoli
110g/¼ lb Zucchini (or any squash
    family vegetable)

110g/¼ lb Baby Corn
45g/13 oz Button Mushrooms
175g/6 oz Tomatoes
4.5g/1 Tbs *Kasoori Methi*/Dried
    Fenugreek Leaf Powder

The Marination

250g/1 cup Yoghurt
6g/1 tsp Ginger Paste (strain)
6g/1 tsp Garlic Paste (strain)
15g/1 Tbs Green Peppercorns
4g/2 tsp *Jeera*/Cumin Seeds (freshly
    roasted)

120ml/½ cup Milk
9g/1 Tbs *Dhania*/Coriander Powder
1.5g/½ tsp *Haldee*/Turmeric Powder
2.25g/1 tsp *Besan*/Gramflour
Salt

The Bases

1 Brinjal (large; round)
90g/6 Tbs Yoghurt
1.5g/½ tsp Red Chilli Powder

Salt
Honey to glaze bases

The Garnish

15g/½ oz Toasted Almond Flakes (optional)

Serves: 4
Preparation Time: 45 minutes
Cooking Time: 40 minutes

Preparation

The Vegetables : Peel, wash and dice carrots and potatoes, (reserve potato dices in water). Clean cauliflower, or broccoli, wash and cut into small florets. Wash and dice zucchini (if using bottle gourd, peel, core and dice.) Remove ears, wash and cut baby corn into thin roundels. Slice the earthy lower bit of the stalks of button mushrooms, wash in running water to remove grit, drain, reserve in water and slice at the time of cooking. Remove eyes, wash, quarter and dice tomatoes.

The Marination : Whisk yoghurt in a large bowl, add the remaining ingredients, mix well, put carrots, potatoes, cauliflower, or broccoli, zucchini, baby corn and mushrooms in the marinade, transfer to a non-stick skillet or frying pan, cover and reserve for 15 minutes.

The Bases : Wash brinjal, cut into ¼" thick slices (take the 4 largest pieces from the middle), evenly sprinkle red chillies and salt on both sides and reserve in a tray for 5 minutes. Whisk yoghurt in a bowl.

Cooking

Uncover the non-stick skillet/frying pan with the marinated vegetables, place it on the stove, bring to a boil over medium heat, reduce to low heat, cover and simmer until the vegetables are *al dente* cooked so as to remain firm when bitten, remove, add tomatoes, stir to mix well. Adjust the seasoning.

Meanwhile, to prepare the bases, spread a teaspoon of yoghurt on one side of the slice of brinjal, place the side so moistened on a non-stick skillet or frying pan and cook for a minute. Apply a teaspoon of the yoghurt on the other side, turn over and repeat the process. Continue in this manner, using 1 teaspoon of yoghurt each time, until the bases are golden brown. Then brush each side with honey and glaze. Remove and arrange a base on each of 4 individual plates.

Spread equal quantities of the vegetables on the brinjal bases, crush the *kasoori methi* between the palms and sprinkle equal quantities on top and garnish with equal quantities of toasted almonds.

EPISODE 004

with Chef Manjit Singh Gill,
WELCOMGROUP

Who says that the vegetarians lack a rich repertoire of *kebab*? The *Harra Kebab* is capable of putting the minced *shahi* to shame.

Harra Kebab

Pan Grilled Spinach Patties stuffed with Nutty Cottage Cheese

Ingredients

300g/1½ cups Spinach
75g/2½ oz Channa Daal/Chick Peas
4 *Chotti Elaichi*/Green Cardamom
2 *Lavang*/Cloves
2 sticks *Daalcheeni*/Cinnamon (1") Powder
Salt
1.5g/½ tsp
1.5g/½ tsp *Chotti Elaichi*/Green
  Cardamom Powder

0.75g/¼ tsp *Javitri*/Mace Powder
0.75g/¼ tsp *Daalcheeni*/Cinnamon
20g/5 tsp Unsalted Butter
  Equal quantities of Butter & Groundnut
  Oil to shallow fry
Red Chilli Powder

The Filling

75g/2½ oz *Paneer*/Casein
30g/1 oz Processed Cheese
12 Cashewnuts

18 Raisins
18 *Chironji*

4 Green Chillies
5g/½" piece Ginger
3.25g/1 Tbs *Taaza Dhania*/Coriander

Salt

Serves: 4 (2 patties/portion)
Preparation Time: 1:20 hours
Cooking Time: 4-5 minutes/set

Preparation

The Spinach : Clean, remove the hard stems and wash in running water. Boil enough water in a *handi*/pan, add spinach and boil until cooked (approx 3-4 minutes). Drain, cool, squeeze out the excess moisture and then grind into a smooth paste, preferably with a *sil-batta* (grinding stone), otherwise in a food processor/blender. Melt half the butter in a *kadhai*/wok, add the spinach paste and *bhunno*/stir-fry until the moisture has completely evaporated and the spinach becomes like a ball. (Only then would the strong aroma of the spinach dissipate.) Remove and spread on a flat surface to cool immediately.

The *Daal* : Pick, wash in running water, drain and then soak in water for at least 30 minutes. Drain, put in a *handi*/pan, add cardamom, cloves, cinnamon and water (approx 240ml/1 cup), boil until cooked and the liquid is absorbed (approx 20-25 minutes). Cool, drain the excess moisture, if any, and then grind into a smooth paste, preferably with a *sil-batta* (grinding stone), otherwise in a food processor/blender. Melt the remaining butter in a *kadhai*/wok, add the lentil paste and *bhunno*/stir-fry until the moisture has completely evaporated and the lentil assumes of a grainy texture (only then would the strong aroma of the lentil dissipate). Remove and cool.

The Spinach-*Daal* Mixture : Put the spinach and lentil pastes in a bowl, add the remaining ingredients, except butter, mix well, divide into 8 equal portions and make balls.

The Filling : Grate *paneer* and cheese in a bowl. Coarsely chop cashewnuts and *chironji*. Remove stems, soak raisins in water for a few minutes, drain and then coarsely chop. Wash green chillies, slit, seed, finely chop and discard the stems. Scrape, wash and finely chop ginger. Clean, wash and finely chop coriander. Mix all the ingredients with the *paneer* and divide into 8 equal portions.

The Stuffing : Flatten each spinach ball between the palms, place a portion of the filling in the middle, make balls again and flatten into ¾″ thick patties.

Cooking

Heat butter and oil on a *tawa*/griddle and shallow fry the patties over medium heat until a crisp layer is formed on both sides. Press with a spatula and remove to absorbent paper to drain the excess fat.

Tandoori Jheenga

Tandoor Grilled Prawns

Ingredients

12 Jumbo Prawns

Butter for basting

The First Marination

60ml/¼ cup Lemon Juice
30g/5 tsp Garlic Paste (strain)
15g/2½ tsp Ginger Paste (strain)

2.25g/¾ tsp *Kashmiri Deghi Mirch* Powder
Salt

The Second Marination

100g/3 oz Chakka Dahi/Yoghurt Cheese
   Hung Yoghurt
60ml/¼ cup Cream
30ml/2 Tbs Lemon Juice
25g/4 tsp Garlic Paste (strain)
15g/2½ tsp Ginger Paste (strain)
A pinch of *Ajwain*/Carom
3g/1 tsp *Kashmiri Deghi Mirch* Powder
A generous pinch of *Chotti Elaichi*/Green
   Cardamom Powder

A generous pinch of *Daalcheeni/*
   Cinnamon Powder
A small pinch of *Lavang*/Clove Powder
A small pinch of *Javitri*/Mace Powder
A small pinch of *Chakriphool*/Star
   Anise Powder
Salt

Serves: 4
Preparation Time: 1:20 hours
Cooking Time: 3-4 minutes

Preparation

The Prawns : Shell, but retain the tails and vein.

The First Marination : Mix all the ingredients in a bowl, evenly rub the prawns with this marinade and reserve for 15 minutes. Then hold the prawns aloft to drain excess moisture.

The Second Marination : Put yoghurt cheese in a bowl, add the remaining ingredients and whisk. Evenly rub the prawns with this marinade and reserve in the refrigerator for 1 hour.

The Oven : Pre-heat to 350°F.

The Skewering : Skewer the prawns (they should touch without overlapping) and keep a tray underneath to collect the drippings.

Cooking

Roast in a moderately hot tandoor, on a charcoal grill or in a pre-heated oven for 1½-2 minutes. Remove, baste with butter and roast again for a minute.

Murgh Malai Kebab

Royal Cumin-flavoured boned breast of Chicken glazed in the tandoor

Ingredients

12 Supremes of Chicken

The First Marination

35g/2 Tbs Ginger Paste (strained)
25g/4 tsp Garlic Paste (strained)

60ml/¼ cup *Sirka*/Malt Vinegar
30ml/2 Tbs White Wine

The Second Marination

260g/1 cup *Chakka Dahi*/Yoghurt Cheese
   Hung Yoghurt
60g/2 oz Cheddar/Processed Cheese
1.5g/½ tsp *Dhania*/Coriander Powder
1.5g/½ tsp *Kashmiri Deghi Mirch*
1.5g/½ tsp *Saunf*/Fennel Powder
0.75g/¼ tsp *Chotti Elaichi*/Green
   Cardamom Powder
0.375g/1/8 tsp *Daalcheeni*/Cinnamom
   Powder

0.375g/1/8 tsp *Javitri*/Mace Powder
0.375g/1/8 tsp *Jaiphal*/Nutmeg Powder
3.25 g/1 Tbs *Taaza Dhania*/Coriander
Salt
120ml/½ cup Cream
0.5g/1 tsp *Zaafraan*/Saffron

Serves: 4
Preparation Time: 1:45 hours
Cooking Time: Up to 15 minutes

Preparation

The Chicken : Clean, bone, cut each breast into 3 equal-sized *tikka*, wash and pat dry.

The First Marination : Mix all the ingredients, rub the chicken pieces with this marinade and reserve for 15 minutes.

The Second Marination : Whisk yoghurt cheese in a bowl. Grate processed cheese and mash. Clean, wash and finely chop coriander. Crush saffron threads with a pestle or the back of a spoon, reserve in 15ml/1 Tbs of cream for 15 minutes and then make a paste. Mix cheese, coriander and remaining ingredients with the yoghurt cheese, whisk, stir-in remaining cream, rub the chicken pieces with the marinade and reserve in the refrigerator for 1 hour.

The Skewering : If cooking in the oven, thread three *tikka* on wooden skewers and keep aside. If cooking in the tandoor or on a charcoal grill, skewer the *tikka* and keep a tray underneath to collect the drippings.

The Oven : Pre-heat to 350°F.

Cooking

Roast in a moderately hot tandoor for approximately 8-10 minutes, on a charcoal grill for about the same time, in a pre-heated oven for 14-15 minutes, basting with butter at regular intervals.

Paneer Tikka

Tandoor Grilled Cottage Cheese cubes

Ingredients

800g/1¾ Ib *Shahi Jeera Paneer* (Royal Cumin imbibed Cottage Cheese)

The Batter

260g/1 cup *Chakka Dahi*/Yoghurt Cheese/
    Hung Yoghurt
30g/1 oz Green Peppercorns
7g/1 Tbs Rice Flour
3/g 1 tps *Peeli Mirch*/Yellow Chilli Powder
2.5g/1 tsp *Ajwain*/Carom
0.375g/ ⅛ tsp *Chotti Elaichi*/Green
    Cardamom Powder

0.375g/ ⅛ tsp *Jaiphal*/Nutmeg Powder
0.375g/ ⅛ tsp *Gulaab Pankhrhi*/Rose Petal
    Powder
Salt
90ml/6 Tbs Single Cream

The *Paneer Tikka Masala*

15g/5 tsp Amchoor[1]
4.5g/1½ tsp *Jeera*/Cumin Powder

3g/1 tsp Black Pepper (freshly roasted &
    coarsely ground)
1.5g/½ tsp *Kaala Namak*/Black Rock Salt

Serves: 4
Preparation Time : 30 minutes
Cooking Time : 30 minutes

Preparation

The *Paneer* (Cottage Cheese) : Cut into 16 equal sized chunks (2″× 2″ × 1″) and let them sweat for 10 minutes.

The Batter : Whisk yoghurt cheese. Drain green peppercorns, pat dry and finely chop. Sift rice flour, add to yoghurt cheese and whisk to remove lumps. Add remaining ingredients, except cream, and whisk again. Fold in cream, dip chunks in this batter, arrange in tray, pour the remaining batter on top of the chunks and reserve in refrigerator for 30 minutes.

The *Paneer Tikka Masala* : Mix all the ingredients and store in a sterilized glass jar.

The Skewering : Skewer *paneer* (cottage cheese) chunks in convenient batches and then skewer a raw onion (to prevent *paneer* from sliding down). Keep a tray underneath to collect drippings.

Cooking

Roast in moderately hot tandoor for 5-6 minutes, on charcoal grill for 6-7 minutes, in pre-heated oven (275°F) for 10-12 minutes.

To Serve

Unskewer onions and *paneer* (cottage cheese), arrange chunks on platter, sprinkle a generous pinch or two of the *Paneer Tikka Masala* and serve hot.

1. Dried slices of unripe green mango, usually available in powdered form.

30

EPISODE 005

with Chef Manjit Singh Gill,
WELCOMGROUP

This episode was dedicated to stuffed specialities. The non-vegetarians were treated to a saffron-touched spring chicken and the vegetarians were given a taste of paradise with jumbo morels imported from the Vale.

Bharwaan Zaafraani Murgh

Stuffed Breast of Chicken in Saffron Gravy

Ingredients

8 Breasts of Chicken (90g/3 oz each)
Butter to grease roasting tray

240ml/1 cup Clear Chicken Stock

The Marination

30g/5¼ tsp Garlic Paste (strain)
20g/3½ tsp Ginger Paste (strain)
30ml/2 Tbs Lemon Juice

3g/1 tsp *Peeli Mirch*/Yellow Chilli Powder
Salt

The Filling

150g/5 oz Chicken Mince
25ml/5 tsp Cream
75g/2½ oz Processed Cheese
1 *Taaza Anaar*/Fresh Pomegranate
10g/1" piece Ginger
3.25g/1 Tbs *Taaza Dhania*/Coriander

4 Green Chillies
1.25g/½ tsp *Shahi Zeera*/Black Cumin
   Seeds
0.5g/½ tsp *Zaafraan*/Saffron
Salt

The Gravy

60g/2 oz *Desi Ghee*/Clarified Butter
4 *Chotti Elaichi*/Green Cardamom
2 *Lavang*/Cloves
2 *Tej Patta*/Bay Leaf
1 stick *Daalcheeni*/Cinnamon (1")
100g/3 oz Boiled Onion Paste
15g/2½ tsp Garlic Paste (strain)
15g/2½ tsp Ginger Paste (strain)
10g/1¼ tsp Green Chilli Paste

250g/1 cup Yoghurt
30g/1 oz Cashewnut Paste
Salt
1.5g/½ tsp *Chotti Elaichi*/Green
   Cardamom Powder
0.75g/¼ tsp *Javitri*/Mace Powder
0.5g/½ tsp *Zaafraan*/Saffron
1 drop *Kewra*

Serves: 4
Preparation Time: 2:15 hours
Cooking Time: 45 minutes

Preparation

The Chicken : Clean, remove the skin, bone, trim, wash and pat dry. Place the breasts, one at a time, between two polythene sheets and flatten with a bat ensuring that the meat is not ruptured and at the same time the shape is retained.

The Marination : Mix all the ingredients in a bowl, evenly rub the flattened chicken breasts with this marinade and reserve for 15 minutes.

The Filling : Grate cheese. Scrape, wash and finely chop ginger. Clean, wash and finely chop coriander. Wash green chillies, slit, seed, finely chop and discard the stems. Crush saffron flakes with a pestle or back of a spoon, reserve in 15ml/1 Tbs of lukewarm water and then make a paste. Add these and the remaining ingredients to the mince, reserving a few pomegranate seeds for garnish. Keep aside.

The Stuffing : Place a portion of the filling at a narrow end of each breast and roll tightly to make paupiettes.

The Oven : Pre-heat to 300°F.

The Roasting : Grease a roasting tray with butter, arrange the breasts with the loose ends touching the bottom of the tray, pour on the chicken stock and roast in the pre-heated oven until evenly light golden. (If an oven is not available, cover the tray with aluminium foil and cook on the regular stove.) Remove paupiettes and reserve the stock.

The Gravy : Whisk yoghurt in a bowl. Crush saffron flakes with a pestle or back of a spoon, reserve in 15ml/1 Tbs of lukewarm water and then make a paste.

Cooking

Heat *ghee* in a *handi*/pan, add green cardamom, cloves, bay leaves and cinnamon, stir over medium heat until cardamom begins to change colour, add onions, *bhunno*/stir-fry until specks of fat begin to appear on the surface, ensuring that they *do not* get coloured. Add garlic and ginger pastes, and *bhunno*/stir-fry until the moisture has evaporated, ensuring the masala does not get coloured. Remove *handi*/pan from heat, stir-in yoghurt, return *handi*/pan to heat and *bhunno*/stir-fry until specks of fat begin to appear on the surface. Then add green chilli and cashewnut pastes, *bhunno*/stir-fry until specks of fat begin to appear on the surface, ensuring the masala does not get coloured. Now add the reserved stock, bring to a boil, reduce to low heat and simmer for 3-4 minutes. Remove and pass the gravy through a fine mesh soup strainer into a saucepan, bring to a boil, reduce to low heat, add the paupiettes, cardamom, mace and saffron, stir, and simmer for 2 minutes. Remove, add *kewra*, stir, and adjust the seasoning.

Bharwaan Zaafraani Guchchi

Stuffed Morels in Saffron Gravy

Ingredients

16/24 *Guchchi*/Morels (large/medium)

The Filling

15g/½ oz Oyster Mushrooms
15g/½ oz Button Mushrooms
30g/1 oz Processed Cheese
12 Cashewnuts
16 Raisins
25g/1 oz Carrots
25g/1 oz Potatoes

5g/½" piece Ginger
2g/2 tsp *Taaza Dhania*/Coriander
2 Green Chillies
A generous pinch of *Shahi Zeera*/Black
 Cumin Seeds
Salt
7.5ml/ ½ Tbs Lemon Juice

The Gravy

60g/2 oz *Desi Ghee*/Clarified Butter
5 *Chotti Elaichi*/Green Cardamom
3 *Lavang*/Cloves
1 stick *Daalcheeni*/Cinnamon (1")
1 *Tej Patta*/Bay Leaf
200g/7 oz Boiled Onion Paste
20g/3½ tsp Ginger Paste (strain)
10g/1¼ tsp Green Chilli Paste
250g/1 cup Yoghurt
15g/1 tsp Cashewnut Paste

15g/1 tsp *Kharbooja*/Melon Seed Paste
1 litre/4¼ cups Vegetable Stock
Salt
30ml/2 Tbs Cream
1.5g/½ tsp *Chotti Elaichi*/Green
 Cardamom Powder
0.75g/¼ tsp *Javitri*/Mace Powder
0.5g/½ tsp *Zaafraan*/Saffron
1 drop *Kewra*

Serves: 4
Preparation Time: 1 hour
Cooking Time: 45 minutes

Preparation

The Morels : Soak in hot water for 10 minutes, drain, carefully wash in running water to remove grit and soak again in hot water for 5 minutes or until they become soft and swollen. Drain, carefully squeeze out the excess water and remove the stems to create pockets for the stuffing.

The Filling : Wash oyster mushrooms in running water, drain, soak (if dried) in lukewarm water for 15 minutes, drain and finely chop. Remove the earthy base of the stalks, wash in running water, drain and finely chop button mushrooms. Grate cheese. Chop cashewnuts. Clean raisins and remove the stems. Peel carrots and potatoes, wash, finely chop, blanch in salted boiling water for 2 minutes, drain, refresh in iced water, drain and pat dry. (The vegetables should be *al dente*, not soft and squishy.) Scrape, wash and finely chop ginger. Clean, wash and finely chop coriander. Wash green chillies, slit, seed, finely chop and discard stems. Put all the ingredients in a bowl, add *shahi jeera*, salt and lemon juice, mix well and divide into 16/24 equal portions.

The Stuffing : Carefully prise open the morels, stuff each with a portion of the filling and refrigerate for 15 minutes.

The Gravy : Whisk yoghurt in a bowl. Crush saffron flakes with a pestle or back of a spoon, reserve in 15ml/1 Tbs of lukewarm water and then make a paste. Reserve 1/4th for garnish.

Cooking

Melt *ghee* in a *handi*/pan, add cardamom, cloves, cinnamon and bay leaf, stir over medium heat until cardamom begins to change colour, add onions and *bhunno*/stir-fry until specks of fat begin to appear on the surface, ensuring that they *do not* get coloured. Add ginger pastes and *bhunno*/stir-fry until the moisture has evaporated, ensuring the masala does not get coloured. Remove *handi*/pan from heat, stir-in yoghurt, return *handi*/pan to heat and *bhunno*/stir-fry until specks of fat begin to appear on the surface. Then add green chilli, cashewnut and melon seed pastes, *bhunno*/stir-fry until specks of fat begin to appear on the surface, ensuring the masala does not get coloured. Now add stock and salt, bring to a boil, reduce to low heat and simmer for 3-4 minutes. Remove and pass the gravy through a fine mesh soup strainer into a saucepan, bring to a boil, reduce to low heat, add the stuffed morels, cardamom, mace and saffron, stir, and simmer for 2 minutes. Remove, add *kewra*, stir, and adjust the seasoning.

36

EPISODE 006

with Chef Manjit Singh Gill,
WELCOMGROUP

Manjit cooked the *Lal Maas* for us in the *Daawat* episode that literally made us see red! For those few who like it hot there can be no peer to this fiery ol' flame. *Rang Rangilo* Rajasthan is resplendent with many hues but it is scarlet red that predominates. *Lal Maas* seeks to evoke its magic.

Milagu Kozhi Chettinad

Chicken in Chettinad Pepper Gravy

Ingredients

12 Chicken Thighs
75ml/5 Tbs Groundnut Oil
5 *Chotti Elaichi*/Green Cardamom
5 *Lavang*/Cloves
2 sticks *Daalcheeni*/Cinnamom (1")
2 *Tej Patta*/Bay Leaf
2g/1 tsp *Zeera*/Cumin Seeds
2g/½ tsp *Methidaana*/Fenugreek Seeds
250g/9 oz Onions
12.5/2 tsp Ginger Paste (strain)

12.5/2 tsp Garlic Paste (strain)
1.5g/½ tsp *Haldee*/Turmeric Powder
9g/1 Tbs *Dhania*/Coriander Powder
1.5g/½ tsp Red Chilli Powder
300g/11 oz Tomatoes
20g/5 tsp Black Pepper (freshly roasted
   & coarsely ground)
Salt
60g/2 oz *Narial*/Coconut Paste
3.25g/1 Tbs *Taaza Dhania*/Coriander

Serves: 4
Preparation Time: 45 minutes
Cooking Time: 35 minutes

Preparation

The Chicken : Clean, remove the skin, trim, wash and pat dry.

The Vegetables : Peel, wash and chop onions. Remove eyes, wash and roughly chop tomatoes. Clean, wash and chop coriander.

Cooking

Heat oil in a *kadhai*/wok, add cardamom, cloves, cinnamon, bay leaves, cumin and fenugreek seeds, stir over medium heat until the cardamom begins to change colour, add onions and *bhunno*/stir-fry until onions are light golden. Then add ginger and garlic pastes, *bhunno*/stir-fry until the onions are golden brown, add turmeric, coriander and red chilli powders—dissolved in 60ml/¼ cup of water—and stir until the moisture evaporates. Add tomatoes, *bhunno*/stir-fry until the fat leaves the sides, add 8g/2 tsp of black peppercorns, stir, add coconut paste and *bhunno*/stir-fry for 2 minutes. Now add chicken and salt, *bhunno*/stir-fry for 3 minutes, add 360ml/1½ cups of water, bring to a boil, reduce to low heat, cover and simmer, stirring occasionally, until the chicken is cooked (approx 10-12 minutes). Uncover and simmer until the moisture has almost evaporated and the chicken is napped. Remove and adjust the seasoning. Garnish with the remaining pepper and coriander.

Laal Maas

Kid/Lamb in fiery Rajasthani Chilli Gravy

Ingredients

1.2kg/2¼ lb *Raan*/Leg of Kid/Lamb
Whole Dried Red Chillies
150g/¾ cup *Desi Ghee*/Clarified Butter
60g/2 oz Garlic
200g/1½ cup Onions
5 *Chotti Elaichi*/Green Cardamom
3 *Motti Elaichi*/Black Cardamom

2g/1 tsp *Zeera*/Cumin Seeds
250ml/1 cup Yoghurt
15g/5 tsp *Dhania*/Coriander Powder
3g/1 tsp *Haldee*/Turmeric Powder
Salt
6.5g/2 Tbs *Taaza Dhania*/Coriander

Serves: 4
Preparation Time: 30 minutes
Cooking Time: 1:45 hours

Preparation

The Kid/Spring Lamb : Clean, cut into 1½ " chunks, wash and pat dry.

The Red Chillies : Wipe clean with moist cloth, slit, seed and remove the stems.

The Vegetables : Peel and slice garlic. Peel, wash and finely slice onions. Clean, wash and chop coriander.

The Cumin : Broil the seeds on a *tawa*/griddle.

The Yoghurt : Whisk in a bowl, add red chillies, cumin, coriander powder, turmeric and salt, mix well and reserve for 10 minutes.

Cooking

Heat ghee in a *handi*/pan, add garlic and *bhunno*/stir-fry over medium heat until light golden, add onion, green cardamom and black cardamom, and *bhunno*/stir-fry until onions are golden brown. Then add meat, increase to high heat *bhunno*/stir-fry to sear for 2-3 minutes. Remove *handi*/pan from heat, stir-in yoghurt mixture, return *handi*/pan to heat and *bhunno*/stir-fry over medium heat until the liquid has evaporated. Add water (approx 1 litre/4¼ cups), bring to a boil reduce to low heat, cover and simmer, stirring occasionally, until the meat is cooked and the gravy is of thin sauce consistency. Remove and adjust the seasoning. Garnish with coriander.

EPISODE 007

with Chef Manjit Singh Gill,
WELCOMGROUP

Then came the mother of all fishy stories. This episode show-cased regional fish favourites covering the entire coastline.

Kekrah Peri-Peri

Lobster in Goan Chilli, Tomato and Vinegar Gravy

Ingredients

550g/1¼ lb Lobster Meat (4 Lobsters)
Salt
30ml/2 Tbs Lemon Juice
45ml/2 Tbs Cooking Oil
120g/1 cup Onions

12 flakes Garlic
175g/1 cup Tomatoes
60ml/¼ cup *Sirka*/Malt Vinegar
3.25g/1 Tbs *Taaza Dhania*/Coriander

The *Peri-Peri* Paste

6 Whole Red Chillies
90ml/6 Tbs *Sirka*/Malt Vinegar
15 Black Peppercorns
10 *Lavang*/Cloves
2 sticks *Daalcheeni*/Cinnamon (1")

2g/1 tsp *Jeera*/Cumin Seeds
25g/2½" piece Ginger
10 flakes Garlic
1.5g/1/2 tsp *Haldee*/Turmeric Powder

Serves : 4
Preparation Time : 1:30 hours
Cooking Time : 35 minutes

Preparation

The Lobster : Remove claws and legs, cut into halves—from head to tail—with the tip of a large, sharp knife and then shell. Clean, vein, wash and pat dry. Sprinkle salt and lemon juice, rub to ensure that the meat is evenly coated and reserve for at least 30 minutes.

Wash 4 shell halves. Half fill a large *handi*/pan with water, put the shell upside down and boil until the colour turns orange. Drain and reserve.

The Vegetables : Peel, wash and finely chop onions, including the bulbs (whites; from the garnish) of the spring onions. Peel and finely chop garlic. Remove eyes, wash and finely chop tomatoes. Clean and finely chop coriander.

The Peri-Peri Paste : Salt, seed and soak the red chillies in vinegar overnight. Scrape, wash and roughly cut ginger. Peel garlic. Put these and the remaining ingredients, including the vinegar, in blender, and make a smooth paste.

Cooking

Heat oil in a *kadhi*/wok, add onions, sauté over medium heat until light golden, add garlic, stir for 30 seconds, add tomatoes and stir. Then add the *Peri-Peri* paste, *bhunno*/stir-fry for a minute, add vinegar and water (60ml/¼ cup), reduce to low heat and simmer until the liquid has evaporated. Now add the marinated lobster, *bhunno*/stir-fry for 1-2 minutes or until the lobster is cooked—it should be soft, **not** overcooked, hard and rubbery. Sprinkle coriander, stir, remove and adjust the seasoning.

Doi Maach

Bengali Fish in Mustard-laced Yoghurt Gravy

Ingredients

600g/1 lb 5 oz Fish (*Rahu/Surmai/Pomfret*)
45ml/3 Tbs
45/1½ oz Onions

4 Green Chillies
3.25g/1 Tbs *Taaza Dhania*/Coriander

The Marination

375g/13 oz Yoghurt
20g/3½ tsp Ginger Paste (strain)
8 Dried Whole Red Chillies·

10g/2" piece *Haldee*/Turmeric Root
25ml/5 tsp Lemon Juice

Serves : 4
Preparation Time : 1:10 hours
Cooking Time : 30 minutes

Preparation

The Fish : Scale, clean, cut into 8 equal size darnes, wash and pat dry.

The Vegetables : Peel, wash and finely chop onions. Wash green chillies, halve lengthways, seed and discard the stems. Clean, wash and chop coriander.

The Marination : Slit, seed, discard the stems and soak the red chillies in water overnight. (If fresh red chillies are available, there will be no need to soak them overnight.) Separately soak turmeric in water overnight. Drain, put red chillies in a blender, add a little water and make a smooth paste. Drain, cut the turmeric into smaller pieces, put in a blender, add a little water and grind into a smooth paste.

Whisk yoghurt in a large bowl, add the two pastes and the remaining ingredients, mix well, evenly rub the darnes with this marinade and reserve for 20 minutes.

Cooking

Heat oil in a *handi*/pan to a smoking point, remove and cool. Reheat the oil, add onions, sauté over medium heat until light golden, add the marinated fish, alongwith the marinade, stir carefully, reduce to low heat, cover and simmer until fish is cooked and napped. Remove and adjust the seasoning. Garnish with coriander.

Bhaarla Saaranga

Konkan Coast's Baked Pomfret stuffed with Roe and Coriander Chutney

Ingredients

4 Pomfret (medium)

Cooking Oil for basting

The Marination

7.5g/1¼ tsp Garlic Paste (strain)
7.5g/1¼ tsp Ginger Paste (strain)
1.5g/½ tsp *Daalcheeni*/Cinnamon Powder
3g/1 tsp Red Chilli Powder

3g/1 tsp *Haldee*/Turmeric Powder
120ml/½ cup Lemon Juice
Salt

The Filling

350g/¾ lb Pomfret Roe/Prawns
1.5g/½ tsp *Haldee*/Turmeric Powder
60ml/¼ cup Cooking Oil
12 flakes Garlic
300g/11 oz Onions
6 Green Chillies
15g/1½" piece Ginger

1 *Narial*/Coconut
35g/1 cup *Taaza Dhania*/Coriander
15g/½ oz *Kokum*
1.5g/½ tsp *Daalcheeni*/Cinnamon
Powder
Salt

Serves: 4
Preparation Time: 45 minutes
Cooking Time: 7-8 minutes

Preparation

The Fish : Place on its side and, using a sharp knife, make an incision from under the tail following the periphery all along the stomach to the neck. Then slide the knife carefully and neatly over the bone ensuring that the skin is not pierced on the other side. Flip the fish over and repeat the procedure on the other side to form a similar pocket. Finally, snip off the bone from the tail and the neck and remove it gently to make a boneless pocket. Now clean, trim, wash and pat dry. With a sharp knife, make three incisions across each side without piercing through to the insides of the pockets.

The Marination : Mix all the ingredients in a bowl, evenly rub the fish with this marinade—inside and out—and reserve for 15 minutes.

46

The Filling : Clean roe carefully ensuring that the membranes do not break and wash just as carefully in running water. Put in a *handi*/pan, add half the turmeric and water (approx 480ml/ 2 cups), blanch for 5 minutes after the first boil and drain carefully to ensure that the membranes do not break. (If roe is not available, shell prawns, vein and blanch for 30 seconds with the same ingredients. Then drain, cool and finely chop.If using tiny prawns, just shell and vein.)

Peel and finely chop garlic. Peel, wash and finely chop onions. Wash green chillies, slit, seed, finely chop and discard the stems. Scrape, wash and finely chop ginger. Remove the brown skin and grate coconut. Clean, wash and chop coriander. Clean, wash and chop *kokum*.

Heat oil in a *kadhai*/wok, add garlic, sauté over medium heat until lightly coloured, add onions and sauté until translucent and glossy. Add green chillies and ginger, stir for a few seconds, add coconut and *bhunno*/stir-fry for a minute. Then add coriander, stir, add the remaining turmeric, salt and *kokum*, *bhunno*/stir-fry for 30 seconds, add the blanched roe and stir for a minute. Sprinkle cinnamon powder, stir, remove and adjust the seasoning. Cool and divide into 4 equal portions.

The Stuffing : Spread a portion of the filling in each pomfret, baste, wrap each in a separate piece of silver foil and arrange in a baking tray.

The Oven : Pre-heat to 350°F.

Cooking

Place the tray in the pre-heated oven and bake the wrapped fish for 5-6 minutes. Remove, uncover the fish on one side, return the tray to the oven and bake until the exposed side is light golden.

Meen Moiley

Red Snapper in Malabar Coconut and Lemon Gravy

Ingredients

12 fillets Red Snapper/Pomfret
30 ml/2 Tbs Coconut Oil
4g/1 Tbs *Sarsondaana*/Mustard Seeds
8 flakes Garlic
10g/1" piece Ginger
6 Green Chillies
150g/5 oz Onions
Salt

24 *Kaari Patta*/Curry Leaf
3 Tomatoes (medium)
1.5g/½ tsp *Haldee*/Turmeric Powder
180ml/¾ cup Coconut Milk
  (III extract)*
180 ml/¾ Coconut Milk (II extract)*
120 ml/½ cup Coconut Milk (I extract)*
15ml/1 Tbs Lemon Juice

Serves: 4
Preparation Time: 35 minutes
Cooking Time: 6-7 minutes

Preparation

The Fish : Wash and pat dry.

The Vegetables : Peel and finely chop garlic. Scrape, wash and cut ginger into juliennes. Wash green chillies, slit, seed cut into juliennes and discard the stems. Peel onions, wash and cut roundels and separate the rings. Clean and wash curry leaf. Remove eyes, wash and cut tomatoes into 8 wedges.

Cooking

Heat oil in a *handi*/pan, add mustard seeds, stir over medium heat until they begin to pop, add garlic and ginger, stir for a minute, add green chillies and stir. Add onions and sauté until translucent and glossy, add turmeric—dissolved in 30ml/2 Tbs of water—and stir until the moisture evaporates. Then add fish and the third extract of coconut milk, bring to a boil, reduce to low heat and simmer, turning carefully once, for 2 to 3 minutes, add salt and stir. Now add curry leaf, tomatoes and the second extract, cover and simmer for 1 to 2 minutes. Uncover, remove *handi*/pan from heat, gently (to make sure that the fillets do not break) stir-in the first extract of coconut milk, return *handi*/pan to heat, bring to just under a boil over low heat, sprinkle lemon juice and stir carefully. Remove and adjust the seasoning.

EPISODE 008

with Chef Manjit Singh Gill,
WELCOMGROUP

Daawat treated its viewers to many innovations, like the Combo dish plating kid and chicken together enhancing eye appeal, and providing variety for the palate. A traditional favourite was accompanied by a debutante dish.

Bharwaan Baingan Mutter Ka Shorva

Stuffed Eggplant in Green Pea Gravy

Ingredients

12 Brinjals (round & small)   Cooking oil to shallow fry Brinjals

The Filling

100g/3 oz *Chakka Dahi*/Yoghurt Cheese/   1.5g/½ tsp *Dhania*/Coriander Powder
   Hung Yoghurt   1.5g/½ tsp Red Chilli Powder
15ml/1 Tbs Cooking Oil   A generous pinch of *Haldee*/Turmeric
2 flakes Garlic   Powder
2.5g/¼" piece Ginger   Salt

The Gravy

360g/2¼ cups Green Peas   6g/2 tsp *Dhania*/Coriander Powder
60ml/¼ cup Cooking Oil   10g/2 tsp *Khus-khus*/Poppy Seed Paste
1 stick *Daalcheeni*/Cinnamon (1")   Salt
130g/1 cup Onions   8.5g/1 tsp Green Chilli Paste
10g/1¾ tsp Ginger Paste (strain)   30ml/2 Tbs Cream
10g/1¾ tsp Garlic Paste (strain)

Serves: 4
Preparation Time: 45 minutes
Cooking Time: 40 minutes

Preparation

The Brinjals : Wash, slit into halves without separating the vegetable from the stems. Carefully scoop out a bit of the vegetable from each of the halves to make small pockets.

The Filling : Whisk yoghurt in a bowl. Scrape, wash and finely chop ginger. Peel and finely chop garlic.

The Gravy : Peel, wash and finely chop onions.

Cooking

To prepare the gravy, heat oil in a *handi*/pan, add cinnamon, stir over medium heat for a few seconds, add onions, sauté until onions are light golden, add ginger and garlic pastes, and *bhunno*/stir-fry until onions are golden. Then add coriander (dissolved in 15ml/1 Tbs of water), *bhunno*/stir-fry until the moisture evaporates, add poppy seed paste, *bhunno*/stir-fry until the fat leaves the sides, add green chilli paste and salt, and stir. Now add peas and water (approx. 180ml/¾ cup), bring to a boil, reduce to low heat and simmer until the peas are cooked. Remove, cool, put in a blender and make a purée. Pass the purée through a fine-mesh soup strainer into a separate *handi*/pan, return gravy to heat, bring to a boil, reduce to low heat, stir-in cream and bring to just under a boil. Remove and adjust the seasoning. Keep warm.

To prepare the filling, heat oil in a frying pan, add garlic, sauté over medium heat until lightly coloured, add ginger and sauté for a few seconds. Then add coriander, red chillies and turmeric (dissolved in 30ml/2 Tbs of water) and *bhunno*/stir-fry until the moisture evaporates. Now add yoghurt and salt, *bhunno*/stir-fry for a few seconds. Divide into 24 equal portions.

To prepare the brinjals, heat oil in a frying pan, add brinjals and shallow fry until soft. Remove to absorbent paper to drain excess fat. Stuff each of the pockets with a portion of the filling.

Make a bed of the gravy and arrange the brinjals on top.

Jheenga Nariyal Kharbooja

Prawn, Coconut and Honeydew Salad in Yoghurt, Honey and Dill Dressing

Ingredients

12 Prawns (B-Grade; 30g/1 oz each)
Salt
30ml/2 Tbs Lemon Juice
6 Black Peppercorns
3 *Chotti Elaichi*/Green Cardamom
2 *Lavang*/Cloves

1 *Tej Patta*/Bay Leaf
4 Dried Whole Red Chillies
150g/5 oz Coconut
150g/5 oz Honeydew Melon
2 Lemons

The Dressing

75g/2½ oz *Chakka Dahi*/Yoghurt Cheese
   Hung Yoghurt
75 ml/5 Tbs Cream
1g/1 tsp *Sua/Soya*/Dill

7.5g/1¼ tsp Red Chilli Paste
5ml/1 tsp Honey
Salt
20ml/4 tsp Lemon Juice

Serves : 4
Preparation Time : 1 hour

Preparation

The Prawns : Shell, but retain the tails, vein, wash and pat dry. Wipe red chillies with moist cloth. Put water in a *handi*/pan, add salt, lemon juice, cardamom, peppercorns, cloves, bay leaf and one red chilli, bring to a boil, add prawns and cook for 1-1½ minutes, drain and refrigerate.

The Remaining Red Chillies : Removes stems and break into small pieces for garnish.

The Coconut : Remove the brown skin and scoop out parisiennes.

The Melon : Halve, remove the seeds and scoop out parisiennes.

The Lemon : Wash and cut into stars.

The Dressing : Clean, wash and chop dill. Whisk yoghurt cheese in a bowl, stir-in cream, add drill, red chilli paste, honey, salt and lemon juice, mix until homogenous. Adjust the seasoning.

To Serve : Spread equal quantities of the dressing in each of 4 individual plates at the 6 o'clock position and sprinkle the reserved red chilli pieces on top. Arrange 3 prawns in the middle of each plate in the standing position by spreading the tails into fan shapes and with the head dipping in the dressing. Stack the coconut and melon parisiennes in pyramids on either side of the prawns. Place a lemon star at the 12 o'clock on each plate and serve.

Bhunna Chooza Aur Chaamp

Grilled·Chicken and Kid/Lamb Chop Duet

Ingredients

4 Spring Chicken (350g/13 oz each)
8 *Chaamp*/Kid/Lamb Chops (2-rib)

Butter to grease roasting tray

The Chicken Marination

45ml/3 Tbs Cooking Oil
30ml/2 Tbs Pineapple Juice
6g/2 tsp *Saunf*/Fennel Powder

3g/1 tsp Black Pepper (freshly roasted
&. coarsely ground)
Salt

The Lamb Marination

60ml/¼ cup Malt Vinegar
15g/2½ tsp Raw Papaya Paste
3g/1 tsp Black Pepper (freshly
roasted &. coarsely ground)

1.5g/½ tsp *Daalcheeni*/Cinnamon
Powder
Salt

The Sauce

3.75g/1½ tsp *Saunf*/Fennel Seeds
3g/1 tsp *Jeera*/Cumin Seeds
1.5g/½ tsp *Kaala Namak*/Black Rock
Salt Powder
17.5g/½ cup *Pudhina*/Mint

Salt
20g/1½ Tbs Butter
125g/½ cup Yoghurt
75ml/5 Tbs Cream

Serves: 4
Preparation Time: 1:15 minutes
Cooking Time: 45 minutes

Preparation

The Kid/Lamb Chops : Clean, remove the excess fat and one rib carefully, trim, wash and pat dry.

The Kid/Lamb Marination : Mix all the ingredients, evenly rub chops with this marinade and reserve for 1 hour.

The Spring Chicken : Clean and remove the skin, wash and pat dry. Then prick the entire surface with a fork.

The Chicken Marination : Mix all the ingredients, evenly rub chicken with this marinade and reserve for 30 minutes.

The Fennel and Mint Paste : Put fennel, cumin, black salt, mint and salt in a blender, add water (approx 15ml/1 Tbs) and make a fine paste. Put yoghurt in a bowl, add the paste and whisk until homogenous.

The Oven : Pre-heat to 300°F.

Cooking

Arrange chicken and chops on a greased roasting tray and roast in the pre-heated oven, basting with the drippings at regular intervals, until cooked.

To prepare the sauce, melt butter in a saucepan, add the fennel and mint paste, and bring to just under a boil over medium heat (approx 5-6 minutes), stirring constantly. Then stir-in cream, bring to just under a boil without increasing heat, reduce to low heat and stir until of sauce consistency. Remove and adjust the seasoning.

Serve chicken and chops on a bed of sauce.

EPISODE 009

with Chef Manjit Singh Gill,
WELCOMGROUP

This episode was devoted to discovering the joys of one-dish meals covering the length and breadth of the subcontinent.

We were surprised how many the "ones" were!

Dum Ki Biryani

Aromatic Basmati Rice with Braised Kid/Lamb from Hyderabad

Ingredients

300g/1½ cups *Basmati* Rice
45ml/3 Tbs *Gulaabjal*/Rose Water
5ml/1 tsp Lemon Juice
Salt
20g/2" piece Ginger
2 Green Chillies
15g/½ oz *Taaza Dhania*/Coriander

15g/½ oz *Pudhina*/Mint
1g/2 tsp Saffron
30m½ Tbs Milk
20g/1½ Tbs *Desi Ghee*/Clarified Butter
15g/½ oz Fried Onions (sliced)
Atta/Whole-wheat dough to seal

The *Bouquet Garni*

5 *Chotti Elaichi*/Green Cardamom

5 *Lavang*/Clove

The Meat

300g/11 oz *Dasti*/Shoulder of Kid/Lamb
8 *Seena*/Spare ribs Kid/Lamb
75g/6 Tbs *Desi Ghee*/Clarified Butter
5 *Chotti Elaichi*/Green Cardamom
3 *Lavang*/Cloves
2 sticks *Daalcheeni*/Cinnamon (1")
2 *Tej Patta*/Bay Leaf
50g/½ cup Onions
30g/5 tsp Garlic Paste (strain)
15g/2½ tsp Ginger Paste (strain)

Salt
125g/½ cup Yoghurt
3g/1 tsp *Peeli Mirch*/Yellow Chilli Powder
30m½ Tbs Lemon Juice
60ml/¼ cup Cream
2.25g/¾ tsp *Chotti Elaichi*/
   Green Cardamom Powder
0.75g/¼ tsp *Javitri*/Mace Powder
1 drop *Ittar*

Serves: 4
Preparation Time: 1:30 hours
Cooking Time: 45 minutes

Preparation

The Rice : Pick, wash in running water and soak for 15 minutes. Drain.

The *Bouquet Garni* : Put both the ingredients in a mortar and pound with a pestle to break the spices, fold in a piece of muslin and secure with enough string for it to hang over the rim of the *handi*/pan.

The Saffron : Crush the threads with pestle or the back of spoon, soak in lukewarm milk and then make a paste.

The Kid/Lamb : Peel, wash and slice onions. Put yoghurt in a bowl, add yellow chillies and whisk to mix well.

The Oven : Pre-heat to 350°F.

Cooking

To prepare the rice, boil 1.5 litres/6½ cups of water in a *handi*/pan, add *bouquet garni* and salt, stir, add rice, bring to a boil, add rose water and lemon juice, continue to boil, stirring occasionally, until the rice is nine-tenths cooked. Remove, drain and discard the *bouquet garni*.

To prepare the kid/lamb, heat *ghee* in a *handi*/pan, add green cardamom, cloves, cinnamon and bay leaf, stir over medium heat until cardamom begins to change colour, add onions, *bhunno*/stir-fry until light golden, add the garlic and ginger pastes, *bhunno*/stir-fry until the moisture evaporates. Then add meat, increase to high heat, *bhunno*/stir-fry to sear for 2-3 minutes, reduce to medium heat, *bhunno*/stir-fry until the fat leaves the sides. Remove *handi*/pan from heat, stir-in the yoghurt mixture, return *handi*/pan to heat, *bhunno*/stir-fry until fat leaves the sides. Add stock (or water) and salt, bring to a boil, reduce to low heat, cover and cook, stirring occasionally, until meat is cooked (approx 20 minutes) and half the liquid has evaporated. Remove the meat and pass the gravy through fine muslin or fine mesh soup strainer into a separate *handi*/pan. Sprinkle lemon juice, stir, add cream and half the saffron, stir, adjust the seasoning and return *handi*/pan to heat. Decent and reserve a quarter to the gravy.

Return meat to the simmering gravy, add green cardamom, mace, rose petal and *ittar*, stir, sprinkle ginger, green chillies and mint, arrange three-fourths of the partially cooked rice around the meat, pour on the decanted gravy, evenly spread the remaining rice, evenly sprinkle the saffron on the rice, evenly pour melted *ghee* on the top, cover with a lid and seal with *atta* dough. Heat a thick *tawa*/griddle, place the *handi*/pan on top, and cook on *dum* over very low heat for 14-15 minutes. Remove and break the seal. This can also be done on a hot plate on a cooking range.

Alternatively, after pouring the melted *ghee*, place moist cloth on top, cover with a lid and seal *handi*/pan with *atta*/whole wheat dough. Then cook on *dum* in the pre-heated oven for 18-20 minutes. Remove and break the seal. Serve with *Burrhani*.

Dhansak

Parsi Kid/Lamb and Lentil Stew Served with Lamb Kavab and Brown Rice

Ingredients

The Mutton

300g/11 oz *Dasti*/Shoulder of Kid/Lamb
300g/11 oz *Seena*/Breast of Kid/Lamb
100g/½ cup *Toor Daal*
100g/½ cup *Masoor Daal*
250g/9 oz *sarson*/Mustard Leaf

100g/3 oz *Baingan*/Brinjals
60g/2 oz *Petha*/Red Pumpkin
15g/½ oz Parsley
4 Lemons

The Tempering

75ml/5 Tbs Cooking Oil
100g/3 oz Onions
175g/1 cup Tomatoes
9g/1 Tbs *Dhansak Masala*

3g/1 tsp *Haldee*/Turmeric Powder
3g/1 tsp Red Chilli Powder
Salt

The *Dhansak Masala*

45g/1½ oz *Lavang*/Cloves
45g/1½ oz *Motti Elaichi*/Black
  Cardamom

45g/1½ oz *Kasoori Methi*/Dried
  Fenugreek Leaf

The Ginger-Garlic Paste

30g/3" piece Ginger
30g/1 oz Garlic

10g/5 tsp *Zeera*/Cumin Seeds
8 Dried Whole Red Chillies

The *Kavab*

300g/11 oz *Kheema*/Kid/Lamb Mince
60g/2 oz Onions
5g/1½ Tbs *Taaza Dhania*/Coriander
5g/2½ Tbs *Pudhina*/Mint
2 Green Chillies
2 slices Bread
5g/1 tsp Ginger Paste (strain)

5g/1 tsp Garlic Paste (strain)
7.5ml/1½ tsp Worcester Sauce
1 Egg
A pinch of *Haldee*/Turmeric Powder
Salt
25g/1 oz Breadcrumbs
Cooking Oil to deep fry

61

The Rice

120g/4 oz *Basmati* Rice
20g/4 tsp Sugar
30m½ Tbs Cooking Oil
100g/3 oz Onions
4 *Chotti Elaichi*/Green Cardamom
4 *Lavang*/Cloves

2 sticks *Daalcheeni*/Cinnamon (1")
2 *Tej Patta*/Bay Leaf
2g/1 tsp *Jeera*/Cumin Seeds
Salt
Cooking Oil to deep fry onions

Serves: 4
Preparation Time: 1:50 hours
Cooking Time: 1:25 hours

Preparation

The Meat : Clean, cut into 1" chunks, wash and pat dry.

The Lentils : Pick, wash in running water and soak both *daal* for 30 minutes. Drain.

The Vegetables : Peel, wash and cut pumpkin into small cubes. Remove stems, wash and cut brinjals into small cubes. Clean, wash and roughly chop mustard leaves and parsley. Wash and cut lemons into wedges.

The Tempering : Peel, wash and slice onions. Remove eyes, wash and chop tomatoes.

The *Dhansak Masala* : Sun-dry cloves and cardamom, put in a mortar and pound with a pestle to make fine powder. Crush fenugreek leaf between the palms and mix with cloves and cardamom. Alternatively, put all the ingredients in a grinder and, employing short pulses, grind to a fine powder. Sift and store in a sterilised, dry and airtight container. Yield: 125g/¼ lb.

The Ginger-Garlic Paste : Scrape, wash and roughly cut ginger. Peel garlic. Wipe red chillies, clean with moist cloth and discard the stems. Put all the ingredients in a blender, add water (approx 30m/½ Tbs), make a paste and remove.

The *Kavab* : Peel, wash and finely chop onions. Clean, wash and chop coriander and mint. Wash green chillies, slit, seed, finely chop and discard the stems. Slice off the edges, soak bread in water and squeeze. Put all the ingredients, except breadcrumbs and oil, in a bowl and mix well. Divide into 20 equal portions, make balls and roll in breadcrumbs.

Heat oil in a *kadhai*/wok and deep fry the *kavab* over low heat until cooked and brown.

The Oven : Pre-heat to 375°F.

The Rice : Pick rice, wash in running water, soak for 15 minutes and drain. Peel, wash and slice onions. Heat oil in a *kadhai*/wok, add half onions and deep fry over medium heat until brown. Remove to absorbent paper to drain excess fat.

Cooking

There are two ways to cook the rice.

The First : Put sugar in a *handi*/pan, caramelise until brown, add water (approx 60ml/¼ cup) and simmer until smooth. Heat oil (30ml/2 Tbs) in a *handi*/pan, add the remaining onions, sauté over medium heat until brown, add cardamom, cloves, cinnamon, bay leaf and cumin, and stir for a few seconds. Then add rice and salt, stir for a minute, add the prepared caramel and water (approx 240ml/1 cup), bring to a boil, reduce to low heat and simmer until the liquid has evaporated. Place moist cloth (muslin or cheesecloth) on top, cover with a lid and keep aside.

The Second : Heat oil in a *handi*/pan, add green cardamom, cloves, cinnamon, bay leaf and cumin, stir over medium heat until the cumin begins to pop, add sugar and caramelise, stirring constantly, until it turns a rich brown, ensuring it does not get burnt and emit an odour. Then add rice and salt, *bhunno*/stir-fry for a minute, add just enough water to cook (the rice should not be soggy). When it comes to a galloping boil, cover the *handi*/pan and pour some water on the lid, reduce to low heat and cook on *dum* for 15 minutes or until rice is done.

To cook the meat, put meat, the two *daal*, mustard leaf, brinjals, pumpkin and parsley in a *handi*/pan, add water (approx 780ml/3¼ cups), bring to a boil, reduce to low heat and simmer, stirring occasionally, until the meat is cooked. Remove *handi*/pan from heat, remove the meat, return *handi*/pan to heat and cook the remaining ingredients over low heat, mashing the lentils and vegetables with the back of a ladle until homogenous. Return meat to *handi*/pan, stir, reduce to very low heat and continue to simmer, stirring occasionally.

To prepare the tempering, heat oil in a *kadhai*/wok, add onions, sauté over medium heat until brown, add the ginger-garlic paste and *bhunno*/stir-fry until the fat leaves the sides. Then add tomatoes, *bhunno*/stir-fry until soft, add *dhansak masala*, turmeric, red chillies and salt, and *bhunno*/stir-fry for a minute. Pour the tempering on the simmering meat, *daal* and vegetable mixture, stir well, bring to a boil, reduce to low heat and simmer, stirring occasionally, for 5 minutes. Remove and adjust the seasoning. Serve with brown rice and *kavab*.

Chutney Pulao

Aromatic Basmati Rice with Potatoes in Mint and Coriander Chutney

Ingredients

300g/1½ cups *Basmati* Rice
Salt
5ml/1 tsp Lemon Juice
5g/½" piece Ginger (juliennes)
12 *Pudhina*/Mint Leaf

200g/7 oz Baby Potatoes
   (peel & boil until *al dente*)
Atta/Whole-wheat dough to seal

The *Bouquet* Garni

3 *Chotti Elaichi*/Green Cardamom

3 *Lavang*/Cloves

The Chutney

100g/3 oz *Taaza Dhania*/Coriander
   (roughly chop)
50g/1½ cups *Pudhina*/Mint
   (roughly chop)
1 *Kairi*/Raw Mango (roughly chop)
4 Green Chillies (slit & seed)

15g/1½ Tbs *Anaardana*/Dried
   Pomegranate Seeds
3g/1 tsp *Zeera*/Cumin Seeds
3g /1 tsp *Saunf*/Fennel Powder
Salt

The Stock

50g/¼ cup *Desi Ghee*/Clarified Butter
360ml/1½ cup Vegetable Stock
1.5g/½ tsp *Peeli*/Yellow Chilli Powder

15ml/1 Tbs Lemon Juice
45ml/3 Tbs Milk

Serves: 4
Preparation Time: 1:15 hours
Cooking Time: 20-25 minutes

Preparation

The Rice : Pick, wash in running water and soak for 15 minutes. Drain.

The *Bouquet Garni* : Put both the ingredients in a mortar and pound with a pestle to break the spices, fold in a piece of muslin and secure with enough string for it to hang over the rim of the *handi*/pan.

The Potatoes : Peel, put in a *handi*/pan, cover with enough water, boil until cooked, ensuring they do not become soft. Drain and cool.

The Chutney : Put all the ingredients in a blender and make a smooth purée. (To bring out the best flavour, make the chutney with a *sil-batta*.) Then add boiled potatoes to the chutney and mix well.

The Jhol : Heat *ghee* in a *handi*/pan, add stock bring to a boil over medium heat, reduce to very low heat, add yellow chillies, stir until fully incorporated, add lemon juice, stir, add cream, stir and remove.

The Oven : Pre-heat to 350°F.

Cooking

To prepare the rice, boil 1.5 litres/6¼ cups of water in a *handi*/pan, add the *bouquet garni* and salt, stir, add rice, bring to a boil, reduce to medium heat, add lemon juice and continue to boil, stirring occasionally, until nine-tenths cooked. Drain, discard the *bouquet garni*. Return the same *handi*/pan to (medium) heat, put half the *jhol* in the same *handi*/pan, spread a third of the boiled rice, arrange half the potatoes and chutney, ginger and mint evenly on top. Spread another third of the rice and arrange the remaining potatoes and chutney, ginger and mint evenly on top. Spread the remaining rice, pour on the remaining *jhol*. Heat a thick *tawa*/griddle, place the *handi*/pan on top, and cook on *dum* over very low heat for 8-10 minutes. Remove and break the seal. This can also be done on a hot plate on a cooking range.

Alternatively, after pouring the remaining *jhol,* place moist cloth on top, cover with a lid and seal *handi*/pan with *atta*/whole wheat dough. Then cook on *dum* in the pre-heated oven for 10–12 minutes. Remove and break the seal.

Daal Baati Churma

Wheat Cakes with Lentils and Candied Sugar

Ingredients

The *Daal*

60g/2 oz *Channa Daal*
60g/2 oz *Masoor Daal*
60g/2 oz *Toor Daal*
60g/2 oz *Moong Daal* (husked)
60g/2 oz *Urad Daal* (husked)
20g/1½ Tbs *Desi Ghee*/Clarified Butter
3g/1½ tsp *Zeera*/Cumin Seeds
50g/½ cup Onions

10g/1¾ tsp Ginger Paste (strain)
10g/1¾ tsp Garlic Paste (strain)
6g/2 tsp *Dhania*/Coriander Powder
4.5g/1½ tsp Red Chilli Powder
1.5g/½ tsp *Haldee*/Turmeric Powder
Salt
6.5g/2 Tbs *Taaza Dhania*/Coriander

The Tempering

20g/1½ Tbs *Desi Ghee*/Clarified Butter
A generous pinch of *Heeng*/Asafoetida

2g/1 tsp *Jeera*/Cumin Seeds

The *Baati*

500g/3½ cups *Atta*/Whole-wheat Flour
6g/1 tsp Baking Powder
7.5g/1½ tsp Salt

100g/½ cup *Desi Ghee*/Clarified Butter
   to soak *Baati*

The *Churma*

145g/1 cup *Atta*/Whole-wheat Flour
45g/1½ oz *Desi Ghee*/Clarified Butter
30ml/2 Tbs Milk
Desi Ghee/Clarified Butter to deep fry
35g/2½ Tbs Castor Sugar

6 Almonds
15g/½ oz *Mishri*/Candied Sugar
5g/1 Tbs Coconut
3g/1 tsp *Chotti Elaichi*/Green Cardamom
   Powder

Serves: 4
Preparation Time: 1:45 hours
Cooking Time: 35-40 minutes

Preparation

The *Daal* : Pick, wash in running water, drain and soak all five *daal* in a panful of water for 30 minutes. Drain at the time of cooking. Peel, wash and slice onions. Clean, wash and chop coriander.

The Tempering : Dissolve asafoetida in 15ml/1 Tbs of water.

The *Baati* : Sift *atta*, baking powder and salt into a *paraat*/tray or onto the work surface, make a bay, add melted *ghee* and start mixing gradually with the tips of the fingers. When fully mixed, add water (approx. for 20 minutes). Then divide into 20 equal portions, make balls, cover with moist cloth and reserve for 10 minutes. Now flatten the balls slightly to make *pedha* (approx. 2½ " diameter). Dust a baking tray with flour, arrange the *pedha* in it, cover with moist cloth and reserve until ready to bake.

The Oven[1]: Pre-heat to 200°F.

The *Churma* : Sift *atta* into a *paraat*/tray or onto the work surface, make a bay, add 30g/1 oz of melted *ghee* and start mixing gradually. When fully incorporated, add milk, knead to make hard dough, make patties, cover with moist cloth and reserve.

Heat *ghee* in a *kadhai*/wok and deep-fry the patties over low-medium heat until golden. Remove, cool, transfer to a mortar and pound into a coarse powder with a pestle. Remove, add 15g/½ oz of the reserved *ghee* and the remaining ingredients, mix well, sprinkle a little water on the mixture, make *laddoo*—balls—with moist hands, cover and keep aside.

Cooking

Uncover and put the baking tray in the pre-heated oven for 30-35 minutes.

To prepare the *daal*, heat *ghee* in a *handi*/pan, add cumin, stir over medium heat until it begins to pop, add onions and sauté until light golden. Add the ginger and garlic pastes, sauté until onions are golden. Then add coriander powder, red chilli and turmeric—dissolved in 30ml/2 Tbs of water—and *bhunno*/stir-fry until the moisture evaporates. Now add 720ml/3 cups of water, stir, add the drained lentils and salt, stir, bring to a boil, reduce to low heat and simmer until cooked (approx 25-30 minutes).

To prepare the tempering, heat *ghee* in a frying pan, add asafoetida, stir over medium heat for a few seconds, add cumin and stir until it begins to pop. Remove, pour over the *daal*, stir, remove and adjust the seasoning. Sprinkle fresh coriander.

Remove the *baati* from the oven, press the top to crack open the crust and soak in melted *ghee* (to soak *baati*). If you are *ghee*-conscious, soak for 10-12 seconds, remove and serve with *daal* and *churma*.

1. The traditional way is to bake the *baati* for 20-25 minutes in *goya*/cow-dung cakes.

EPISODE 010

with Chef R.P.S. Malhotra,
WELCOMGROUP

Most of us have forgotten that Mughlai cuisine is not confined to meaty fare. The Mughal influence is strong in use of fruit specially pomegranate to enhance the sensuous delight. This episode played around nostalgically with Kandahari *anaar*.

Mahi Dum Anaari

Baby Pomfret stuffed with Squid, Scallops and Pomegranate in Fenugreek-tempered Yoghurt Gravy

Ingredients

8 fillets Baby Pomfret

The Marination

30g/5¼ tsp Garlic Paste (strain)   30ml/2 Tbs Lemon Juice
20g/3½ tsp Ginger Paste (strain)   Salt

The Filling

120g/¼ lb Prawns   2 Green Chillies
90g/3 oz Squid   1.5g/1½ tsp Fresh Oregano
90g/3 oz Scallops   2 slices White Bread
60g/2 oz *Taaza Anaar*/Fresh Pomegranate 30ml/2 Tbs Cream
5g/½" piece Ginger   Salt
3.25g/1 Tbs *Taaza Dhania*/Coriander

The Gravy

45ml/3 Tbs Mustard Oil   30g/2 Tbs Fried Garlic Paste
1g/¼ tsp *Methidaana*/Fenugreek Seeds   1 litre/4¼ cups Fish Stock
30g/5¼ tsp Garlic Paste (strain)   Salt
15g/2½ tsp Ginger Paste (strain)   1.5g/½ tsp *Chotti Elaichi*/Green
3g/1 tsp *Haldee*/Turmeric Powder   Cardamom Powder
1.5g/½ tsp Red Chilli Powder   1g/⅓ tsp *Javitri*/Mace Powder
120g/½ cup Yoghurt   20m/¼ tsp Cream
80g/5 Tbs Fried Onion Paste

Serves: 4
Preparation Time: 1:45 hours
Cooking Time: 25 minutes

Preparation

The Fish Fillets : Clean, trim, wash and pat dry.

The Marination : Mix all the ingredients, evenly rub the fish fillets with this marinade and reserve for 10 minutes.

The Filling : Shell prawns, vein, wash and pat dry. Clean squid and scallops, wash and pat dry. Put these ingredients in a food processor/mincer and make a coarse mousse. Scrape, wash and finely chop ginger. Clean, wash and finely chop coriander and oregano. Wash green chillies, slit, seed, finely chop and discard stems. Remove the crust, soak bread in cream and then mash. Put these ingredients in a bowl, add the remaining ingredients, mix well and divide into 4 equal portions.

The Stuffing : Spread a portion of the filling on 4 of the fish fillets, cover with the remaining fillets to make "sandwiches" and keep aside. Pre-heat a charcoal/electric grill, brush the grill with oil, arrange the "sandwiches" on top and grill each side for 2 minutes, turning every minute to obtain criss-crossed grill marks. Remove and keep aside.

The Gravy : Whisk yoghurt in a bowl.

Cooking

Heat mustard oil to a smoking point in a *handi*/pan, remove *handi*/pan from heat and sprinkle a little water carefully to bring the temperature down (alternatively, remove and cool the oil). Reheat the oil, add fenugreek, stir over medium heat until it begins to pop, add the garlic and ginger pastes, *bhunno*/stir-fry for a minute, add turmeric, red chillies and salt (all dissolved in 30ml/2 Tbs of water), and stir until liquid has evaporated. Remove *handi*/pan from heat, stir-in yoghurt, return handi/pan to heat and *bhunno*/stir-fry until fat leaves the sides. Now add fried onion paste, stir for a few seconds, add fried garlic paste and *bhunno*/stir- fry until fat leaves the sides. Then add fish stock, bring to a boil, reduce to low heat and simmer, stirring occasionally, until reduced by half. Remove and pass gravy through a fine mesh soup strainer into a separate *handi*/pan. Return gravy to heat, gently add the grilled fish and bring to a boil. Sprinkle cardamom and mace, and stir carefully. Stir-in cream, remove and adjust the seasoning.

72

Phaldari Kofta

Raw Banana Kofta stuffed with Morels and Oyster Mushrooms in Cashewnut and Tomato Gravy

Ingredients

200g/7 oz Raw Bananas
150g/5 oz Potatoes
3g/1 tsp *Amchoor*/Mango Powder
1.5g/½ tsp Red Chilli Powder
1.5g/½ tsp *Chotti Elaichi*/Green
   Cardamom Powder

0.75g/¼ tsp *Daalcheeni*/Cinnamon
   Powder
0.75g/¼ tsp *Javitri*/Mace Powder
Salt
Sesame/Cooking Oil to deep fry *kofta*

The Filling

8 Morels (large)
60g/2 oz Oyster Mushrooms
60g/2 oz Button Mushrooms
15ml/1 Tbs Sesame Oil
3.25g/1 Tbs *Taaza Dhania*/Coriander
   (or 12.5g/1Tbs Butter)

10g/1" piece Ginger
2 Green Chillies
3g/1 tsp Five Spice Powder
Salt

The Gravy

60/2 oz *Desi Ghee*/Clarified Butter
5 *Chotti Elaichi*/Green Cardamom
3 *Lavang*/Cloves
2 sticks *Daalcheeni*/Cinnamon (1")
2 *Tej Patta*/Bay Leaf
20g/3½ tsp Garlic Paste (strain)
20g/3½ tsp Ginger Paste (strain)
1.5g/½ tsp Red Chilli Powder

45g/3 Tbs Cashewnut Paste
80g/5 Tbs Fried Onion Paste
360ml/1½ cups Fresh Tomato Purée
60ml/¼ cup Cream
1.5g/½ tsp *Chotti Elaichi*/Green
   Cardamom Powder
A generous pinch of *Kasoori Methi*/Dried
   Fenugreek Leaf

Serves : 4
Preparation Time : 2:15 hours
Cooking Time : 45 minutes

Preparation

The Raw Bananas & Potatoes : Boil, cool, peel, mash, mix, add the remaining ingredients, mix well, divide into 8 equal portions and make balls.

73

The Filling : Remove stems, wash morels in running water to remove grit, drain, soak in lukewarm water for 15 minutes, drain and chop. Remove the earthy base of the oyster and button mushrooms' stalks, wash in running water to remove grit, drain and chop. Scrape, wash and finely chop ginger. Wash green chillies, slit, seed, finely chop and discard stems. Clean, wash and finely chop coriander.

Heat oil (or melt butter) in a frying pan, add ginger and green chillies, stir over medium heat for a minute, add all the mushrooms, and cook until the liquid has evaporated. Then add five spice powder and salt, stir, add coriander, stir, remove and adjust the seasoning. Divide into 8 equal portions.

The Stuffing : Flatten each ball between the palms, place a portion of the filling in the middle, make oval-shaped *kofta*.

The Kofta : Heat oil in a *kadhai*/wok and deep fry over medium heat until golden brown. Remove to absorbent paper to drain the excess fat.

Cooking

Heat *ghee* in a *handi*/pan, add cardamom, cloves, cinnamon and bay leaves, stir over medium heat until cardamom begins to change colour, add the garlic and ginger pastes (dissolved in 100ml/7 Tbs of water), and *bhunno*/stir-fry until the moisture has evaporated. Then add red chillies (dissolved in 30ml/2 Tbs of water), *bhunno*/stir-fry until the fat leaves the sides and the masala becomes grainy, add cashewnut paste and *bhunno*/stir-fry until the fat leaves the sides. Now add fried onion paste, *bhunno*/stir-fry until fat leaves the sides, add tomato purée and salt, *bhunno*/stir-fry until a sheen appears on the surface. Remove, pass through a fine mesh soup strainer into a separate *handi*/pan, return gravy to heat, add *kofta*, bring to a boil, reduce to low heat and stir-in cream. Sprinkle cardamom and *kasoori methi*, stir carefully, remove and adjust the seasoning.

74

Seekh-e-Dum Pukht

Tandoor Grilled Chicken Sausage stuffed with Crab Meat

Ingredients

200g/7 oz Chicken Mince (10% fat)
4 flakes Garlic
2.5g/¼ " piece Ginger
1 Green Chilli
1g/1 tsp *Taaza Dhania*/Coriander
A generous pinch of *Shahi Jeera*/Black
  Cumin Seeds

A pinch of *Chotti Elaichi*/Green
  Cardamom Powder
A pinch of *Javitri*/Mace Powder
Salt

The Mousse

120g/4 oz Crab Meat
90g/3 oz Prawns (small)
15ml/1 Tbs Sesame/Cooking Oil
1g/¼ tsp *Sarsondaana*/Black
  Mustard Seeds

1 Whole Red Chilli (preferably fresh)
8 *Kaari Patta*/Curry Leaf
1.5g/½ tsp *Chakriphool*/Star
  Anise Powder
Salt

The Sauce

240ml/1 cup Clear Chicken Stock
30ml/2 Tbs Cream
A pinch of *Shahi*
A pinch of *Chotti Elaichi*/Green
  Cardamom Powder

A pinch of Black Pepper (freshly roasted
& coarsely ground)
1 drop of *Kewra*
Salt

Serves : 4
Preparation Time : 1:30 hours
Cooking Time : 15 minutes

Preparation

The Chicken Mince : Peel and finely chop garlic. Scrape, wash and finely chop ginger. Wash green chillies, slit, seed, finely chop and discard stems. Clean, wash and finely chop coriander. Mix these and the remaining ingredients with the mince in a bowl and make a ball.

The Skewering : Using a moist hand, spread the ball by pressing along the length of the skewer (1½″ diameter) and then, moistening the hands again, smoothen the surface and shape the edges.

The Grilling : Roast in a moderately hot *tandoor* for 3 minutes or until light golden. Or on a moderately hot grill for approximately the same time. Or, in a pre-heated oven, (275°F) for 3-4 minutes. Remove the *kebab* from the skewer and keep aside.

The Mousse : Shell prawns, vein, wash, pat dry, put in a bowl, add crab meat and mix well. Put the mixture in a food processor/blender and make a smooth mousse. Wash red chillies, slit, seed, chop and discard stems. (If using dried red chilli, refresh in water until soft.) Clean, wash and chop curry leaf.

Heat oil in a frying pan, add mustard seeds and stir over medium heat until they begin to crackle, add red chillies and curry leaves, stir for a few seconds, remove and pour over the crab and prawn mixture. Sprinkle the remaining ingredients and mix well. Remove, adjust the seasoning and transfer to a piping bag. Then pipe the mousse into the chicken *seekh* and wrap tightly in cling film.

Cooking

To finish the *seekh*, boil water in *iddli* or any other steamer and steam the wrapped *kebab* for 10-12 minutes. Remove, and cut into 4 equal size pieces.

Meanwhile, to prepare the sauce, put chicken stock in a *handi*/pan, bring to a boil, reduce to low heat and simmer, removing scum at regular intervals, until reduced by a third. Stir-in cream, add the remaining ingredients, stir, remove and adjust the seasoning. Pour the sauce over the *kebab* and serve.

Paneer Kandahari

Cottage Cheese "Sandwiches" in Yoghurt and Tomato Gravy

Ingredients

The Paneer

16 slices Paneer (3½" x 2½" x 1/8")
30g/1 oz Flour

30g/1 oz Cornflour
Cooking Oil to deep fry *paneer*

The Filling

60g/2 oz Pomegranate
60g/1 oz *Paneer*/Cottage Cheese
45g/3 oz Cheese (processed/cheddar)
3.25g/1 Tbs *Taaza Dhania*/Coriander
5g/½" piece Ginger
4 Green Chillies

1g/¾ tsp *Shahi Jeera*/Black Cumin Seeds
1.5g/½ tsp Black Pepper (freshly roasted
& coarsely ground)
Salt
0.25g/½ tsp *Zaafraan*/Saffron

The Gravy

45ml/3 Tbs Mustard Oil
20g/3½ tsp Garlic Paste (strain)
10g/1¾ tsp Ginger Paste (strain)
3g/1 tsp *Dhania*/Coriander Powder
3g/1 tsp Yellow Chilli Powder
1.5g/½ tsp *Haldee*/Turmeric Powder
60g/¼ cup Yoghurt
90g/3 oz Fried Onion Paste
90g/3 oz Fresh Tomato Purée

Salt
1.5g/½ tsp *Moti Elaichi*/Black
Cardamom Powder
0.75g/¼ tsp *Daalcheeni*/Cinnamon
Powder
A generous pinch of *Kasoori Methi*/Dried
Fenugreek Leaf Powder
30ml/2 Tbs Cream

The Garnish

30g/1 oz Pomegranate

Serves : 4
Preparation Time : 1 hour
Cooking Time : 45 minutes

Preparation

The *Paneer* : Cut the slices with an oval cutter and reserve the trimmings for the stuffing. Sift flour and cornflour into a bowl, add water (approx. 60ml/¼ cup) and mix to make a thin batter.

The Filling : Mash *paneer*. Grate cheese. Clean, wash and finely chop coriander. Scrape, wash and finely chop ginger. Wash green chillies, slit, seed, finely chop and discard stems. Sun-dry saffron and then grind into a powder. Put these ingredients in a bowl, add the remaining ingredients, mix well and divide into 8 equal portions.

The Stuffing : Spread a portion of the filling on 8 of the *paneer* ovals, cover with the remaining ovals to make "sandwiches" and keep aside. Heat oil in a *kadhai*/wok, dip the "sandwiches" in the batter and deep fry over medium heat until light golden. Remove to absorbent paper to drain excess fat.

The Gravy : Whisk yoghurt in a bowl.

Cooking

Heat mustard oil to a smoking point in a *handi*/pan, remove *handi*/pan from heat and sprinkle a little water carefully to bring the temperature down (alternatively, remove and cool the oil). Reheat the oil, add the garlic and ginger pastes, *bhunno*/stir-fry until the moisture evaporates, add coriander, yellow chilli and turmeric powders, (dissolved in 45ml/3 Tbs of water), *bhunno*/stir-fry until the moisture evaporates. Remove *handi*/pan from heat, stir-in yoghurt, return *handi*/pan to heat and *bhunno*/stir-fry until the fat leaves the sides. Add the fried onion paste, *bhunno*/stir-fry until the fat leaves the sides, add tomato purée and *bhunno*/stir-fry until the fat leaves the sides. Then add water (approx. 1 litre/4¼ cups) and salt, bring to a boil, reduce to low heat and simmer, stirring occasionally, until of medium-thick sauce consistency. Now gently add the fried paneer "sandwiches" and simmer until the gravy is of sauce consistency. Sprinkle black cardamom, cinnamon powders and *kasoori methi*, stir carefully, stir-in cream, remove and adjust the seasoning. Garnish with pomegranate.

EPISODE 011

with Chef R.P.S. Malhotra,
WELCOMGROUP

There was a time when the city of Lahore was considered the Paris of the orient. The seat of empire attracted men of talent in diverse fields and not surprisingly became the Mecca of foodlovers. Mastercooks here matched the best in the land in their creativity. A touch of elegance became the halmark of the city's cuisine and transformed the simplest to the sublime. *Lahori Aloo* is one such dish.

Pista ka Saalan is a dish that has a reputation of being the favourite of the princes. The recipe is purloined from the repertoire of a hakim who used it not to cure the jaded palate of his patients but to restore to them their vigour and vitality!

Gushtaba is the crowning glory of the Kashmiri *waazvan*. The dish is conventionally made with mutton painstakingly pounded with a wooden mallet. We prepared this for vegetarians with nadru — lotus stems — much favoured by the residents of the valley. Raminder Malhotra's exertions were amply rewarded by the ecstatic sighs that saluted the sublime dish.

Lahori Aloo

Potatoes in Fried Onion and Yoghurt Gravy

Ingredients

8 Potatoes (medium)
Mustard Oil to deep fry
50g/¼ Cup *Desi Ghee*/Clarified Butter
2g/1 tsp *Jeera*/Cumin Seeds
15g/2½ tsp Garlic Paste (strain)
10g/1¾ tsp Ginger Paste (strain)
200g/7 oz Yoghurt
3g/1 tsp Red Chilli Powder
30g/1 oz Almond Paste

120g/4 oz Fried Onion Paste
Salt
1.5g/½ tsp *Chotti Elaichi*/Green
   Cardamon Powder
0.75g/¼ *Javitri*/Mace Powder
8 Almonds
12 Raisins
3.25g/1 Tbs *Taaza Dhania*/Coriander

Serves: 4
Preparation Time: 1 hour
Cooking Time: 30 minutes

Preparation

The Potatoes : Peel, wash, halve, cut the edges and soak in water for 10 minutes.

Heat oil in a *kadhai*/wok to a point, carefully sprinkle a little water to bring down the temperature or remove *kadhai*, cool, reheat, drain and add potatoes, deep fry over medium heat until light golden, remove to absorbent paper to drain the excess fat.

The Yoghurt : Put in a bowl, add red chillies and whisk until homogenous.

The Garnish : Blanch almonds for 5-6 minutes, drain, cool, peel and slice. Soak raisins in water for 10 minutes and drain. Clean, wash and chop coriander.

Cooking

Melt *ghee* in a *handi*/pan, add cumin, stir over medium heat until it beings to pop, add garlic and ginger pastes, stir for a minute. Remove *handi*/pan from heat, stir-in the yoghurt mixture, return *handi*/pan to heat and *bhunno*/stir-fry until specks of fat begin to appear on the surface.

Then add almond paste, stir until fully incorporated, add fried onion paste, *bhunno*/stir-fry until the fat leaves the sides, add salt, stir, add water (approx 480ml/2 cups), bring to a boil, reduce to low heat and simmer, stirring occasionally, for 4-5 minutes. Now add the fried potatoes, bring to a boil, reduce to low heat, sprinkle cardamom and mace, stir carefully, cover with a lid, seal with *atta* (whole-wheat) dough and simmer for 5-6 minutes. Remove *handi*/pan from heat, break the seal and adjust the seasoning.

Pista Ka Saalan

Kid/Lamb in Pistachio Gravy

Ingredients

900g/2 lb *Raan*/Leg of Kid/Lamb
225g/8 oz Pistachios
75g/6 Tbs *Desi Ghee*/Clarified Butter
5 *Chotti Elaichi*/Green Cardamom
3 *Lavang*/Cloves
2 sticks *Daalcheeni*/Cinnamon (1")
1½ flower *Javitri*/Mace
90g/3 oz Onions
30g/5¼ tsp Garlic Paste (strain)
20g/3½ tsp Ginger Paste (strain)
Salt

160g/5 oz Yoghurt
4.5g/1½ tsp *Dhania*/Coriander Powder
3g/1 tsp *Peeli Mirch*/Yellow Chilli Powder
1.5g/½ tsp *Haldee*/Turmeric Powder
60g/2 oz Fried Onion Paste
1 litre/4¼ cups Kid/Lamb Stock (or water)
1.5g/½ tsp *Chotti Elaichi*/Green
    Cardamom Powder
0.75g/¼ *Javitri*/Mace Powder
0.5g/½ tsp *Zaafraan*/Saffron
1 drop *Kewra*

Serves: 4
Preparation Time: 1 hour
Cooking Time: 1:30 minutes

Preparation

The Kid/Lamb : Clean, bone, cut into 1½ cubes, wash and pat dry.

The Pistachio : Blench in boiling water for 3 minutes, drain, cool, peel, put half in a blender, add 45 ml/3 Tbs of water and make a smooth paste. Halve the remaining pistachio and reserve for garnish.

The Gravy : Peel, wash and slice onions. Put yoghurt in a bowl, add coriander, yellow chillies and turmeric, and whisk to homogenize. Crush the saffron threads with a pestle or back of spoon, reserve in 30 ml/2 Tbs of lukewarm water and then make a paste.

Cooking

Melt *ghee* in a *handi*/pan, add green cardamon, cloves, cinnamon and mace, stir over medium heat until the cardamom beings to change colour, add onions, sauté until translucent and glossy, add the garlic and ginger paste, *bhunno*/stir-fry to sear for 2-3 minutes, reduce to low heat, and salt, stir, cover and simmer, stirring occasionally, for 15 minutes, adding a little water if required. Uncover, increase to medium heat and *bhunno*/stir-fry until the liquid, if any, evaporates. Remove *handi*/pan from heat, stir-in the yoghurt mixture, return *handi*/pan to heat, *bhunno*/stir-fry until the fat leaves the sides. Now add fried onion paste, *bhunno*/stir-fry until the fat leaves the sides, add the pistachio paste, *bhunno*/stir-fry for a minute, add stock (or water), bring to a boil, reduce to low heat, cover and simmer, stirring occasionally, until the meat is cooked. Uncover, remove the meat pieces and pass the gravy through a fine mesh soup strainer into a separate *handi*/pan. Return gravy to heat, bring to a boil, reduce to low heat, return meat pieces to gravy and simmer, stirring occasionally, until gravy is of medium thick sauce consistency. Sprinkle the cardamom and mace powders, stir, remove, add saffron and *kewra*, stir and adjust the seasoning. Sprinkle the reserved pistachio at the time to serve.

Nadar "Gushtaba"

Lotus Stem Kofta stuffed with Figs and Walnuts in Almond Gravy

Ingredients

The Kofta

4 *Nadru/Bhein*/Lotus Roots
400g/14 oz *Paneer*/Cottage Cheese
30ml/2 Tbs Lemon Juice
9g/1 Tbs *Saunf*/Fennel Powder
3g/1 tsp *Saunth*/Dried Ginger Powder

3g/1 tsp Black Pepper (freshly roasted & coarsely ground)
6.5g/1 Tbs *Arrowroot*/Cornflour
Salt

The Filling

1.25g/½ tsp *Motti Elaichi*/Black Cardamom Seeds
0.5g/1 tsp *Zaafraan*/Saffron
15ml/1 tsp Milk
8 *Anjeer*/Figs (dried)

8 Walnut Halves
3.25g/1 Tbs *Taaza Dhania*/Coriander
2 Green Chillies
Rind of ½ lemon

The Gravy

50g/¼ cup *Desi Ghee*/Clarified Butter
4 *Lavang*/Cloves
2 *Tej Patta*/Bay Leaf
20g/3½ tsp Ginger Paste (strain)
15g/2½ tsp Green Chilli Paste
150g/5 oz Boiled Onion Paste
45g/1½ oz Almond Paste

180g/¾ cup Yoghurt
Salt
1.5g/1/2 tsp *Chotti Elaichi*/Green Cardamon Powder
30 ml/2 Tbs *Gulaabjal*/Rose Water
30ml/2 Tbs Cream

Serves: 4
Preparation Time: 2:00 hours
Cooking Time: 45 minutes

Preparation

The Lotus Roots : Peel, rinse thoroughly, finely grate, put in a *handi*/pan, add lemon juice and enough water, boil until tender. Drain, cool and then squeeze in a napkin to ensure it is completely devoid of moisture.

The Kofta Mixture : Grate *paneer* in a bowl, add the moisture-free *nadar* and the remaining ingredients, mix well. Divide into 12 equal portions, make balls and keep aside.

The Filling : Crush saffron threads with a pestle or the back of spoon, reserve in lukewarm milk and then make a paste. Clean and finely chop figs. Quarter walnut halves. Clean coriander, wash and chop. Wash green chillies, slit, seed, finely chop and discard stems. Grate lemon rind. Put these ingredients in a bowl, add black cardamom seeds, mix well and divide ito 12 equal portions.

The Stuffing : Flatten the *kofta* between the palms, place a portion of the filling in the middle of each and make balls again.

The Frying : Heat oil in a *kadhai*/wok, add the stuffed *kofta* and deep fry over medium heat until cooked, ensuring they do not get coloured (approx 2 minutes). Remove to absorbent paper to drain excess fat.

The Gravy : Whisk yoghurt in a bowl.

Cooking

Melt *ghee* in a *handi*/pan, add cloves and bay leaves, stir over medium heat until cloves begin to pop, add ginger paste, *bhunno*/stir-fry for a few seconds, ensuring it does not get coloured. Then add green chilli paste, stir, add boiled onion paste and *bhunno*/stir-fry until specks of fat begin to appear on the surface, ensuring that the masala does not get coloured. Add almond paste, *bhunno*/stir-fry until specks of fat begins to appear on the surface, ensuring that the masala does not get coloured. Remove *handi*/pan from heat, stir-in yoghurt, return *handi*/pan to heat and *bhunno*/stir-fry until specks of fat begin to appear on the surface, ensuring that the masala does not get coloured. Add water (approx 720 ml/3 cups), bring to a boil, reduce to low heat and simmer for 2-3 minutes. Remove and pass the gravy through a fine mesh soup strainer into a separate *handi*/pan. Return gravy to heat, add salt and cardamom powder, stir, add the fried *kofta* and simmer over medium heat until gravy is of medium thick sauce consistency. Stir-in rosewater and cream, remove and adjust the seasoning.

Murgh Shahi Qorma

Chicken Drumsticks wrapped in Saffron, Poppy Seeds and Clotted Cream Masala

Ingredients

12 Chicken Drumsticks
1g/2 tsp *Zaafraan*/Saffron
260g/1 cup *Chakka Dahi*/Yoghurt Cheese/
    Hung Yoghurt
90g/1 oz Fried Onion Paste

30g/1 oz Fried Garlic Paste
1.5g/½ tsp Red Chilli Powder
90g/3 oz *Malai* (skimmed off milk)/Cream
    (if *malai* is not available)

The Marination

20g/3½ tsp Garlic Paste (strain)
20g/3½ tsp Ginger Paste (strain)

Salt

The *Shahi Paste*

30g/1 oz Raisins
30g/1 oz Almonds

15g/½ oz Pistachio
15g/½ oz *Khus-khus*/Poppy Seeds

The *Shahi Masala*

10g/5 tsp *Jeera*/Cumin Seeds
8 *Chotti Elaichi*/Green Cardamom
5 *Lavang*/Cloves
5 sticks *Daalcheeni*/Cinnamon (1")

10 Black Peppercorns
1 flower *Javitri*/Mace
¼ *Jaiphal*/Nutmeg
20 *Gulaabpankhrhi*/Dried Rose Petals

Serves: 4
Preparation Time: 1:30 hours
Cooking Time: 25 minutes

Preparation

The Marination : Mix all the ingredients in a bowl, evenly rub chicken drumsticks with this marinade and reserve for 20 minutes.

The Saffron : Crush the threads with a pestle or back of a spoon, reserve in 30ml/2 Tbs of lukewarm water, and then make a paste.

The *Shahi* Paste : Wash raisins and soak to refresh. Blanch almonds and pistachio in boiling water for 2 minutes, cool and peel. Soak poppy seeds in lukewarm water for 10 minutes. Put all the ingredients in a blender, add 90 ml/6 Tbs of water and make a smooth paste. Remove the paste, and keep aside.

The *Shahi* Masala : Sun-dry the spices, put in a mortar and pound with a pestle to make fine powder. Alternatively, put the spices in a grinder and, employing short pulses, grind to a fine powder. Sift and reserve.

The *Qorma* Paste : Put saffron paste, yoghurt cheese, the fried onion and garlic pastes, red chilli powder, salt, *Shahi Paste* and *Shahi Masala* in a large bowl and mix well. Hold aloft the chicken drumsticks to drain the excess marinade, evenly rub the drumsticks with *Qorma paste*, arrange in a *lagan*/flat pan or a large *handi*/pan with a suitable gap between each drumstick and pour on the excess paste. Then evenly spread the *malai* on top.

The Oven : Pre-heat to 300°F.

Cooking

Put *lagan*/flat pan or *handi*/pan on the stove and *bhunno*/stir-fry over medium heat until the paste begins to boil. Remove, cover with a lid, seal with *atta*/whole-wheat dough, transfer to the pre-heated oven and cook on *dum* for 15 minutes.

Remove, break the seal and adjust the seasoning.

EPISODE 012

with Chef Praveen Anand,
WELCOMGROUP

Daawat was as much about celebrating our glorious diversity as our unity. In the country okra (lady's finger) is enjoyed as a dry dish. In *Bendakai Pulusu*, an unusual South Indian curry, its charms as a gravy dish are unveiled.

Thengenkai Kori

Chicken Breast in Coconut and Yoghurt Gravy

Ingredients

8 Breasts of Chicken
75ml/5 Tbs Cooking Oil
5 *Chotti Elaichi*/Green Cardamom
5 *Lavang*/Cloves
2 sticks *Daalcheeni*/Cinnamon (1")
180g/1½ cups Onions
(or First Extract of Milk)
40g/7 tsp Garlic Paste (strain)

20g/3½ tsp Ginger Paste (strain)

150g/5 oz Yoghurt
6g/2 tsp Red Chilli Powder
1.5g/½ tsp *Haldee*/Turmeric Powder
720ml/3 cups Clear Chicken Stock
Salt
120ml/½ cup *Narial*/Coconut Cream

1.5g/½ tsp *Chotti Elaichi*/Green
    Cardamom Powder
10g/4 tsp *Narial*/Coconut

Serves: 4
Preparation Time: 20 minutes
Cooking Time: 30 minutes

Preparation

The Chicken : Clean breasts of chicken bone but retain the winglet bones, wash and pat dry.

The Marination : Mix all the ingredients, evenly rub the chicken breasts and reserve for 15 minutes.

The Gravy : Peel, wash and chop onions. Put yoghurt in a bowl, add red chillies and turmeric, and whisk until well mixed.

The Coconut : Remove the brown skin and grate

Cooking

Heat oil in a *handi*/pan, add green cardamom, cloves and cinnamon, stir over medium heat until cardamom begins to change colour, add onions and sauté until light golden. Then add the garlic and ginger pastes, *bhunno*/stir-fry until onions are golden. Remove *handi*/pan from heat, stir-in the yoghurt mixture, return *handi*/pan to heat and *bhunno*/stir-fry until the fat begins to appear on the surface. Now add chicken stock, bring to a boil, reduce to low heat, add chicken and salt, and simmer until chicken is cooked.

Remove the breasts and keep aside. Pass the gravy through a fine mesh soup strainer into a separate *handi*/pan, return gravy to heat, add the cooked chicken and coconut cream (or milk), and bring to just under a boil, ensuring that it does not come to a bubble (or the coconut cream/milk will curdle). Sprinkle cardamom powder and stir. Remove and adjust the seasoning. Garnish with grated coconut at the time of service.

Bendakai Pulusu

Okra in Tomato and Tamarind Gravy

Ingredients

400g/14 oz Okra

The Gravy

60ml/¼ cup Cooking Oil
120g/1 cup Onions
200ml/7 oz Tomato Purée (canned)
Salt
2 Green Chillies
7.5g/1¼ tsp Garlic Paste (strain)

6g/2 tsp *Dhania*/Coriander Powder
3g/1 tsp Red Chilli Powder
1.5g/½ tsp *Haldee*/Turmeric Powder
15g/½ oz *Imlee*/Tamarind Pulp
5g/1 tsp Sugar

The Tempering

15ml/1 Tbs Cooking Oil
2.5g/1 tsp *Rai*/Mustard Seeds

2.25g/½ tsp *Methidaana*/Fenugreek
  Seeds
16 *Kaari Patta*/Curry Leaf

Serves: 4
Preparation Time: 30 minutes
Cooking Time: 20 minutes

Preparation

The Okra : Wash in running water, pat dry, and slice off the caps and the tips. Heat oil in a *kadhai*/wok, add 120ml/½ cup of water and bring to a boil over high heat. Then add okra and *bhunno*/stir-fry for a minute or until the moisture is absorbed.

The Gravy : Peel, wash and chop onions. Wash green chillies, slit, seed, finely chop and discard stems.

The Tamarind Pulp : Put in a small pan, add 120ml/½ cup of water, bring to a boil, reduce to low heat and simmer until reduced to one-third.

The Tempering : Clean, wash and pat dry.

Cooking

Heat oil in a *handi*/pan, add onions and a little salt, sauté over medium heat until translucent and glossy, add garlic paste, and sauté until onions are light golden. Add green chillies, stir for 30 seconds, add coriander, red chilli and turmeric powders (all dissolved in 30m/½ Tbs of water), and stir until the moisture evaporates. Then add tomato purée (canned), *bhunno*/stir-fry until fat begins to appear on the surface, add tamarind, *bhunno*/stir-fry for a minute, add water (approx 180ml/¾ cup), sugar and salt, bring to a boil, reduce to low heat and simmer for 2-3 minutes. Now add okra and simmer until the tempering is ready.

To prepare the tempering, heat oil in a frying pan, add mustard seeds, stir over medium heat until they begin to pop, add fenugreek seeds and curry leaf, stir until the leaf stop spluttering, and pour over the simmering okra. Remove and adjust the seasoning.

Erha-Meen Mulakittathu

Prawn and Sole Combo in Fennel Gravy

Ingredients

8 Fillet of Sole/Pomfret
8 Prawns (large)

Cooking oil to shallow fry fish and prawns

The Marination

40g/7 tsp Garlic Paste (strain)
20g/3½ tsp Ginger Paste (strain)
45ml/3 Tbs Lemon Juice

1.5g/½ tsp *Haldee*/Turmeric Powder
Salt

The Gravy

30m½Tbs Cooking Oil
2.5g/1 tsp *Saunf*/Fennel Seeds
1.25g/½ tsp *Rai*/Mustard Seeds
1g/¼ tsp *Methidaana*/Fenugreek Seeds
120g/1 cup Onions
40g/7 tsp Garlic Paste (strain)
4 Green Chillies
24 *Kaari Patta*/Curry Leaf

6g/2tsp *Dhania*/Coriander Powder
4.5g/1½ tsp Red Chilli Powder
1.5g/¼ tsp *Haldee*/Turmeric Powder
400ml/¼ oz Tomato Purée (canned)
30g/1 oz *Imlee*/Tamarind Pulp
3.25g/1 Tbs *Taaza Dhania*/Coriander
10g/4 tsp *Narial*/Coconut

Serves: 4
Preparation Time: 1 hour
Cooking Time: 45 minutes

Preparation

The Fish : Clean, trim, wash and pat dry.

The Prawns : Shell but retain the tails, vein, wash and pat dry. Then pierce the prawn with wooden skewers from tail to head.

The Marination : Mix all the ingredients, evenly rub the fish and prawns and reserve for 30 minutes.

95

The Gravy : Peel, wash and slice onions. Wash green chillies, slit, seed, finely chop and discard stems. Clean and wash curry leaf. Put tamarind pulp in a small pan, add 180ml/¾ cup of water, bring to a boil, reduce to low heat and simmer until reduced to one-third. Clean, wash and roughly chop coriander. Remove brown skin and grate coconut.

Cooking

Heat oil in a *handi*/pan, add fennel, mustard and fenugreek seeds, and stir over medium heat until they begin to pop. Add onions, sauté until light golden, add garlic paste and *bhunno*/stir-fry until onions are golden. Then add the green chillies and curry leaf, stir for 30 seconds, add the coriander, red chilli and turmeric powders (all dissolved in 30ml/½ Tbs of water) and *bhunno*/stir-fry until the moisture evaporates. Now add tomato purée (canned), *bhunno*/stir-fry until specks of fat begin to appear on the surface, add tamarind pulp and *bhunno*/stir-fry for a minute. Now add water (approx 360ml/1½ cups), bring to a boil, reduce to low heat and simmer until the fish and prawns are shallow fried.

Heat a little oil in a frying pan, add fish and shallow-fry over medium heat turning once until evenly coloured—approx. a minute for each side—and transfer to the gravy. Heat a little more oil in the same pan, add prawns and shallow fry over medium heat turning once until evenly coloured— approx. a minute for each side—and transfer to the gravy. Once the fish and prawns have been added to the gravy, bring to a boil, remove and adjust the seasoning. Garnish with coriander and coconut at the time of service.

Koorina Kakarakaya

Stuffed Bitter Gourd in Mustard Seed and Coconut Gravy

Ingredients

12 *Karela*/Bitter Gourd
Salt
20g/ ⅔oz *Imlee*/Tamarind Pulp
30g/2 Tbs Sugar

0.75g/¼ tsp Red Chilli Powder
A pinch of *Haldee*/Turmeric Powder
Cooking oil to shallow-fry stuffed gourd

The Filling

120g/¼ lb Potatoes
120g/¼ lb Carrots
30ml½ Tbs Cooking Oil
1g/½ tsp *Jeera*/Cumin Seeds
20g/2″ piece Ginger
Salt

8 flakes Garlic
4 Green Chillies
120g/¼ lb Onions
3.25g/2 Tbs *Taaza Dhania*/Coriander
10ml/2 tsp Lemon Juice

The Gravy

30ml½ Tbs Cooking Oil
2.5g/1 tsp *Saunf*/Fennel Seeds
1.25g/½ tsp *Rai*/Mustard Seeds
1g/¼ tsp *Methidaana*/Fenugreek Seeds
24 *Kaari Patta*/Curry Leaf
120g/1 cup Onions
20g/3½ tsp Ginger Paste (strain)

20g/3½ tsp Garlic Paste (strain)
3g/1 tsp *Dhania*/Coriander Powder
3g/1 tsp Red Chilli Powder
0.75g/¼ tsp *Haldee*/Turmeric Powder
400ml/14 oz Tomato Purée (canned)
Salt
30g/2 Tbs Sugar

Serves: 4
Preparation Time:
Cooking Time:

Preparation

The Bitter Gourd : Wash, slit, rub with salt, arrange on a tilting tray and reserve for at least 2 hours. (This is done to reduce the bitterness. If you think you cannot handle even this little bitterness, reserve the bitter gourd overnight).

Put 720ml/3 cups of water in a *handi*/pan, add tamarind pulp, sugar, red chilli powder, turmeric powder and salt, bring to a boil, reduce to medium heat, add bitter gourd and cook until the liquid has almost evaporated (approximately 15 minutes). Drain and keep aside.

The Filling : Wash potatoes, boil, cool, peel and cut into ⅛″ dices. Peel carrots, halve lengthwise, boil, cool and cut into ⅛″ dices. Peel, wash and finely chop onions. Scrape, wash and finely chop ginger. Peel and finely chop garlic. Wash green chillies, slit, seed, finely chop and discard stems. Clean, wash and finely chop coriander.

Heat oil in a frying pan, add cumin seeds, stir over medium heat until they begin to pop, add ginger, garlic and green chillies, and sauté until garlic is lightly coloured. Add onions and sauté until translucent and glossy. Then add the potatoes, carrots and salt, *bhunno*/stir-fry for a minute. Remove, cool, add coriander and lemon juice, and mix well. Divide into 12 equal portions.

The Stuffing : Pack a portion in each of the boiled bitter gourd and secure with string.

Cooking

Heat a little oil in a non-stick frying pan, add the stuffed bitter gourd and shallow fry over medium heat until lightly coloured and crisp. Remove to absorbent paper to drain the excess fat.

To prepare the gravy, heat oil in a saucepan, add fennel, mustard and fenugreek, stir over medium heat until they begin to pop, add curry leaf and stir until they stop spluttering. Add onions, sauté until light golden, add the ginger and garlic pastes, *bhunno*/stir-fry until the moisture evaporates. Then add coriander, red chillies and turmeric (all dissolved in 30ml/2 Tbs of water), *bhunno*/stir-fry until the moisture evaporates, add tomato purée and salt, and *bhunno*/stir-fry, until specks of fat begin to appear on the surface. Add water (approximately 480 ml/2 cups), bring to a boil, reduce to low heat and simmer until reduced by half. Now add the fried bitter gourd and sugar, bring to a boil, reduce to low heat and simmer for 2-3 minutes. Remove and adjust the seasoning.

EPISODE 013

with Chef Praveen Anand,
WELCOMGROUP

The harvest festival accords top priority to feasting and *Pongal* is cooked both sweet and savoury, leaving a lingering after-taste.

Venn Pongal

Savoury Rice and Moong Lentil

Ingredients

250g/1¼ cups Rice
100g/½ cup *Moong Daal* (husked)
100g/½ cup *Desi Ghee*/Clarified Butter
Salt
3g/1 tsp *Jeera*/Cumin Seeds

20g/2" piece Ginger
24 *Kaari Patta*/Curry Leaf
6g/1¼ tsp Black Pepper (freshly roasted
    and coarsely ground)
12 Cashewnuts

Serves: 4
Preparation Time: 45 minutes
Cooking Time: 30 minutes

Preparation

The Rice : Pick, wash in running water, drain, soak for 30 minutes and drain.

The *Moong Daal* : Pick, wash in running water, drain, soak for 30 minutes and drain.

The Ginger : Scrape, wash and finely chop.

The Curry Leaf : Clean and wash.

The Cashewnuts : Split into halves.

Cooking

Melt 25g/2 Tbs of *ghee* in a *handi*/pan, add *daal*, and *bhunno*/stir-fry for 2 minutes. Add rice, stir, add 840ml/3½ cups of water, bring to a boil, reduce to low heat and cook, stirring at regular intervals, until the mixture is three-fourths cooked, ensuring it does not stick to the bottom of the *handi*/pan. Then add salt, stir, add 50g/¼ cup of *ghee* and cook until the mixture is of a slightly dry *khichri* (porridge) consistency. Remove and keep aside.

Melt the remaining *ghee* in a frying pan, add cumin, stir over medium heat until they begin to pop, add ginger and *bhunno*/stir-fry for a few seconds. Then add curry leaf, stir until spluttering stops, add pepper and cashewnuts, and stir until the cashewnuts begin to change colour. Remove and pour over the *Pongal* and stir until fully incorporated.

Chakkara Pongal

Jaggery-sweetened Rice and Moong Lentil

Ingredients

250g/1¼ cups Rice
75g/3 oz *Moong Daal* (husked)
100g/½ cup *Desi Ghee*/Clarified Butter
240ml/1 cup Milk (full fat)
120g/15 oz *Gurh*/Jaggery
Salt
0.5g/1 tsp *Zaafraan*/Saffron
30ml½ Tbs Milk

2.25g/¾ tsp *Chotti Elaichi*/Green
 Cardamom Powder
0.75g/¼ tsp *Jaiphal*/Nutmeg Powder
A pinch of *Karpoor*/Camphor
18 Cashewnuts
36 Raisins

Serves : 4
Preparation Time : 45 minutes
Cooking Time : 30 minutes

Preparation

The Rice : Pick, wash in running water, drain, soak for 30 minutes and drain.

The *Moong Dal* : Pick, wash in running water, drain, soak for 30 minutes and drain.

The Saffron : Reserve in lukewarm milk.

The Cashewnuts : Split into halves.

The Raisins : Remove stems, wash in running water, drain and pat dry.

Cooking

Melt 25g/2 Tbs of *ghee* in a *handi*/pan, add *daal*, *bhunno*/stir-fry for 2 minutes, add rice, and stir. Then add milk and water (600ml/2½ cups), bring to a boil, reduce to low heat and cook, stirring at regular intervals, until the mixture is three-fourths cooked, ensuring it does not stick to the bottom of the *handi*/pan.

Meanwhile, boil 120ml/½ cup of water in a *handi*/pan, add jaggery and stir until the jaggery melts and the mixture is homogenous. Remove and pass through a fine mesh soup strainer onto the cooking rice and stir. Then add a pinch of salt, stir, add 50g/¼ cup of *ghee* and cook until the

102

mixture is of a slightly dry *khichri* (porridge) consistency. Remove, add saffron, cardamom and nutmeg powders, stir until fully incorporated. Sprinkle camphor and stir until incorporated.

Melt the remaining *ghee* in a frying pan, add the cashewnut halves and raisins, stir over medium heat until the cashewnuts are light golden. Remove and pour over the *Pongal* and stir until fully incorporated.

Aezhethan Kozhambu

Vegetable and Lentil Stew tempered with Curry Leaf

Ingredients

150g/¾cup *Arhar/Toor Daal*
2 Potatoes (large)

4 *Arbi/Coloccasia*
75g/2½ oz *Zimikand/Yam*
1 Drumstick
75g/2¼ oz French Beans

2 Raw Bananas
Chaas/Buttermilk (thin) to reserve
    bananas
Salt
1.5g/½tsp *Haldee/Turmeric Powder*
15g/2 oz *Imlee/Tamarind Pulp*

The *Masala*

110g/1 cup Coconut
10ml/2 tsp Cooking Oil
4 Red Chillies

15g/½ oz *Channa Daal*
15g/7½ tsp *Dhania/Coriander Seeds*
1g/¼ tsp *Methidaana/Fenugreek Seeds*

The Tempering

20ml/4 tsp Cooking Oil
4 Red Chillies
1.25g/½ tsp *Rai/Mustard Seeds*

1g/¼ tsp *Methidaana/Fenugreek Seeds*
24 *Kaari Patta/Curry Leaf*
A pinch of *Heeng/Asafoetida*

The Garnish

3.25g/1 Tbs *Taaza Dhania/Coriander*

24 Cashewnuts

Serves: 4
Preparation Time: 30 minutes
Cooking Time: 20 minutes

Preparation

The *Arhar/Toor Daal* : Pick, wash in running water, drain, put in a *handi*/pan, add 480ml/2 cups of water, bring to a boil, reduce to low heat, cover and simmer, stirring occasionally, until cooked. Then mash with a ladle to a custard consistency. Continue to cook over very low heat, stirring at regular intervals to prevent sticking.

The Vegetables : Peel, wash and scoop out 16 parisiennes each of potatoes and carrots. Peel, wash, halve and turn coloccasia. Scrape, wash and cut yam into ¼″ cubes. String drumstick and beans, cut drumstick into 1½″ piece and the beans into 1″ pieces.

The Bananas : Peel quarter, turn and reserve in bowl of thin buttermilk.

The *Masala* : Remove the brown skin and grate coconut. Remove stems and wipe the red chillies clean with a moist cloth. Pick *channa daal*, wash in running water, drain and pat dry. Heat oil in a frying pan, add red chillies, *channa daal*, coriander and fenugreek seeds, stir over medium heat until the *daal* begins to change colour. Then add coconut and stir until coconut is golden brown. Remove to a grinder, add 60ml/¼ cup of water and make a fine paste.

The Tempering : Remove stems and wipe the red chillies clean with a moist cloth. Clean and wash curry leaf.

The Garnish : Clean, wash and finely chop coriander. Split cashewnut into halves. Heat enough oil in a *kadhai/wok*, add cashewnuts and deep fry over medium heat until light golden. Remove to absorbent paper to drain the excess fat.

Cooking

Put 1 litre/4¼ cups of water in a *handi*/pan, add salt and turmeric, bring to a boil, add the vegetables and the bananas, bring to a boil, reduce to low heat, cover and simmer, stirring occasionally, until the vegetables are half cooked. Then add tamarind pulp—dissolved in 240ml/ 1 cup of water—cover and simmer, stirring occasionally, until the vegetables are cooked. Now add the masala, stir, add the cooked *daal*, stir, cover and simmer, stirring occasionally, until the tempering is ready.

To prepare the tempering, heat oil in a frying pan, add red chillies, stir over medium heat until they begin to change colour, add mustard and fenugreek seeds, and stir until they begin to pop. Add curry leaf, stir until they stop spluttering, add asafoetida, stir, remove and pour over the simmering *Kozhambu*. Garnish with coriander and cashewnuts at the time of service.

Masala Vadai

Lentil "Donut" with Thin Tomato Gravy

Ingredients

The Vadai

250g/1¼ cups Channa Daal
2.5g/1 tsp *Saunf*/Fennel Seeds
4 Red Chillies
120g/1 cup Onions

5g/½" piece Ginger
24 *Kaari Patta*/Curry Leaf
Salt
Cooking oil to deep fry *vadai*

The *Rassam*

75g/2½ oz Tomato
15g/½oz *Arhar*/Toor Daal
10g/5 tsp *Dhania*/Coriander Seeds
6g/1 Tbs *Zeera*/Cumin Seeds
8g/2 tsp Black Pepper
  (freshly roasted & coarsely ground)
30g/1 oz *Imlee*/Tamarind Pulp
0.75g/¼ tsp *Haldee*/Turmeric Powder

Salt
3 flakes Garlic
10ml½ tsp Cooking Oil
2 Red Chillies
2.5g/1tsp *Rai*/Mustard Seeds
1g/½ tsp *Zeera*/Cumin Seeds
A pinch of *Heeng*/Asafoetida
24 *Kaari Patta*/Curry Leaf

Serves : 4
Preparation Time : 2:45 hours
Cooking Time : 5 minutes

Preparation

The Vadai : Pick *channa daal*, wash in running water and drain. Remove stems and wipe red chillies clean with a moist cloth. Put *daal* in a *handi*/pan, add fennel seeds and red chillies, cover with enough water and reserve for 2 hours. Peel, wash and finely chop onions. Scrape, wash and finely chop ginger. Clean, wash and chop curry leaf. Remove and reserve 50g/2 oz of the soaked *channa daal*. Drain and put the remaining *daal*, fennel and red chillies in the blender and grind into a coarse paste. Remove, add all the other ingredients, including the reserved *daal*, and salt, mix well, divide into 16 equal portions and flatten between the palms into patties of 2½" diameter.

  The Rassam : Remove eyes, wash and chop tomato. Peel and crush garlic. Heat a *tawa*/griddle, add *arhar/toor daal*, coriander, cumin and pepper, broil until they emit their unique aroma. Remove to a grinder and make a coarse powder. Remove and keep aside. Remove stems and wipe red chillies clean with a moist cloth. Clean and wash curry leaf.

Put 600ml/2½ cups of water in a *handi*/pan, add tamarind, tomatoes, turmeric and salt, stir well, bring to a boil, reduce to low heat and simmer, stirring occasionally, for 8-10 minutes. Then add the crushed garlic and the prepared coarse powder, stir, cover and cook over medium heat until it begins to boil. Reduce to low heat and simmer until the tempering is ready.

To prepare the tempering, heat oil in a frying pan, add red chillies, mustard and cumin, stir over medium heat until the seeds begin to pop, add asafoetida and curry leaf, stir until the leaf stops spluttering, pour over the *Rassam* and mix well.

Cooking

Heat enough oil, add the *Vadai* patties and deep fry over medium heat until golden brown. Remove to absorbent paper to drain the excess fat. Serve with *Rassam*.

EPISODE 014

with Chef Murali,
THE LEELA

Murali was flown in from Mumbai, to render the *Kolhapuri Mutton*, the pride of martial Maratha. He also treated us to the *Undhiya* to give us a taste of neighbouring Gujarat.

Tarlleli Surmai

Kingfish in tangy Spinach Gravy from coastal Maharastra

Ingredients

4 darnes *Surmai*/Kingfish (200g/7 oz each)   Cooking oil to shallow fry fish

The Marination

30ml/½ Tbs Lemon Juice
15g/2½ tsp Ginger Paste (strain)
15g/2½ tsp Garlic Paste (strain)

9g/1 Tbs Red Chilli Powder
Salt

The Gravy

30g/¼ cup Onions
4 Green Chillies
20g/¼ lb *Ambat Chuka* *
30g/1 oz Spinach
30m½ Tbs Cooking Oil

2.5g/1 tsp *Sarsondaana*/Black Mustard
  Seeds
A generous pinch of *Heeng*/Asafoetida
4 Dried Red Chillies

Serves: 4
Preparation Time: 40 minutes
Cooking Time: 30 minutes

Preparations

The Fish : Clean, trim, wash and pat dry.

The Marination : Mix all the ingredients, evenly rub the darnes with this marinade and reserve for 15 minutes.

The Gravy : Peel, wash and finely chop onions. Wash green chillies, slit, seed, finely chop and discard stems.

Clean, remove stems, wash *ambat chuka* in running water to remove grit, and drain. Heat 10ml/2 tsp of oil in a frying pan, add *ambat chuka* and sauté over medium heat until the leaves are soft. Remove to a blender, add 60ml/¼ cup of water and make a smooth purée. Remove and keep aside.

Clean, remove stems, wash spinach in running water to remove grit and drain. Then blanch in salted boiling water for 30 seconds, drain, refresh in iced water, drain, transfer to a blender, add 30ml/2 Tbs of water and make a smooth purée.

Wipe red chillies, clean with moist cloth, slit, seed and discard the stems.

Cooking

Heat the remaining oil in a *handi*/pan, add mustard, stir over medium heat until it begins to pop, add asafoetida and the red chillies and stir until the chillies become bright red. Then add *ambat chuka* and spinach, *bhunno*/stir-fry until the fat leaves the sides, add 480ml/2 cups of water, bring to a boil, reduce to low heat and simmer, stirring occasionally, until the fish is fried.

To fry the fish, heat enough oil in a frying pan, add the darnes and shallow fry over medium heat, turning once, until evenly coloured. Remove to absorbent paper to drain the excess fat. Add to the gravy, stir carefully, and simmer for 1½-2 minutes. Remove and adjust the seasoning.

*A tangy, leafy vegetable intrinsic to the Deccan.

Kolhapuri Mutton

Maharashtrian Kid/Lamb Chops in Chilli, Sesame and Poppy Seed Gravy

Ingredients

16 *Chaamp*/Kid/Lamb Chops (2-rib)

The Marination

30g/5 tsp Ginger Paste (strain)
30g/5 tsp Garlic Paste (strain)
10m/½ tsp Cooking Oil

3g/1 tsp *Haldee*/Turmeric Powder
Salt

The *Kolhapuri Masala*

90g/3 oz Onions
75g/2½ oz *Narial*/Coconut
30m/½ Tbs Cooking Oil
15g/½ oz *Dhania*/Coriander Seeds
6g/1 Tbs *Jeera*/Cumin Seeds

5g/1½ tsp *Safaed Til*/Sesame Seeds
4.5g/1½ tsp *Khus-khus*/Poppy Seeds
Rasampati/Red Chillies
8 *Kashmiri Deghi Mirch*
4 *Lavang*/Cloves

The Gravy

75ml/3 Tbs Cooking Oil
120g/1 cup Onions

3.25g/1 Tbs *Taaza Dhania*/Coriander

Serves: 4
Preparation Time: 2 hours
Cooking Time: 1 hour

Preparation

The Kid/Lamb Chops : Clean, trim, wash and pat dry.

The Marination : Mix all the ingredients, evenly rub the chops with this marinade and reserve in the refrigerator for 1:30 hours.

The *Kolhapuri Masala* : Peel, wash and finely chop onions. Remove the brown skin and grate coconut. Wipe red chillies, clean with the moist cloth, slit, seed and discard the stems. Heat oil in a frying pan, add coriander seeds, cumin seeds, sesame seeds, poppy seeds, red chillies and cloves, stir over medium heat until they begin to pop. Then add onions and coconut and sauté until onions are translucent and glossy. Remove to a blender, add 60ml/¼ cup of water and make a coarse paste. Remove and keep aside.

The Gravy : Peel, wash and finely chop onions. Clean, wash and chop coriander.

Cooking

Heat oil in a *handi*/pan, add onions and sauté over medium heat until golden. Increase to high heat, add the marinated meat, *bhunno*/stir-fry to sear for 2-3 minutes. Reduce to medium heat, and *bhunno*/stir-fry until the liquor evaporates and the fat leaves the sides. Then add 30ml/2 Tbs of water and *bhunno*/stir-fry until the fat leaves the sides. Repeat the process of adding water and stir-frying until the meat is three-fourths cooked. Then add the *Kolhapuri Masala*, *bhunno*/stir-fry until the fat leaves the sides, add 720ml/3 cups of water, bring to a boil, reduce to low heat, cover and simmer, stirring occasionally, until the meat is cooked. Remove and adjust the seasoning. Garnish with coriander at the time of service.

Undhiya

Cooked Vegetables and Raw Bananas served with Fenugreek and Gramflour Dumplings—from Gujarat

Ingredients

200g/7 oz *Surati Papadi* (Small Beans)
2.5g/1 tsp *Ajwain*/Carom
A generous pinch of Soda Bi-carb
10ml/2 tsp Cooking Oil

200g/7 oz *Shakkarkandi*/Sweet Potato
4 Potatoes (Medium)
3 Raw Bananas
16 Baby Brinjals

The *Muthia*

50g/2 oz *Methi*/Fenugreek Leaves
5g/1 tsp Sugar
Salt
2 Green Chillies

5g/1½ tsp *Safaed Til*/Sesame Seeds
55g/½ cup *Besan*/Gramflour
10ml/½ tsp Cooking Oil
Cooking oil to deep fry *Muthia*

The Masala

80g/¾ cup*Narial*/Coconut
50g/1 cup *Taaza Dhania*/Coriander
4 Green Chillies
20g/2/3 oz *Imlee*/Tamarind Pulp

3g/1 tsp *Haldee*/Turmeric Powder
5g/1 tsp Sugar
Salt

Serves: 4
Preparation Time: 50 minutes
Cooking Time: 30 minutes

Preparations

The Vegetables and Bananas : String *surati papadi*, wash and keep aside. Peel potatoes, wash, cut into ¼" cubes and reserve in water. Peel *shakkarkandi*, wash, cut into ¼" cubes and reserve in water. Peel bananas, cut into ½" thick roundels and reserve in water. Remove cap, wash brinjals, make criss-cross slits leaving them attached at the stalk end and reserve in water.

The *Muthia* : Remove stems, chop fenugreek, wash in running water to remove grit, drain and then squeeze in muslin to reduce the bitterness. Wash green chillies, slit, seed, finely chop and discard stems. Sift *besan* into a bowl, add remaining ingredients and knead to make hard dough. Divide into 20 equal portions and make olive shaped dumplings.

Heat oil in a *kadhai*/wok, add the dumplings and deep fry over medium heat until cooked and golden. Remove to absorbent paper to drain the excess fat. Reserve the oil.

The *Masala* : Remove the brown skin and grate coconut. Clean, wash and finely chop coriander. Wash green chillies, slit, seed, finely chop and discard stems. Put these and the remaining ingredients in a bowl and mix well.

Cooking

Reheat the reserved oil, add sweet potato, deep fry over medium heat until half cooked and remove to absorbent paper to drain the excess fat. Reheat the oil, add potatoes, deep fry over medium heat until half cooked and remove to absorbent paper to drain the excess fat. Reheat the oil, add raw bananas, deep fry over medium heat until half cooked and remove to absorbent paper to drain the excess fat. Reheat the oil, add brinjals, deep fry over medium heat until half cooked and remove to absorbent paper to drain the excess fat.

Put 480ml/2 cups of water in a *handi*/pan, add *ajwain*, soda bi-carb and oil (10ml/2 tsp), bring to a boil, add *surati papadi* and continue to boil until half cooked. Then add the fried vegetables in the same order in which they were fried, and boil until all the ingredients are cooked. Then add the *masala*, stir, reduce to low heat, cover and simmer, stirring occasionally, for 4-5 minutes. Remove and adjust the seasoning. Serve with *Muthia*.

116

Aloo-Papaya Chaat with Avocado

Potato, Papaya and Avocado Salad with Fennel and Jaggery Dressing

Ingredients

4 Potatoes (large)
1 Papaya

4 Avocado
2 Pomegranate

The Chutney

20m/¼ tsp Cooking Oil
4 Red Chillies
15g/2 Tbs *Saunf*/Fennel Seeds

20g/2/3 oz *Gurh*/Jaggery
Salt

Serves: 4
Preparation Time: 1 hour

Preparation

The Potatoes : Wash, boil, cool, peel and cut into ½" cubes.

The Papaya : Halve, seed and obtain as many parisiennes as possible.

The Avocado : Halve, remove the stone and cut into slices.

The Pomegranate : Remove the fruit.

The Chutney : Wipe the red chillies clean with a moist cloth. Grate jaggery.

Heat oil in a saucepan to a smoking point, add the red chillies and stir until bright red. Then add fennel seeds, stir for 30 seconds, add jaggery and water (approx 240ml/1 cup), bring to a boil, reduce to low heat and simmer until of coating consistency. Remove and adjust the seasoning.

Assembling

Place the potatoes in the middle of the plate, arrange the sliced avocado, overlapping, on either side of the potatoes, place the papaya parisiennes at the open end of the arranged avocado and spread the pomegranate seeds around the papaya. Pour the chutney on the potatoes and the papaya.

EPISODE 015

with Chef Murli,
THE LEELA

Devinder Kumar assisted us with another interesting *Daawat* episode. This time the idea was to present stuffed fare. *Bharwaan Jheenga Zaafraan* and *Patra Roulade* were served to the viewers. Both the fillings and the 'containers' received acclaim for their novelty.

Bharwaan Jheenga Zaafraan

Stuffed Prawns in Carom and Cardamom Gravy

Ingredients

12 Tiger Prawns

The Marination

250g/1 cup Yoghurt
10g/1¾ tsp Garlic Paste (strain)
10g/1¾ tsp Ginger Paste (strain)
4.5g/¾ tsp Red Chilli Paste
10ml/2 tsp Lemon Juice
2.5g/1 tsp *Ajwain*/Carom
A small pinch of *Chotti Elaichi*/Green Cardamom Powder
A small pinch of *Daalcheeni*/Cinnamon Powder

A small pinch of *Javitri*/Mace Powder
A small pinch of Black Pepper (freshly roasted & coarsely ground)
A small pinch of *Saunf*/Fennel Powder
A small pinch of *Saunth*/Dried Ginger Powder
A small pinch of *Gulaabpankhrhi*/Rose Petal Powder
Salt

The Filling

20ml/4 tsp Cooking Oil
60g/½ cup Onions
2 Green Chillies
85g/½ cup Potatoes
75g/½ cup Carrots

75g/2½ oz Brinjals
1.5g/½ tsp *Dhania*/Coriander Powder
1.5g/½ tsp Red Chilli Powder
0.75g/¼ tsp *Haldee*/Turmeric Powder
Salt

The Gravy

20ml/4 tsp Cooking Oil
3 *Chotti Elaichi*/Green Cardamom
3 *Lavang*/Cloves
1 stick *Daalcheeni*/Cinnamon (1")
8 Black Peppercorns
1.25g/½ tsp *Ajwain*/Carom
10g/1¾ tsp Garlic Paste (strain)
10g/1¾ tsp Ginger Paste (strain)

125/½ cup Yoghurt
30g/1 oz Cashewnut Paste
90g/3 oz Boiled Onion Paste
0.5g/1 tsp *Zaafraan*/Saffron
3g/1 tsp *Chotti Elaichi*/Green Cardamom Powder
Salt

Serves: 4
Preparation Time: 1 hour
Cooking Time: 50 minutes

Preparation

The Prawns : Shell but retain the tails, vein, slit along the vein without cutting through, flatten just enough with a wooden bat to make it look like a butterfly, wash and pat dry.

The Marination : Whisk yoghurt in a bowl, add the remaining ingredients, mix well, evenly rub prawns with this marinade and reserve in the refrigerator for 30 minutes.

The Filling : Peel, wash and chop onions. Wash green chillies, slit, seed, finely chop and discard stems. Peel, wash and cut carrots and potatoes into brunnoise. Remove stems, wash and cut brinjal into brunnoise.

Heat oil in a frying pan, add onions, sauté over medium heat until translucent and glossy, add green chillies and sauté until onions are light golden. Add carrots and potatoes, sauté for a minute, add brinjals and sauté for a minute. Then add coriander, red chilli and turmeric powders (dissolved in 30ml/2 Tbs of water), *bhunno*/stir-fry until the moisture evaporates, add 180ml/¾ cup of water, bring to a boil, reduce to low heat, cover and simmer, stirring occasionally, until the vegetables are *al dente*. Uncover, increase to medium heat, add salt and *bhunno*/stir-fry until the liquid evaporates. Remove, adjust the seasoning, cool and divide into 12 equal portions.

The Stuffing : Place a portion of the filling at the top end of each prawn, roll (like a Swiss Roll), pierce 2 toothpicks horizontally and 1 vertically between the tail and then press just a fraction to enable the roll to stand on the plate with the tail pointing up. Now wrap the prawns in foil, arrange on a baking tray and keep aside.

The Oven : Pre-heat to 200°F.

The Gravy : Put yoghurt in a bowl, add cashew and boiled onion pastes, and whisk to mix well. Crush saffron with pestle or back of spoon, reserve in 30ml/2 Tbs of lukewarm water and then make a paste.

Cooking

Heat oil in a saucepan, add green cardamom, cloves, cinnamon and black peppercorns, stir over medium heat until the cardamom begins to change colour, add *ajwain*, and stir for a few seconds. Then add ginger and garlic pastes, dissolved in 60ml/¼ cup of water and *bhunno*/stir-fry until the moisture evaporates, add yoghurt-cashew-boiled onion mixture and *bhunno*/stir-fry until the fat leaves the sides. Now add 240ml/1 cup of water, bring to a boil, reduce to low heat and simmer, stirring occasionally, for 2 minutes. Remove and pass the gravy through a fine mesh soup strainer into a separate *handi*/pan, return gravy to heat, bring to a boil, reduce to low heat, add saffron and green cardamom powder, stir, remove and adjust the seasoning.

Meanwhile to cook the prawns, place the baking tray in the pre-heated oven and bake for 3 minutes. Remove and keep aside.

Serve prawns on a bed of the sauce.

Patra Roulade

Sautéed Vegetables in Colocassia Leaves

Ingredients

10 *Arbi*/Colocassia Leaves

The Batter

6g/1 Tbs Cumin Seeds

150g/6 oz *Besan*/Gramflour

The Filling

30ml/2 Tbs Cooking Oil

175g/6 oz Carrots

2g/1 tsp Cumin Seeds

175g/6 oz French Beans

10ml/2 tsp Lemon Juice

90g/3 oz Parmesan Cheese

10g/1" piece Ginger

10g/3 Tbs Coriander

2 Green Chillies

The Gravy

20ml/4 tsp Cooking Oil

10ml/2 tsp Lemon Juice

20g/2" piece Ginger

6.5g/1 tsp Cornflour

5ml/1 tsp Honey

The Garnish

16 Asparagus Spears

¼ Beetroot

8 sprigs Coriander

2 Star Fruit

8 Black Olives (without pits)

Serves: 4
Preparation Time: 1:30 hours
Cooking Time: 45 minutes

Preparation

The *Arbi*/Colocassia Leaves : Clean, remove the stems and large veins with a knife, wash and pat dry.

The Batter : Heat a pan, add cumin seeds, broil over medium heat until they emit their unique aroma, add of gramflour and *bhunno*/stir until gramflour is lightly coloured. Remove to a bowl, add 480ml/2 cups of water to make a batter of coating consistency. Pass the batter through a fine mesh soup strainer into a separate bowl, reserve 2/3 oz or 20 g to seal the leaves and divide the rest into 2 equal portions.

The Filling : Scrape, wash and finely chop ginger. Wash green chillies, slit, deseed, finely chop and discard the stems. Peel, wash and cut carrots into brunnoise. String, wash and cut beans into brunnoise. Grate parmesan or, if that is not available, processed cheese. Clean, wash and finely chop coriander.

Heat oil in a frying pan, add cumin seeds, stir over medium heat until they begin to crackle, add ginger and green chillies, *bhunno*/stir-fry for a minute, add carrots and *bhunno*/stir-fry for a minute. Then add beans and salt, stir for a minute, add 60 ml/¼ cup of water, stir, cover and cook for 2 minutes. Uncover and *bhunno*/stir-fry until the liquid evaporates. Remove to a bowl, add lemon juice, cheese and coriander, mix well, divide into 2 equal portions and keep aside.

The Roulade : Place 5 *arbi* leaves overlapping and spreading across to a width of 10". Repeat the process with the remaining leaves. Evenly apply a portion of the gramflour batter on the 2 sets of *arbi* leaves. Divide each portion of the filling into 4 unequal parts, spread the largest portion (approx 80g/2$\frac{2}{3}$ oz), 1" wide, at the broad end, roll like a Swiss roll, spread the second largest portion (approx. 60g/2 oz), 1" wide, roll again, spread the next portion (approx 40g/1$\frac{1}{3}$ oz), 1" wide, roll again, spread the smallest portion (approx 20g/$\frac{2}{3}$ oz), 1" wide and roll the remaining portion of the leaves to make a roulade. Seal the ends with the remaining batter. (Cut into half if the steamer is not wide enough.) Repeat the process with the other set of leaves. Do not cut this roulade. Keep aside.

The Gravy : Scrape, wash and finely chop ginger. Dissolve cornflour in 15ml/1 Tbs of water.

Cooking

Put the roulades in the steamer and cook for 15 minutes.

Meanwhile, to prepare the gravy, heat oil in a saucepan, add ginger and sauté over medium heat for 30 seconds, add honey, stir until the mixture is homogenous (approx 45 seconds), add 240 ml/1 cup of water, bring to a boil, stirring constantly without increasing the heat. Then add lemon juice, stir, add cornflour and stir until of sauce consistency. Sprinkle salt and stir. Remove and pass through a fine mesh soup strainer into a bowl and keep aside.

Now remove the *patra*, trim the edges and cut into 1½" thick pieces. Pour on the gravy and serve.

125

EPISODE 016

with Pratap Reddy,
WELCOMGROUP

There are those to whom the world is an oyster, and those who have tasted the *Muru Curry* for whom no other world exists beyond the oyster.

Avanasa Sasam

Pineapple Salad in Coconut and Jaggery Dressing

Ingredients

2 Pineapples (medium)   110g/½ cup Sugar

The Dressing

2 *Narial*/Coconut (medium)   Salt
4 Red Chillies (dried)   4.5g/2 tsp *Sarsondaana*/Black Mustard
30g/1 oz *Gurh*/Jaggery   Seeds

The Tempering

16 *Kaari Patta*/Curry Leaf   4.5g/2 tsp *Sarsondaana*/Black Mustard
15ml/1 Tbs Cooking Oil   Seeds

Serves : 4
Preparation Time : 1:45 hours

Preparation

The Pineapples : Wash, halve, carefully scoop out the fruit leaving approximately ½″ of the fruit and the skin to make "boats". Cut the scooped fruit into ½″ cubes.

The Syrup : Put the sugar in a pan, add 240ml/1 cup of water, bring to a boil, reduce to low heat, remove the scum and then simmer until the syrup is of one-string consistency. Remove and cool.

The *Sasam* : Add pineapple cubes to the syrup and reserve for at least an hour and drain. Put equal quantities of *Sasam* in the "boats" and refrigerate until ready to serve.

The Dressing : Remove the brown skin, wash and grate coconuts. Wipe red chillies clean with moist cloth and dry broil on a griddle or in a frying pan for a minute, remove and keep aside. Grate jaggery. Crush mustard seeds with a pestle.

Put the coconut and the red chillies in a blender, add 45ml/3 Tbs of water and make a coarse paste. Remove to a bowl, add jaggery and salt, mix until fully incorporated. Then add crushed mustard to the coconut paste and mix well.

The Tempering : Clean and wash curry leaf. Heat oil in a frying pan, add mustard seeds and curry leaves, stir over medium heat until the seeds begin to crackle.

Remove the boats from the refrigerator, spread the coconut mixture on top, powder equal quantities of the tempering over the *Sasam* and serve.

Chenaikandae Masala Barthathu

Tamarind-marinated Yam in Tomato Gravy

Ingredients

1 Kg/2¼ lb Zimikand/Yam

The Marination

15ml/½ oz *Imlee*/Tamarind Pulp
15g/2½ tsp Garlic Paste (strain) Powder
15g/2½ tsp Ginger Paste (strain)
3g/1 tsp *Dhania*/Coriander Powder

3g/1 tsp Red Chilli
Salt
Cooking Oil to shallow fry *Zimikand*/Yam

The *Masala*

60g/2 oz Onions
4 Green Chillies
15g/1½" piece Ginger
10 flakes Garlic
4g/1 tsp Black Peppercorns
3g/1 tsp *Khus-khus*/Poppy Seeds

2g/1 tsp *Zeera*/Cumin Seeds
1g/¼ tsp *Methidaana*/Fenugreek Seeds
2 sticks *Daalcheeni*/Cinnamon (1")
2 *Chotti Elaichi*/Green Cardamom
2 *Lavang*/Cloves
0.75g/¼ tsp *Haldee*/Turmeric Powder

The Gravy

75g/6 Tbs *Desi Ghee*/Clarified Butter
120g/1 cup Onions
120g/4 oz Tomatoes

Salt
75g/1¼ cups *Taaza Dhania*/Coriander
12.5g/1 Tbs Butter

Serves : 4
Preparation Time : 1 hour
Cooking Time : 25 minutes

Preparation

The Yam : Peel, wash, cut into ½" thick slices, and then cut into 16 roundels.

The Marination : Put all the ingredients in a bowl, mix well, evenly smear the marinade on the yam roundels and reserve for 10 minutes. Put water in a steamer and steam the roundels until *al dente*. Remove and keep aside.

131

The Masala : Peel, wash and roughly chop onions. Wash green chillies, slit, seed, roughly chop and discard stems. Scrape, wash and roughly chop ginger. Peel and roughly chop garlic. Put these ingredients in a blender, add the remaining ingredients, except turmeric, add 60ml/¼ cup of water, and make a smooth paste. Remove, add turmeric, mix well and keep aside.

The Gravy : Peel, wash and roughly chop onions. Remove eyes, wash and roughly chop tomatoes. Clean, wash and roughly chop coriander. Then add the *masala*, *bhunno*/stir-fry until the fat leaves the sides, add tomatoes and salt, *bhunno*/stir-fry until the fat leaves the sides, add 480ml/2 cups of water, bring to a boil, reduce to low heat and simmer, stirring occasionally, until reduced by half. Then add the coriander paste, stir, add butter, and stir until a sheen appears on the surface (approx 2-3 minutes). Remove and adjust the seasoning. Serve yam on a bed of gravy.

Coondapur Koli Thalna

Chicken Legs in piquant Mangalorean Pepper and Chilli Gravy

Ingredients

4 Chicken Legs
30ml/2 Tbs Lemon Juice

Salt
Desi Ghee/Clarified Butter to shallow fry
  chicken

The *Coondapur* Masala

125g/½ lb Red Chillies
60g/2 oz *Dhania*/Coriander Seeds
10g/2½ tsp Black Peppercorns

3.75g/1½ tsp *Methidaana*/Fenugreek
  Seeds
12 flakes Garlic
3g/1 tsp *Haldee*/Turmeric Powder

The Gravy

50g/¼ cup *Desi Ghee*/Clarified Butter
6 flakes Garlic
120g/1 cup Onions
1/2 *Narial*/Coconut

360ml/1½ cups Coconut Milk (Second
  extract)
60ml/¼ cup Coconut Milk (First
  extract)
Salt

Serves: 4
Preparation Time: 1 hour
Cooking Time: 35 minutes

Preparation

The Chicken : Halve the chickens lengthways and bone carefully, leaving the 'ankle knob' intact. Then place the halves between dry towels and flatten with a heavy steak hammer/bat/cleaver/rolling pin.

The *Coondapur* Masala : Individually roast red chillies and coriander on a *tawa*/griddle over very low heat until each emits its unique aroma. Roast peppercorns until they begin to puff up. Roast fenugreek seeds until they begin to change colour. **Do not** peel the garlic. Put all these ingredients into a mortar and pound with a pestle to obtain a coarse powder. Remove, add turmeric, mix well and preserve in a sterilised and airtight container. **Shelf life:** 6 months

The Marination : Mix 9g/1 Tbs of *Coondapur Masala* with lemon juice and salt, evenly rub the chicken legs with this marinade and reserve for 30 minutes.

The Gravy : Remove the brown skin, wash and grate coconut, remove to a blender, add 30ml/ 2 Tbs of water, make a smooth paste, remove and keep aside. Peel, wash and finely chop onions. Peel and finely chop garlic.

Cooking

Heat half the *ghee*, add garlic, sauté over medium heat until it begins to change colour, add onions and sauté until onions are translucent and glossy. Then add 18g/2 Tbs of *Coondapur Masala*, stir, add coconut paste and the second extract of coconut milk, bring to a boil, reduce to low heat, cover and simmer, stirring occasionally, until reduced by half. Remove *handi*/pan from heat, stir-in the first extract of coconut milk, bring to just under a boil, ensuring that it does not come to a bubble (or the coconut milk will curdle), reduce to low heat and simmer until the gravy is medium thick. Remove and adjust the seasoning.

Heat half the *ghee* in a frying pan, arrange the marinated chicken legs, two at a time, in it, cover and grill over very low heat, turning at regular intervals, for 5-6 minutes or until cooked. Remove to absorbent paper to drain excess fat. Serve chicken on a bed of gravy.

Muru Curry

Oysters in velvety Coconut Gravy

Ingredients

24 Oysters
75ml/5 Tbs Coconut Oil
1.25g/½ tsp *Sarsondaana*/Black
   Mustard Seeds
7.5g/¾ " Ginger

6 flakes Garlic

6 Green Chillies

120g/1 cup Onions
1.5g/½ tsp *Haldee*/Turmeric Powder
24 *Kaari Patta*/Curry Leaf

360ml/1½ cups Coconut Milk (Second
   extract)
240ml/1 cup Coconut Milk
   (First extract)
Salt

Serves: 4
Preparation Time: 45 minutes
Cooking Time: 15 minutes

Preparation

The Oyster : Rinse shells, scrub with a brush, open oysters, remove the flesh and reserve on a bed of ice. Reserve the shells.

The Ginger : Scrape, wash and finely chop.

The Garlic : Peel and finely chop.

The Green Chillies : Wash green chillies, slit, seed, finely chop and discard stems.

The Onions : Peel, wash and finely chop.

The Curry Leaf : Clean and wash.

Cooking

Heat 3 Tbs or 45ml of coconut oil in a *handi*/pan, add mustard, stir over medium heat until it begins to pop, add ginger, garlic and green chillies and sauté over medium heat for a few seconds. Then add onions, sauté until translucent and glossy, add turmeric—dissolved in 15ml/1 Tbs of water—and *bhunno*/stir-fry until the moisture evaporates. Add curry leaf, stir, add the second

135

extract of coconut milk, bring to a boil, reduce to low heat, cover and simmer, stirring occasionally, until reduced by half. Remove *handi*/pan from heat, stir-in the first extract of coconut milk, bring to just under a boil, ensuring that it does not come to a bubble (or the coconut milk will curdle), reduce to low heat and simmer until the gravy is medium thin.

To cook the oysters, heat the remaining coconut oil, add the oysters and sauté over medium heat until they begin to release their juices. Add to the simmering gravy, stir carefully, remove and adjust the seasoning.

EPISODE 017

with Chef Pratap Reddy,
WELCOMGROUP

Indians have a penchant for barbecues—*tandoor, sigarhi* and *bhatti*. It is not surprising that the Anglo-Indian fare is a national favourite. This episode show-cased the gems from the Anglo-Indian grill.

Grilled Chicken Leg with BBQ Sauce

Ingredients

8 Leg of Chicken (thigh & drumstick)
30g/5¼ tsp

Salt
Garlic Paste (strain)

The Barbecue Sauce

300ml/11 oz Tomato Purée
100g/3 oz Bacon (chop)
2 Chotti Elaichi/Green Cardamom
2 Lavang/Cloves
1 stick Daalcheeni/ Cinnamon
2g/1 tsp Dhania/Coriander Seeds
2g/1 tsp Jeera/Cumin Seeds
100g/3 oz Onions (roughly chop)
10 flakes Garlic (roughly chop)
100g/3 oz Celery (roughly chop)
100g/3 oz Leeks (roughly chop)

100g/3 oz Carrots (roughly chop)
45g/1½ oz Parsley (roughly chop)
30g/1 oz Taaza Dhania/Coriander
 (roughly chop)
10g Taaza Pudhina/Mint (roughly chop)
4 Fresh/Dried Red Chillies (finely chop)
Salt
1.5g/½ tsp Chotti Elaichi/Green
 Cardamom Powder
0.75g/¼ Jaiphal/Nutmeg Powder

Serves: 4
Preparation Time: 5.30 hours
Cooking Time: 25 minutes

Preparation

The Chicken : Make a slit on the inner side of the leg, carefully pry out the thigh and drumstick bones without splitting the skin (ask the butcher in case you cannot do it; you can cook the dish without the skin as well). Clean, wash and pat dry.

The First Marination : Rub the chicken legs evenly with garlic paste and salt, and reserve until the barbecue sauce is ready.

The Barbecue Sauce : Put green cardamom, cloves, cinnamon and coriander seeds in a mortar and pound with a pestle to break the spices into smaller pieces. If using dried chillies, soak in water for 15 minutes and then finely chop.

Toss bacon over medium heat in a saucepan until the fat leaves the meat completely, add the broken spices and cumin seeds, stir until cumin begins to crackle. Then add onions and garlic, sauté for a minute, add the remaining ingredients except salt, cardamom powder and nutmeg, and sauté for 2-3 minutes. Now add tomato purée and a little water, if necessary, bring to a boil, reduce to low heat and reduce until of a thin sauce consistency.

Remove and force through a fine mesh sieve into a separate saucepan, return the sauce to heat and allow to simmer to ketchup consistency. Remove, add salt, cardamom powder and nutmeg, stir. Adjust the seasoning. Reserve a fourth of the sauce for basting.

The Second Marination : Rub the chicken legs evenly with the barbecue sauce and reserve in the refrigerator for 4 hours, turning often.

Cooking

Arrange the marinated chicken legs on a mesh grill and roast over medium heat, turning and basting with butter at regular intervals until cooked.

Serve with the reserved barbecue sauce.

Bangalooru Grilled Lobster

Ingredients

4 Lobster (large)
Melted Butter to baste
60ml/¼ cup White Wine

4 springs *Soya/Sua/*Dill
Salt

The Masala

60g/2 oz Onions
6 Whole Red Chillies
15g/1½ piece Ginger
10 flakes Garlic
4g/1 tsp Black Peppercorns

2g/ 1tsp *Jeera/*Cumin Seeds
2 sticks *Daalcheeni/*Cinnamon (1")
2 sticks *Chotti Elaichi/*Green Cardamom
2 sticks *Lavang/*Cloves

Serves: 4
Preparation Time: 4:30 minutes
Cooking Time: 5-6 minutes

Preparation

The Lobster : Split lobster down the middle, vein carefully, wash and pat dry. Clean, wash and chop dill leaves.

The Masala : Peel, wash and roughly chop onions. Refresh red chillies, pat dry, split, seed, roughly chop and discard stems. Scrape, wash and roughly chop ginger. Peel and roughly chop garlic. Put these ingredients in a blender, add the remaining ingredients, pulse to make a coarse masala. Remove, add wine, dill and salt, mix well and keep aside.

The Marination : Rub the exposed lobster meat evenly with the masala and reserve in the refrigerator for 30 minutes.

Cooking

Arrange the lobster on a mesh grill, shell-side up and roast over medium heat, basting with butter at regular intervals until cooked (approx 3-4 minutes). Turn once to 'colour' the shell.

Mustard Chutney Marinated Grilled Bataer

Ingredients

12 Japanese Quails

Butter for basting

The Marination

120ml/½ cup *Kashundi* (Bengali bottle mustard)
90g/3 oz *Chakka Dahi*/Yoghurt Cheese/Hung Yoghurt
60g/2 oz Processed/Cheddar Cheese
30ml/2 Tsp Toddy/Malt Vinegar
20 ml/4 tsp Lemon Juice
15 ml/ 1Tsp Rum
10 ml/2 Tsp Worcester Sauce
20g/3¼ tsp Garlic Paste (strain)

15g/2½ tsp Ginger Paste (strain)
A generous pinch *Kaala Namak*/ Black Rock Salt Powder
Salt
3g/1 tsp Black Pepper (freshly roasted & coarsely ground)
1.5g/½ tsp *Chotti Elaichi*/Green Cardamom Powder
Lavang/Clove Powder
A pinch of *Javitri*/Mace Powder

Serves: 4
Preparation Time: 1:45 hour
Cooking Time: In Tandoor—10 minutes
In Oven—12 minutes

Preparation

The Quails : Clean, remove the skin, carefully cut the breastbone down the middle to flatten and open like a book. Then make slanting incisions—2 on each breast, 2 on each thigh and 1 on each drumstick.

The Marination : Whisk the yoghurt cheese in a bowl. Grate and then mash the cheese with the base of the palm. Mix cheese and the remaining ingredients with the yoghurt cheese, and rub the quails evenly with this marinade. Reserve for 1 hour.

Cooking

Arrange quails on a mesh grill, ribcage-side down and roast over medium heat, turning and basting with butter at regular intervals until cooked (approx 8-9 minutes).

Grilled Broccoli

Ingredients

4 Broccoli (150g/5 oz each)
8 Cheese slices

1g/½ tsp *Shahi Jeera*/Black cumin seeds
Cooking oil to grease baking tray

The Seasoning

65g/2¼ oz Cumin Seeds
65g/2¼ oz Black Peppercorns
60g/2 oz *Kaala Namak*/Black Salt
30g/1 oz Dry Mint Leaves
5g/2 tsp *Ajwain*/Carom

5g/ 1 tsp Asafoetida/Heeng
4g/¾ tsp Tartric
150g/5¾ oz Mango Powder
20g/¾ oz Ginger Powder
20g/¾ oz *Peeli Mirch*/Yellow Chilli
   Powder

The Filling

60g/2 oz Paneer
60g/2 oz Cheese (cheddar/processed)
60g/2 oz Marscapone Cheese
16 Almonds
30g/ 1 oz Pomegranate
8 Stuffed Olives

2 Green Chillies
1g/¾ tsp Black Pepper (freshly roasted
   & coarsely ground
1.5g/½ tsp *Chotti Elaichi*/Green
   Cardamom Powder
Salt

Serves: 4
Preparation Time: 45 minutes
Cooking Time: 7-8 minutes

Preparation

The Broccoli : Remove the thick stems and leaves, clean, wash to remove grit, blanch in salted boiling water for 2-3 minutes. Drain, refresh in iced water, drain and pat dry.

The Seasoning : Put all ingredients, except mango powder, salt, ginger powder and yellow chilli powder, in mortar and pound with pestle to make fine powder. Transfer to clean, dry bowl, add remaining ingredients and mix well. Sift and store in sterilised, dry and airtight container. Yield : 450g/1 lb.

    Place the broccoli, stem side up, on a tray. Sprinkle 4.5g/1½ tsp of the seasoning on each of the florets and let them 'sweat' for 10 minutes.

The Filling : Grate *paneer* and cheese in a bowl and blend both with marscapone. Blanch almonds, cool, peel and chop. Chop stuffed olives. Remove stems, slit, seed, wash and finely chop green chillies. Add these and the remaining ingredients to the marscapone mixture, mix well and divide into 4 equal portions.

The Stuffing : Place the broccoli on the greased baking tray stem side up, stuff a portion of the filling carefully between the florets, ensuring they do not break. Turn the florets over and keep aside.

The Oven : Pre-heat to 275°F.

Cooking

Place the baking tray in the pre-heated oven and grill for 3-4 minutes.

Finishing

Remove florets from baking tray, wrap 2 cheese slices around each floret, sprinkle black cumin seeds and grill in the oven under top heat or under a salamander until the cheese melts.

EPISODE 018

with Chef Ashok Sharma,
THE HYATT

Paneer — cottage cheese — although a dairy produce, is reckoned as a 'vegetable' in India. It is encountered in many equally tempting forms — plain, as fritters, grilled, curried, stir-fried, scrambled, as a filling, 'stuffed' and paired with a mind boggling variety of real vegetables. No *Daawat* is complete without the *paneer*. How could we do without it? We devoted an entire episode to *paneer* specialities and explain how *paneer* can be made at home. Manjit worked with us on this one.

Til Ki Tikki

Cottage Cheese Croquettes rolled in Sesame Seeds

Ingredients

The Croquette

400g/14 oz *Paneer*
250g/9 oz *Bhein/Nadru/*Lotus Roots
15ml/1 Tbs Lemon Juice
120g/4 oz Green Peas

120g/4 oz Carrots
30g/1 oz Green Peppercorns
15g/1½" piece Ginger

8 *Guchchi/*Morels
60g/2 oz Flour of Roasted *Channa/*Gram
2g/1 tsp *Jeera/*Cumin Seeds
3g/1 tsp Black Pepper (freshly roasted &
  coarsely ground)
Salt
*Safaed Til/*Sesame Seeds to prinkle
Cooking oil to deep fry

The Sauce

500g/1 lb 2 oz Tomatoes
90ml/6 Tbs Cooking Oil
60g/2 oz Onions
8 flakes Garlic
15g/½" piece Ginger
30g/1 oz Carrots
8 Black Peppercorns

2 *Tej Patta/*Bay Leaf
1.5/½" tsp Black Pepper (freshly
  roasted & coarsely ground)
Salt
7.5/1¼ tsp Red Chilli Paste
10g/1½ tsp *Beurre Manie*

Serves: 4
Preparation Time: 1 hours
Cooking Time: 45 minutes

Preparation

The *Paneer* : Grate in a bowl.

The Lotus Roots : Peel, rinse thoroughly, grate, put in a *handi*/pan, add lemon juice and enough water, boil until tender. Drain, cool, squeeze in a napkin to ensure there is no moisture and then coarsely mince.

The Remaining Vegetables : Boil peas until *al dente*, drain, refresh in iced water and drain when ready to cook. Peel carrots, wash, finely chop, blanch in salted boiling water for 8-10 minutes, drain, refresh in iced water and drain when ready to cook. Peel, wash and finely chop ginger.

The Green Pepper Corns : Drain and pat dry.

The Morels : Soak in hot water for 10 minutes, drain, wash in running water to remove grit, soak again in hot water for 5 minutes. Drain and finely chop.

The Croquette : Put all the ingredients, mix well, divide into 20 equal portions, make croquettes, roll in sesame seeds and refrigerate.

The Sauce : Remove eyes, wash and roughly chop tomatoes. Peel, wash and roughly chop onions and carrots. Peel garlic. Scrape, wash and roughly chop ginger.

Cooking

To prepare the sauce, heat oil in a pot, add onions and garlic, sauté over medium heat until onions are translucent and glossy, add the carrots, ginger, peppercorns and bay leaves, stir for 5-6 minutes, add tomatoes, stir, cover and cook, stirring occasionally, until mashed. Then add 1 litre of water, bring to a boil, reduce to low heat, cover and simmer, stirring occasionally, until reduced by half. Remove and force through a soup strainer into a saucepan. Return sauce to heat, add pepper and salt, stir, reduce to low heat, add chilli paste and *beurre manie*, stir and then simmer, stirring at regular intervals, until of sauce consistency. Remove, adjust the seasoning and keep warm.

Heat oil in a *kadhai*/wok, add the croquettes and deep fry over medium heat until golden. Remove to absorbent paper to drain the excess fat. Keep warm. Arrange croquettes on the sauce and serve.

Talahua Paneer Pasanda

Tamarind-marinated Yam in Tomato Gravy

Ingredients

24 roundels *Paneer* (Cottage Cheese)
  2" diameter; ⅜" thick

Cooking oil to deep fry
12 sprigs Coriander

The Filling

45g/1½ oz *Paneer* (Cottage Cheese)
Laal Shimla Mirch/Red Bell Peppers
30g/1 oz Spinach
30g/1 oz Butter
1.25g/½ tsp *Shahi Zeera*/Black Cumin
  Seeds

30g/1 oz Cheese (Cheddar/Processed)
45g/1½ oz Carrots
3g/1 tsp Black Pepper (freshly roasted
  and coarsely ground)
A pinch of *Jaiphal*/Nutmeg Powder
Salt

The Batter

100g/3 oz Rice Flour
2 Green Chillies
4.5g/1½ tsp *Saunf*/Fennel Powder

0.5g/1 tsp *Zaafraan*/Saffron
Salt

The Sauce

500g/3 cups Tomatoes
90ml/6 Tbs Cooking Oil
60g/½ cup Onions
8 flakes Garlic
30g/1 oz Carrots
8 Black Pepper (freshly roasted
  and coarsely ground)

2 *Tej Patta*/Bay Leaf
A few *Taaza Dhania*/Coriander Stems
1.5g/½ tsp Black Pepper (freshly roasted
  and coarsely ground)
Salt
10g/1½ tsp *Beurre Manie*

Serves: 4
Preparation Time: 1 hour
Cooking Time: 45 minutes

Preparation

The Paneer : Trim the roundels and reserve the trimmings for the filling.

149

The Coriander : Clean, wash, snip off the stems and reserve for the sauce. Keep the sprigs in a pan of iced water for garnish. Drain at the time of plating.

The Filling : Grate *paneer* and cheese. Peel carrots, wash and cut into the smallest possible dices. Wash red bell pepper, seed and cut into the smallest possible dices. Remove stems, wash spinach in running water to remove grit, blanch in salted boiling water for 2 minutes, drain and refresh in iced water. Drain and finely chop.

Melt butter in a frying pan, add black cumin, stir over medium heat for 2-3 seconds, add the vegetables and toss over medium heat until devoid of moisture. Put all the ingredients in a bowl, mix well and divide into 12 equal portions.

The Stuffing : Place half the *paneer* roundels on a work surface, spread a portion of the filling evenly on top, cover with the remaining roundels to make "sandwiches" and keep aside.

The Batter : Wash green chillies, slit, seed, finely chop and discard stems. Crush saffron with a pestle or back of spoon, reserve in 15ml/1 Tbs of lukewarm water for 5 minutes and then make a paste. Put rice flour in a bowl, add the remaining ingredients and 120ml/½ cup of water, and make a smooth batter.

The Sauce : Remove eyes, wash and roughly chop tomatoes. Peel, wash and roughly chop onions and carrots. Peel and crush garlic. Clean and wash coriander stems including the reserved ones.

Cooking

To prepare the sauce, heat oil in a *handi*/pot, add onions and garlic, sauté over medium heat until onions are translucent and glossy, add the carrots, peppercorns and bay leaves, stir for 1½-2 minutes, add tomatoes, stir, cover and cook, stirring occasionally, until mashed. Then add 1 litre/4¼ cups of water and coriander, bring to a boil, reduce to low heat, cover and simmer, stirring at regular intervals, until reduced by half. Remove and force through a soup strainer into a saucepan. Return sauce to heat, add pepper and salt, stir, reduce to low heat, add *beurre manie* and simmer until of sauce consistency. Remove, adjust the seasoning and keep warm.

To prepare the accompaniments, melt butter in a frying pan, add sugar and 15ml/1 Tbs of water and stir over low heat until the mixture is of syrupy consistency. Then add the mushrooms and vegetables, stir, add pepper and salt and stir for 3-4 minutes or until glazed. Remove, sprinkle lemon juice, stir, adjust the seasoning and keep warm.

To prepare the *paneer*, heat oil in a *kadhai*/wok, dip the paneer "sandwiches" in the batter and deep fry over medium heat until golden. Remove to absorbent paper to drain excess fat, serve the "sandwiches" on a bed of sauce.

150

Khatta Murgh

Cottage Cheese-stuffed Breast of Chicken in Yoghurt Cheese Gravy

Ingredients

8 Breasts of Chicken (large)
175g/6 oz *Chakka Dahi*/Yoghurt-
   Cheese/Hung Yoghurt
30g/1 oz Almond Paste
15g/2½ tsp Green Chilli Paste
3g/1 tsp White Pepper Powder
Salt

90ml/6 Tbs Single Cream
20g/1½ Tbs Butter (unsalted)
15ml/1 Tbs Lemon Juice
3g/1 tsp *Chotti Elaichi*/Green Cardamom
   Powder

The Marination

30g/5¼ tsp Garlic Paste (strain)
20g/3½ tsp Ginger Paste (strain)

15ml/1 Tbs Lemon Juice
Salt

The Filling

200g/7 oz Cheese (Cheddar/Processed)
180g/1½ cups Spring Onions (Bulbs)
10g/1" piece Ginger
Seeds

4 Green Chillies
16 *Taaza Pudhina*/Mint Leaf
2.5g/1 tsp *Shahi Jeera*/Black Cumin

The Garnish

0.5g/1 tsp *Zaafraan*/Saffron
15ml/1 Tbs Milk

8 *Taaza Pudhina*/Mint Leaf

Serves: 4
Preparation Time: 50 minutes
Cooking Time: 30 minutes

Preparation

The Chicken : Clean, remove the skin, bone but retain the winglet bones, wash and pat dry. With a sharp knife make a deep slit along the thick edge of each breast to make a pocket, taking care not to penetrate the flesh on the other side.

The Marination : Mix all the ingredients in a bowl, evenly rub the breasts with this marinade and reserve for 20 minutes.

The Filling : Grate cheese in a bowl. Wash and cut spring onions into thin roundels. Scrape, wash and finely chop ginger. Wash green chillies, slit, seed, finely chop and discard stems. Wash mint leaves. Mix these ingredients and cumin with cheese, and divide into 8 equal portions.

The Stuffing : Pack a portion of the filling in the pockets of the marinated breasts and then seal each with the tip of a knife, ensuring that the flesh is not pierced.

The Yoghurt Cheese Mixture : Put yoghurt cheese in a large bowl, add half the cream and the remaining ingredients, except lemon juice and butter, and whisk to mix well. Coat the stuffed chicken with this mixture. Reserve the remaining mixture.

The Garnish : Crush saffron threads with pestle or back of spoon, reserve in lukewarm milk for 5 minutes and then make a paste. Clean, wash and pluck mint leaves, discard the stems.

The Cooking

Arrange the breasts, alongwith the marinade, in a non-stick frying pan, pour on the reserved yoghurt cheese mixture, place little knobs of butter on top, cover with aluminium foil and cook over medium heat until cooked but not coloured (approx 12-15 minutes). Remove the chicken breasts and keep aside. Pass the gravy through a fine mesh soup strainer into a separate saucepan. Return the gravy to heat, add the remaining cream and bring to just under a boil over medium heat, stirring continuously, until of sauce consistency. Remove, stir-in lemon juice and adjust the seasoning. Garnish with equal quantities of saffron and mint and serve warm.

Dhingri Dulma

Cottage Cheese Scramble with Champignon and Bell Peppers

Ingredients

200g/7 oz Button Mushrooms
450g/1 lb *Paneer*/Cottage Cheese
1 *Laal Shimla Mirch*/Red Bell
  Peppers *(large)*
1 *Harri Shimla Mirch*/Green Bell
  Peppers (large)
1 *Peeli Shimla Mirch*/Yellow Bell
  Peppers (large)
50g/¼ cup *Desi Ghee*/Clarified Butter
2.5g/1 tsp *Shahi Jeera*/Black Cumin Seeds
4 Spring Onions
25g/4 tsp Ginger Paste (strain)
25g/4 tsp Garlic Paste (strain)
4.5g/1½ tsp Red Chilli Powder
175g/1 cup Tomatoes
Salt

3g/1 tsp Black Pepper (freshly roasted &
  coarsely ground)
A generous pinch of *Chotti Elaichi*/Green
  Cardamom Power
A generous pinch of *Lavang*/Clove
  Powder
A generous pinch of *Jaiphal*/Nutmeg
  Powder
A generous pinch of *Kasoori Methi*/
  Fenugreek Leaf Powder
A generous pinch of *Kala Namak*/Black
  Rock Salt Powder
15g/1½ " piece Ginger
12.5g/¼ cup *Taaza Dhania*/Coriander

Serves: 4
Preparation Time: 30 minutes
Cooking Time: 15 minutes

Preparation

The Mushrooms : Remove the earthy base of the stalks, slice and wash just prior to cooking.

The *Paneer* : Crumble with the fingers.

The Remaining Vegetables : Wash bell peppers, quarter, seed, cut into 1/8″ thick strips and discard stems. Peel the outer layer of the spring onions, remove whiskers, wash, chop the white bulbs and slice the greens. Remove eyes, wash tomatoes, quarter, seed and dice. Scrape, wash and cut ginger into juliennes. Clean, wash and chop coriander.

Cooking

Heat *ghee* in a *kadhai*/wok, add cumin and stir over medium heat until it begins to pop, add the chopped onions, sauté until light golden, add the ginger and garlic pastes, *bhunno*/stir-fry until the moisture evaporates. Then add red chillies, stir, add tomatoes, *bhunno*/stir-fry until the moisture evaporates, add mushrooms and *bhunno*/stir-fry until the mushroom liquor evaporates. Now add bell peppers, *bhunno*/stir-fry for 15-20 seconds, add *paneer* and salt, *bhunno*/stir-fry for a minute, add pepper, green cardamom, clove, nutmeg, *kasoori methi* and rock salt, stir, remove and adjust the seasoning. Garnish with ginger and coriander.

154

EPISODE 019

with Chef Ashok Sharma,

THE HYATT

An entire episode was dedicated to that almost forgotten delicacy — quails. Don't get us wrong. We remember that *bataer* is an endangered species and forbidden, but the ban does not apply to farm bred birds and this is what we use and recommend. Once the supplier was identified one did not have to be the proverbial blind man to be gifted the most delicious morsel by lady luck — *andhe ke haath bataer* — and we could serve the *bataer* in myriad forms, stuffed, as a filling in refreshing emerald drape, *harra masala*, and more. Ashok Sharma handled the *bataer* on the set.

Bataer Kofta

Stuffed with Tartare of Prawns in Pepper Gravy

Ingredients

800g/1¾ lb Mince of *Bataer*/Quails
50g/2 oz Chicken Fat
10g/1" piece Ginger
6.5g/2 Tbs *Taaza Dhania*/Coriander
2 Green Chillies

3g/1 tsp *Jeera*/Cumin Powder
2g/1 tsp *Motti Elaichi*/Black
  Cardamom Seeds
Salt
Cooking oil to pan grill *kofta*

The Filling

12 Prawns (medium)
60ml/¼ cup *Taaza Anaar*/Fresh
  Pomegranate Juice or Lemon Juice
7.5g/1¼ tsp Ginger paste (strain)

7.5g/1¼ tsp Garlic paste (strain)
Salt
30g/1 oz/¼ cup Cheese (processed/
  cheddar)

The Gravy

60ml/¼ cup Cooking oil
3 *Chotti Elaichi*/Green Cardamom
3 *Lavang*/Cloves
1 stick *Daalcheeni*/Cinnamon (1")
1 *Tej Patta*/Bay Leaf
3g/1½ tsp *Jeera*/Cumin Seeds
250g/9 oz Onions
12.5g/2 tsp Ginger paste (strain)
12.5g/2 tsp Garlic paste (strain)
9g/1 Tbs *Dhania*/Coriander Powder

1.5g/½ tsp *Haldee*/Turmeric Powder
1.5g/½ tsp Red Chilli Powder
225g/8 oz Tomato Purée (fresh)
9g/1 Tbs Black Pepper (freshly roasted
  & coarsely ground)
1 litre/4¼ cups Chicken Stock
Salt
60ml/¼ cup Coconut Cream
A few Green Peppercorns (canned;
  for garnish)

Serves: 4
Preparation Time: 1:45 hours
Cooking Time: 45 minutes

Preparation

The Mince : Chop chicken fat, mix with the quail mince and mince again. Scrape, wash and finely chop ginger. Clean, wash and finely chop coriander. Wash green chillies, slit, seed, finely chop and discard stems. Crush (do not powder) black cardamom seeds. Mix these ingredients, cumin seeds and salt with the mince and divide into 8 equal portions, make balls and refrigerate for 30 minutes.

The Filling : Shell, vein, wash, pat dry and cut each prawn into 8 pieces. Put the remaining ingredients, except cheese, in a bowl, mix well and reserve the prawns in this marinade for 20 minutes. Remove prawns and hold aloft to drain the excess marinade. Grate and add cheese to the prawns, mix well and divide in 8 equal portions.

The *Kofta* : Flatten each mince ball between the palms, place a portion of the filling in the middle, make oval shaped *kofta* and refrigerate for 15 minutes. Heat a little oil in a frying pan and grill *kofta* over medium heat until evenly golden. Remove to absorbent paper to drain excess fat.

The Gravy : Peel, wash and grate onions.

Cooking

Heat oil in a *handi*/pan, add cardamom, cloves, cinnamon, bay leaf and cumin seeds, stir over medium heat until cardamom begins to change colour, add onions, *bhunno*/stir-fry until light golden, add the ginger and garlic pastes, *bhunno*/stir-fry until onions are golden. Then add coriander, turmeric and red chillies (all dissolved in 60ml/¼ cup of water), *bhunno*/stir-fry until the moisture evaporates, add tomato purée and *bhunno*/stir-fry until fat leaves the sides. Now add chicken stock, bring to a boil, reduce to low heat and simmer, stirring occasionally, until reduced by half. Remove and force gravy through a fine mesh soup strainer into a separate *handi*/pan. Return gravy to heat, bring to a boil, reduce to low heat, carefully add the *kofta* and pepper, cover and simmer, turning and stirring occasionally, for 2-3 minutes. Stir-in coconut cream, bring to just under a boil, remove and adjust the seasoning. Garnish with green peppercorns.

Bataer-Bharra Murgh Pasanda

Breast of Chicken stuffed with Tartare of Prawns in Pepper Gravy

Ingredients

8 Breasts of Chicken
8 *Bataer*/Quails

Cooking oil to shallow fry chicken

The Marination

60ml/¼ cup Lemon Juice
30g/5¼ tsp Garlic Paste (strain)

15g/2½ tsp Ginger Paste (strain)
Salt

The Stock

1 litre/4¼ cups Chicken Stock

¼ *Khus* Root

The Filling

60g/½ cup Bulbs of Spring Onions
12 *Taaza Dhania*/Coriander Stems
5g/½" piece Ginger
2 Green Chillies
7.5g/1 Tbs *Saunf*/Fennel Seeds

24 Black Peppercorns
24 Pistachios
50g/½ cup Cheese (processed/cheddar)

The Gravy

50g/¼ cup *Desi Ghee*/Clarified Butter
5 *Chotti Elaichi*/Green Cardamom
3 *Lavang*/Cloves
2 sticks *Daalcheeni*/Cinnamon (1")
2 *Tej Patta*/Bay Leaf
30g/5¼ tsp Garlic Paste (strain)
15g/2½ tsp Ginger Paste (strain)
4.5g/1½ tsp *Dhania*/Coriander Powder
1.5g/½ tsp Red Chilli Powder

200g/7 oz Yoghurt
90g/3 oz Fried Onion Paste
30g/1 oz Cashewnut Paste
120ml/½ cup Fresh Tomato Purée
Salt
0.75g/¼ tsp *Jaiphal*/Nutmeg Powder
15ml/1 Tbs Lemon Juice
1g/2 tsp *Zaafraan*/Saffron

Serves: 4
Preparation Time: 1:45 hours
Cooking Time: 45 minutes

Preparation

The Chicken : Clean, remove the skin, bone but retain the winglet bones, wash and pat dry. With a sharp knife make a deep slit along the thick edge of each breast to make a pocket, taking care not to penetrate the flesh on the other side.

The Marination : Mix all the ingredients, rub the chicken breasts—inside and out—and reserve for 30 minutes.

The Stock : Put stock in a *handi*/stock pot, add the *khus* root, bring to a boil, reduce to low heat and simmer for 15 minutes. Remove and pass through a fine mesh soup strainer into a separate *handi*/pan.

The Filling : Clean quails, bone, wash, pat dry and mince. Peel outer layer, wash and finely chop spring onions. Clean, wash and finely chop coriander. Scrape, wash and finely chop ginger. Wash green chillies, slit, seed, finely chop and discard stems. Put fennel and peppercorns in a mortar and crush with a pestle to obtain a coarse powder. Blanch pistachios, cool, remove the skin and halve. Grate cheese in a large bowl. Add all the ingredients to the cheese, mix well and transfer to a piping bag.

The Stuffing : Pack a portion of the filling in the pockets of the chicken breasts and then seal using the blunt edge of a knife.

The Gravy : Whisk yoghurt in a bowl. Crush saffron with pestle or back of spoon, reserve in 30ml/2 Tbs of lukewarm water for 5 minutes and then make a paste.

Cooking

Heat *ghee* in a *handi*/pan, add cardamom, cloves, cinnamon and bay leaf, and stir over medium heat until cardamom begins to change colour. Add the ginger and garlic pastes (dissolved in 100ml/7 Tbs of water), *bhunno*/stir-fry until the moisture evaporates, add coriander powder and red chillies (dissolved in 30ml/2 Tbs of water), *bhunno*/stir-fry until the fat comes to the surface completely and the masala becomes grainy. Remove *handi*/pan from heat, stir-in yoghurt, *bhunno*/stir-fry until the fat leaves the sides, add fried onion paste and *bhunno*/stir-fry until fat leaves the sides, add cashewnut paste, *bhunno*/stir-fry until the fat leaves the sides, add tomato purée and *bhunno*/stir-fry until the fat leaves the sides. Then add stock and salt, bring to a boil, reduce to low heat and simmer, stirring occasionally, until reduced by a third. Remove, pass through a fine mesh soup strainer into a separate *handi*/pan, return gravy to heat, add chicken, bring to a boil, add the chicken breasts, reduce to low heat and simmer, stirring occasionally, until chicken is cooked and gravy is of medium thick sauce consistency. Now add nutmeg, stir, add lemon juice, stir, add saffron, stir, remove and adjust the seasoning.

Duck Moiley

Cubes of Duck in East Indian Bottle Masala Gravy

Ingredients

8 Breasts of Duck
200g/7 oz Potatoes

Cooking oil to fry duck and potatoes

The Gravy

90ml/6 Tbs Cooking Oil
16 flakes Garlic
15g/1½" Ginger
4 Green Chillies
6g/2 tsp *Bottle Masala*

Salt
60ml/¼ cup *Sirka*/Malt Vinegar
1.5g/½ tsp *Chotti Elaichi*/Green
    Cardamom Powder
1.5g/½ tsp *Lavang*/Clove Powder

The *Bottle Masala*

200g/7 oz Whole Dried Red Chillies
150g/5 oz *Kashmiri Deghi Mirch*
150g/5 oz *Dhania*/Coriander Seeds
60g/2 oz *Haldee*/Turmeric Root
30g/1 oz *Khus-khus*/Poppy Seeds
30g/1 oz *Safaed Til*/Sesame Seeds
30g/1 oz *Peeli Rai*/Yellow Mustard Seeds
30g/1 oz *Jeera*/Cumin Seeds
30g/1 oz Black Peppercorns
15g/½ oz *Chotti Elaichi*/Green Cardamom
15g/½ oz *Daalcheeni*/Cinnamon
15g/½ oz *Lavang*/Cloves

15g/½ oz *Gehun*/Whole Wheat
15g/½ oz *Channa Daal*
2 *Jaiphal*/Nutmeg
7.5g/¼ oz *Shahi Jeera*/Black Cumin Seeds
7.5g/¼ oz *Tej Patta*/Bay Leaf
7.5g/¼ oz *Daalcheeni*/Cinnamon Flowers
7.5g/¼ oz *Safaed Til*/Sesame Flowers
7.5g/¼ oz *Javitri*/Mace
7.5g/¼ oz *Kebab Cheeni*/Allspice
5g/⅙ oz *Heeng*/Asafoetida

Serves: 4
Preparation Time: 1:45 hours
Cooking Time: 30 minutes

Preparation

The Duck : Clean, remove the skin, bone, wash, pat dry and cut into 1½" cubes. Heat enough oil in a frying pan, add the duck cubes, sear over medium heat until lightly coloured, remove to absorbent paper to drain excess fat. Strain and reserve the oil to fry the potatoes.

The Potatoes : Peel, wash and cut into ½" cubes. Reheat the reserved oil (add more if necessary), add the potatoes, deep fry over medium heat until golden, remove to absorbent paper to drain excess fat. Strain and reserve the oil for the gravy.

The Gravy : Peel, wash and slice onions into thin roundels. Peel and finely chop garlic. Scrape, wash and finely chop ginger. Wash green chillies, slit, seed, finely chop and discard the stems.

The *Bottle Masala* : Put all the ingredients in a mortar and pound with a pestle to make a fine powder. (Alternatively, put the spices in a blender and grind in short pulses to make a fine powder). Sift and store in a sterilised, dry and airtight container.

Cooking

Heat 90ml/6 Tbs of the reserved oil, add onions, sauté over medium heat until translucent and glossy, add garlic, ginger and green chillies, and stir for 30 seconds. Add *bottle masala* and salt, stir, add 240ml/1 cup of water, bring to a boil and *bhunno*/stir-fry until fat leaves the sides. Then add duck, stir, add 360ml/1½ cups of water, bring to a boil, reduce to low heat, and simmer, stirring occasionally, until the duck is cooked. Now add vinegar, simmer, stirring at regular intervals, until fat leaves the sides, add potatoes, stir for a minute, sprinkle cardamom and cloves, stir, remove and adjust the seasoning.

Bataer Harra Masala

Quails marinated and cooked in Pomegranate, Coriander and Mint Chutney

Ingredients

8 *Bataer*/Quails

The Marination

25g/4 tsp Garlic Paste (strain)
10g/1¾ tsp Ginger Paste (strain)

30ml/2 Tbs Lemon Juice
Salt

The *Harra Masala*

100g/2 cups *Taaza Dhania*/Coriander
35g/1 cup *Pudhina*/Mint
4 Green Chillies

15g/½ oz *Anaardana*/Dried Pomegranate
  Seeds
4g/2 tsp *Jeera*/Cumin Seeds

The Gravy

60ml/¼ cup Cooking Oil
5 *Chotti Elaichi*/Green Cardamom
3 *Lavang*/Cloves
2 sticks *Daalcheeni*/Cinnamon (1")
2 *Tej Patta*/Bay Leaf

20g/2" piece Ginger
100g/3 oz Boiled Onion Paste
90g/3 oz Yoghurt
Salt

The Stock

720ml/3 cups Chicken Stock

20 *Pudhina*/Mint Leaves

The Garnish

10g/1" piece Ginger

30ml/2 Tbs Lemon Juice

Serves: 4
Preparation Time: 1 hour
Cooking Time: 30 minutes

Preparation

The Quails : Clean, remove the skin, trim, wash and pat dry.

The Marination : Mix all the ingredients, evenly rub the quails with this marinade and reserve for 30 minutes.

The *Harra Masala* : Clean, wash and roughly chop coriander and mint. Wash green chillies, slit, seed, roughly chop and discard the stems. Put these and the remaining ingredients in a blender, make a smooth paste, remove to a bowl and keep aside.

The Gravy : Scrape, wash and finely chop ginger. Whisk yoghurt in a bowl.

The Stock : Put chicken stock in a *handi*/pan, add mint leaves, bring to a boil, reduce to low heat and simmer until reduced by half. Remove and keep aside.

The Garnish : Scrape, wash and cut ginger into fine juliennes. Reserve the juliennes in lemon juice.

Cooking

Heat oil in a large *pateela*/pot, add cardamom, cloves, cinnamon and bay leaves, stir over medium heat until cardamom begins to change colour, add ginger and *bhunno*/stir-fry until the moisture evaporates. Then add boiled onion paste, *bhunno*/stir-fry until specks of fat begin to appear on the surface. Remove *pateela*/pot from heat, stir-in yoghurt, return *pateela*/pot to heat, *bhunno*/stir-fry until fat leaves the sides, add quails alongwith the marinade, and *bhunno*/stir-fry for 6-7 minutes. Now add *harra masala*, stir for a minute, add stock, bring to a boil, reduce to low heat and simmer, stirring occasionally, for 2-3 minutes or until the quails are cooked. Remove quails and keep aside. Pass the gravy through a fine mesh soup strainer into a saucepan, return gravy to heat, bring to a boil, reduce to low heat, add quails and simmer, stirring occasionally, until quails are napped. Remove and adjust the seasoning. Garnish with pickled ginger juliennes.

164

EPISODE 020

with Chef Davinder Kumar,
LE MERIDIEN

heenga Murgh Jugalbandi sought to 'fuse' crayfish with the fowl. What was music for the ears became a delicious duet for the palate on the sets of Daawat. The Combo won many adherents immediately.

Shanks are very popular with sub-continental meat eaters and Nalliwala Meat was included in the Daawat selection in due deference. This dish is labeled differently in different menus but as the bard said, what is there in the name, a nalliwalla is a nalliwala is a nalliwalla. One of the incomparable simple joys of life.

Bharta is a lipsmacking dish but is usually kept out of a party menu — due to lack of eye appeal. We had long wondered how this ugly duckling could somehow be transformed into a beautiful swan. The challenge lay in matching the taste with appearance. Daawat provided us with the opportunity to do this with Baingan Tower.

Jheenga Murgh Jugalbandi

Smoked Prawns and Chicken in Pumpkin Gravy

Ingredients

8 Chicken Breasts
16 Prawns (large)

Butter to baste

The Marination

25g/4 tsp Garlic Paste (strain)
15g/2½ tsp Ginger Paste (strain)
1.5g/½ tsp *Haldee*/Turmeric Powder

1.5g/½ tsp Red Chilli Powder
Salt
30ml/2 Tbs Lemon Juice

The *Dhuanaar*

2 sticks *Daalcheeni*/Cinnamon (1″)

4g/1 tsp *Desi Ghee*/Clarified Butter

The Gravy

75ml/5 Tbs Cooking Oil
5 *Chotti Elaichi*/Green Cardamom
2 sticks *Daalcheeni*/Cinnamon (1″)
2 *Tej Patta*/Bay Leaf
30g/5¼ tsp Ginger Paste (strain)
15g/2½ tsp Garlic Paste (strain)
60g/¼ cup Yoghurt

1.5g/½ tsp *Haldee*/Turmeric Powder
150g/5 oz Red Pumpkin
1.5g/½ tsp Red Chilli Powder
Salt
1 litre/4¼ cups Chicken Stock
1 Raw Mango (large)
30ml/2 Tbs Cream

The Tempering

12.5g/1 Tbs Butter

1.25g/½ tsp *Shahi Jeera*/Black
Cumin Seeds

The Garnish

Sua/Soya/Dill

Serves: 4
Preparation Time: 1:15 hours
Cooking Time: 45 minutes

Preparation

The Chicken : Clean, bone and slice horizontally from the narrower end to the thicker without slicing through. Then open the flap like the page of a book, wash, pat dry and gently flatten with a mallet.

The Marination : Mix all the ingredients, evenly rub the chicken with this marinade and reserve for 20 minutes.

The Prawns : Shell but retain the tails, slit, vein, wash and pat dry.

The *Dhuanaar* : Put 4-5 tiny glowing embers of charcoal in a small metal bowl and arrange in a large *handi*/pot. Place the prawns around the bowl. Put cinnamon in the metal bowl, pour on *ghee*, cover with a lid as soon as the smoke begins to rise and reserve for 20 minutes. Remove and keep aside.

The Assembling : Intertwine 2 prawns into an S shape with the tails on the outside, wrap the middle of the prawns (where the two heads meet) in the chicken breasts as tightly as possible, basting the prawns with butter as you wrap. Refrigerate for 30 minutes.

The Gravy : Put yoghurt in a bowl, add turmeric and whisk to mix well. Peel pumpkin, remove the seeds, roughly chop and boil until cooked and soft, drain, put in a blender and make a smooth purée. Peel the raw mango, halve, remove the stone, put in a blender and make a smooth purée.

Th Garnish : Clean dill, wash, drain and reserve in iced water.

Cooking

Heat oil in a *handi*/pan, add cardamom, cinnamon and bay leaf, stir over medium heat until cardamom begins to change colour, add the ginger and garlic pastes, and *bhunno*/stir-fry until the moisture evaporates. Remove *handi*/pan from heat, stir-in the yoghurt, return *handi*/pan to heat and *bhunno*/stir-fry until specks of fat begin to appear on the surface. Then add pumpkin purée, *bhunno*/stir-fry until fat leaves the sides, add red chillies and salt, stir for a minute, add chicken stock, bring to a boil, reduce to low heat, add the assembled chicken and prawns, cover and simmer, stirring occasionally, for 4-5 minutes or until cooked. Remove the assembled chicken and prawns, halve and keep warm. Now add mango purée to the gravy, cook for a minute, remove and pass through a fine mesh soup strainer into a separate *handi*/pan. Return gravy to heat, bring to a boil, reduce to low heat and simmer, stirring at regular intervals, until of sauce consistency. Stir-in cream, remove and adjust the seasoning. Keep warm.

To prepare the tempering, melt butter in a frying pan, add *shahi jeera*, stir over medium heat until it begins to pop and pour over the gravy. Garnish with dill.

Nalliwala Meat

Lamb Shanks in Saffron and Poppy Seed Gravy

Ingredients

12 *Nalli*/Shanks of Kid/Lamb
90g/7 Tbs *Desi Ghee*/Clarified Butter
6 *Chotti Elaichi*/Green Cardamom
4 *Motti Elaichi*/Black Cardamom
3 *Lavang*/Cloves
2 sticks *Daalcheeni*/Cinnamon (1")
1 *Tej Patta*/Bay Leaf
3g/1½ tsp *Jeera*/Cumin Seeds
200g/7 oz Onions
15g/2½ tsp Garlic Paste (strain)

10g/1¾ tsp Ginger Paste (strain)
4.5g/1½ tsp *Dhania*/Coriander Powder
4.5g/1½ tsp Red Chilli Powder
30g/2 Tbs *Khus-khus*/Poppy Seed Paste
125g/½ cup Fresh Tomato Purée
3g/1 tsp *Chotti Elaichi*/Green Cardamom
  Powder
1g/2 tsp *Zaafraan*/Saffron
Salt
Cooking Oil to grease roasting tray

The Marination

250g/1 cup Yoghurt
15g/2½ tsp Garlic Paste (strain)
10g/1¾ tsp Ginger Paste (strain)

0.75g/¼ tsp *Jaiphal*/Nutmeg Powder
  (freshly grated)
Salt

The Stock

1.5 litres/6½ cups Kid/Lamb Stock
10g/¼ cup *Pudhina*/Mint

½ *Khus* Root

The Garnish

4 sprigs *Taaza Dhania*/Coriander

Serves: 4
Preparation Time: 3:30 hours
Cooking Time: 1:45 hours

Preparation

The Kid/Lamb : Clean, remove the sinews, wash and pat dry. (Ask the butcher for *nalli* or shanks, ensuring they are open-ended on both sides.) Then remove the meat by carefully scraping along the length of the shanks, starting at the narrower end to expose the bone, leaving an inch

169

from the other end. (This is done so that when the meat is braised, it shrivels at the unexposed end, making the shank easy to cut at the time of eating. Also, it makes the dish more attractive.)

The Onions : Peel, wash and slice onions.

The Marination : Put yoghurt in a large bowl, add the remaining ingredients and whisk to mix well. Evenly rub the *nalli* and the boneless meat with this marinade and reserve for 3 hours.

The Stock : Clean and wash mint. Put kid/lamb stock in a *handi*/pan, bring to a boil, add mint and *khus*, reduce to low heat and simmer for 15-20 minutes. Remove, pass the stock through a fine mesh soup strainer into a separate *handi*/pan and keep aside.

The Saffron : Crush threads with pestle or back of spoon, reserve in 30ml/2 Tbs of lukewarm water and then make a paste.

The Garnish : Clean and wash coriander.

Cooking

Melt *ghee* in a *handi*/pan, add black and green cardamom, cloves, cinnamon and bay leaf, stir over medium heat until green cardamom begins to change colour, add cumin and stir until it begins to pop. Add onions, sauté until light golden, add the ginger and garlic pastes, sauté until onions are golden, add meat (reserve the marinade), increase to high heat and *bhunno*/stir-fry to sear for three minutes. Reduce to low heat, cover and cook, stirring occasionally, for 20 minutes (add a little stock to prevent sticking, if necessary). Uncover, *bhunno*/stir-fry until the moisture has evaporated, add coriander powder and one-fourth of the marinade, *bhunno*/stir-fry until the moisture has evaporated, add another fourth of the marinade and keep repeating the process until the marinade is used up. Now add red chillies (dissolved in 30ml/ 2 Tbs of water), stir for a minute, add poppy seed paste, *bhunno*/stir-fry until fat leaves the sides, add tomato purée and *bhunno*/stir-fry until the fat leaves the sides again. Add stock, increase to medium heat, bring to a boil, reduce to low heat, cover and simmer, stirring occasionally, until meat is cooked. Uncover and remove the meat. Pass the gravy through a fine mesh soup strainer into a separate *handi*/pan, return gravy to heat, add the meat, bring to a boil, reduce to low heat and simmer, stirring at regular intervals, until gravy is of medium-thin sauce consistency. Add cardamom powder and saffron, stir, remove and adjust the seasoning. Garnish with pickled ginger and coriander.

Bharwaan Gobhipatta Akhrot Ki Tarri

Cabbage Leaves stuffed with Peppered Vegetables in Walnut Gravy

Ingredients

1 head Iceberg Lettuce or Cabbage Butter to grease and baste (large)

The Filling

2 Carrots (medium)
1 Potato (medium)
60g/2 oz Peas
100g/3 oz Button Mushrooms
25g/2 Tbs Butter
2g/1 tsp *Jeera*/Cumin Seeds

100g/3 oz *Paneer*/Cottage Cheese
60g/2 oz Cheddar/Processed Cheese
3.25g/1 Tbs *Taaza Dhania*/Coriander
3g/1 tsp Black Pepper (freshly roasted
   & coarsely ground)
Salt

The Gravy

60g/5 Tbs *Desi Ghee*/Clarified Butter
15g/2½ tsp Ginger Paste (strain)
15g/2½ tsp Garlic Paste (strain)
480ml/2 cups Fresh Tomato Purée
10g/1" piece Ginger
6g/1 tsp Red Chilli Paste

Salt
45g/1½ oz *Akhrot*/Walnut Paste
90ml/6 Tbs *Anaar*/Pomegranate Juice
10g/3 Tbs *Tulsi*/Basil (fresh)
90ml/6 Tbs Cream

Serves: 4
Preparation Time: 1 hour
Cooking Time: 10 minutes

Preparation

The Lettuce/Cabbage : Remove the outer leaves, wash in running water to remove grit, remove of the 8 largest leaves, remove stems, blanch in salted boiling water for 15 seconds, drain and refresh in iced water. Shred ¼ of the remaining head and keep aside.

The Filling : Peel carrots and potatoes, wash, cut into ⅛" dices, blanch in salted boiling water for 2 minutes, drain, refresh in iced water, drain and pat dry. Boil peas in salted water until *al dente*. Remove the earthy lower bits of the stalks, wash mushrooms in running water to remove grit, and cut into ⅛" dices. Grate *paneer* and cheese in a large bowl.

Melt butter in a frying pan, add cumin, stir over medium heat until it begins to pop, add mushrooms, sauté until the moisture evaporates, add the blanched vegetables and stir for a minute. Remove, cool, add the reserved lettuce or cabbage and the remaining ingredients, mix well and divide into 8 equal portions.

The Stuffing : Pat the blanched lettuce or cabbage leaves, dry and gently flatten with the back of a ladle. Arrange a leaf in a round ladle, place a portion of the filling in the middle, roll into a pouch and carefully invert on a greased roasting tray. Repeat the process with the remaining leaves and portions of the filling.

The Gravy : Scrape, wash and cut ginger into fine juliennes. Clean, wash and chop basil.

The Oven : Pre-heat to 275°F.

Cooking

Put the tray in the pre-heated oven and bake for 3-4 minutes.

Melt *ghee* in a *handi*/pan, add the ginger and garlic pastes, and *bhunno*/stir-fry over medium heat until the moisture evaporates and the *masala* acquires a grainy texture. Then add tomato purée, bring to a boil, reduce to low heat, add ginger juliennes, red chilli paste and salt, cook, stirring occasionally, for 2-3 minutes. Add walnut paste and cook, stirring constantly, for 2 minutes. Now add pomegranate juice, simmer for 2-3 minutes, add basil, stir and continue to simmer until of thick sauce consistency. Remove, stir-in cream and adjust the seasoning.

Make a bed of the sauce in a shallow dish and arrange the baked stuffed lettuce or cabbage leaves on top.

Baghare Baingan Tower

*Eggplant Concasse layered between Aubergine slices
in Peanut, Tamarind and Basil Gravy*

Ingredients

6 Brinjals (large)
Mustard oil to deep fry Brinjals
90ml/6 Tbs Mustard Oil
20g/3½ tsp Garlic Paste (strain)
15g/2½ tsp Ginger Paste (strain)
3g/1 tsp *Haldee*/Turmeric Powder

3g/1 tsp Red Chilli Powder
Salt
200g/7 oz Fresh Tomato Purée
60g/2oz *Imlee*/Tamarind Pulp
1.5g/½ tsp *Jeera*/Cumin Powder
10g/1" piece Ginger

The Paste

75g/½ cup Roasted Peanuts
75g/¾ cup *Kopra*/Desiccated Coconut

45g/4½ Tbs *Safaed Til*/Sesame Seeds
250g/2 cups Onions

The Tempering

5ml/1 tsp *Sarson*/Mustard Oil
1.5g/⅓ tsp *Sarsondaana*/Black
   Mustard Seeds

16 *Kaari Patta*/Curry Leaf

The Concasse

45ml/3 Tbs *Sarson*/Mustard Oil
4g/2 tsp *Jeera*/Cumin Powder
90g/3 oz Onions
5g/½" piece Ginger

4 Green Chillies
85g/½ cup Tomatoes
Salt
6.5g/2 Tbs *Taaza Dhania*/Coriander

Serves: 4
Preparation Time: 2:30 hours
Cooking Time: 40 minutes

Preparation

The Brinjals : Remove stems, wash and pat dry. Cut brinjals into ¼" thick roundels. Reserve 8 of these of equal diameter from the middle for the *timbale* and the rest for the concasse, after removing the skin.

Heat enough mustard oil to a smoking point in a *kadhai*/wok, sprinkle a little water (to bring the temperature down quickly, though this must be done carefully or the splattering may cause burns), reheat, add the brinjal roundels and deep fry over medium heat until soft (approx. 3-4 minutes). Remove to absorbent paper to drain excess fat. In the same oil, add the peeled roundels, deep fry over medium heat until soft. Remove to absorbent paper to drain excess fat, cool and chop. Strain and reserve the oil.

The Ginger : Scrape, wash and cut into juliennes.

The Paste : Heat a *tawa*/griddle or a non-stick frying pan, roast coconut and sesame seeds, separately, over very low heat until each emits its unique aroma (approx. 1-1½ minutes in each case). Peel, wash and roughly chop onions. Put these ingredients in a blender, add peanuts and 180ml/¾ cup of water, make a smooth paste. Remove and keep aside.

The Tempering : Clean and wash curry leaf.

The Concasse : Peel, wash and chop onions. Scrape, wash and chop ginger. Wash green chillies, slit, seed, finely chop and discard the stems. Remove eyes, wash and roughly chop tomatoes. Clean, wash and finely chop coriander.

Heat mustard oil in a frying pan, add cumin, stir over medium heat until it begins to pop, add onions, sauté until translucent and glossy, add ginger and green chillies, and stir for a few seconds. Then add the tomatoes, *bhunno*/stir-fry until the fat leaves the sides, add the chopped brinjals and salt, *bhunno*/stir-fry until the concasse acquires a sheen (approx. 8-9 minutes). Remove, cool, add coriander, mix well and divide into 8 equal portions.

The Timbale : Arrange 4 rings of 4″ diameter on a roasting tray and place a fried brinjal roundel at the bottom of each. Place a portion of the concasse on top and level with a spatula. Place a second roundel on the concasse, top with the remaining portions of the concasse and level with a spatula.

The Oven : Pre-heat to 200°F

Cooking

To prepare the gravy, reheat 120ml/½ cup of the reserved mustard oil in a *handi*/pan, add the garlic and ginger pastes, and *bhunno*/stir-fry over medium heat until the moisture evaporates. Add turmeric and red chillies (dissolved in 30ml/2 Tbs of water) and *bhunno*/stir-fry until the moisture evaporates. Then add the paste, *bhunno*/stir-fry until the fat leaves the sides (adding a little water towards the end, if necessary, to ensure that the masala does not stick and burn), add tomato

174

purée and *bhunno*/stir-fry until the fat leaves the sides. Now add salt, stir, add tamarind pulp, cook for 4-5 minutes, stirring constantly, add 400ml/1²⁄₃ cups of water, bring to a boil, reduce to low heat and simmer until the gravy is of sauce consistency. Sprinkle cumin powder, stir, remove and adjust the seasoning.

To prepare the tempering, reheat 5ml/1 tsp of the reserved mustard oil, add mustard seeds, stir over medium heat until they begin to crackle, add curry leaf, stir until they stop spluttering. Pour over the gravy and stir.

Put the roasting tray in the pre-heated oven and bake for 2–3 minutes.

EPISODE 021

with Chef Vikrant Kapoor,
WELCOMGROUP

What can be more enticing than braids of lush hair dancing on the back of a beautiful maiden? Enamoured by the sight poets in different languages have gone into raptures. One such verse inspired the *gosht ki parandi* crafted for *Daawat*. Gastronomic license in the realm of poetry never yielded better results.

Baingan—brinjal—is often made the butt of jokes as the archetypal opportunist rolling along on the *thali* or derided as *be-gun*, devoid of any qualities. Ayurved, however, ascribes to it many beneficial properties. Many have been verified by modern science. *Khatte Baingan*, originally from Kashmir, was given a special beauty treatment to enhance eye appeal.

Gosht Ki Parandi

Braided Kid/Lamb fillets in Green Peppercorn and Star Anise Gravy

Ingredients

12 Fillets of Kid/Lamb (from the *raan*)   30ml/2 Tbs Coconut Oil

The Marination

20g/3½ tsp Raw Papaya Paste   4.5g/1½ tsp Black Pepper (freshly
10ml/2 tsp Cooking Oil   roasted & coarsely ground)
7.5ml/1½ tsp Ginger Juice   3g/1 tsp Saltpetre Powder
6g/2 tsp *Chakriphool*/Star Anise Powder   Salt

The Gravy

30ml/2 Tbs Coconut Oil   360ml/1½ cups Clear Lamb Stock
150g/5 oz Onions   240ml/1 cup Coconut Cream
3 *Chakriphool*/Star Anise   Salt
5g/2 tsp *Saunf*/Fennel Seeds   32 Green Peppercorns
8 Green Chillies   1.5g/½ tsp *Chotti Elaichi*/Green
10g/1" piece Ginger   Cardamom Powder
16 *Kaari Patta*/Curry Leaf

Serves: 4
Preparation Time: 2:30 hours
Cooking Time: 35 minutes

Preparation

The Meat : Clean, remove the tissue, trim the silver side (so called because it shines), wash and pat dry.

The Marination : Mix all the ingredients, rub the fillets with the mixture and reserve for at least ninety minutes. (Ideally, it should be left overnight in the refrigerator.)

The *Parandi* : Take 3 fillets and tie all three at one end with a string to prevent unwinding, make a plait or *parandi* and then tie the other end. Repeat the process to make a total of 4 plaits.

179

The Braising : Heat coconut oil in a large frying pan/skillet, add *parandi* and *bhunno*/sear over high heat until the meat changes colour (this is done to seal the juices). Reduce to low heat, cover and continue to cook, turning at regular intervals, until cooked (approx. 20 minutes). Remove, cut each into half and keep aside.

The Gravy : Peel, wash and finely slice onions. Break star anise into small pieces. Wash green chillies, slit, seed, finely chop and discard the stem. Scrape, wash and finely chop ginger. Wash curry leaf. Wash and pat dry green peppercorns.

Cooking

Heat coconut oil in a *handi*/pan, add onions and sauté over medium heat until translucent and glossy. Add star anise and fennel, stir for 30 seconds, add green chillies, ginger and curry leaf, until the leaf stop spluttering. Then add stock, bring to a boil, reduce to low heat and simmer, stirring occasionally, until reduced by half. Remove and pass gravy through a fine mesh soup strainer into a separate *handi*/pan. Return *handi*/pan to heat, add *parandi*, bring to a boil, reduce to low heat, stir in coconut cream, and bring to just under a boil. Now add green peppercorns and green cardamom powder, stir, remove and adjust the seasoning.

Khatte Baingan

Eggplant in Tamarind and Tomato Gravy

Ingredients

8 Brinjals (round; medium)

The Marination

1.5g/½ tsp *Haldee*/Turmeric Powder
Salt

30ml/2 Tbs Lemon Juice
Cooking Oil to deep fry

The Paste

15g/2½ tsp Ginger Paste (strain)
15g/2½ tsp Garlic Paste (strain)
9g/1 Tbs *Dhania*/Coriander Powder

10g/1¾ tsp Red Chilli Paste
3g/1 tsp *Haldee*/Turmeric Powder

The Gravy

30ml/2 Tbs Cooking Oil
6 *Lavang*/Cloves
2 sticks *Daalcheeni*/Cinnamon (1″)

90ml/3 oz Tomato Purée
30g/1 oz *Imlee*/Tamarind Pulp
30g/4½ tsp Fried Onion Paste

Serves: 4
Preparation Time: 1:20 hours
Cooking Time: 30 minutes

Preparation

The Brinjals : Wash, halve and make 'fans'.

The Marination : Mix all the ingredients, evenly rub the brinjal fans with the mixture and reserve for 30 minutes.

The Frying : Heat enough oil in a *kadhai*/wok, add marinated fans and deep fry over medium heat until cooked. Remove to absorbent paper to drain excess fat.

The Paste : Put all the ingredients in a bowl, add 60ml/¼ cup of water and mix well.

The Gravy : Put tamarind pulp in a *handi*/pan, add 120ml/½ cup of water, bring to a boil, reduce to low heat and simmer until reduced by half.

Cooking

Heat oil (30ml/2 Tbs) in a saucepan, add cloves and cinnamon, stir over medium heat for a few seconds, add the paste, *bhunno*/stir-fry until fat leaves the sides. Then add tomato purée, *bhunno*/stir-fry for 2-3 minutes, add tamarind pulp, *bhunno*/stir-fry for a minute, add fried onion paste and *bhunno*/stir-fry until fat leaves the sides. Now add 240ml/1 cup of water, bring to a boil, reduce to low heat and simmer, stirring occasionally, until gravy is of thin sauce consistency. Remove and pass gravy through a fine mesh soup strainer into a separate saucepan, return gravy to heat, add the brinjal 'fans' carefully and simmer until the gravy is of sauce consistency. Remove and adjust the seasoning.

Paalak Ki Potli

Spinach Pouches stuffed with Cottage Cheese and Mushrooms in Lentil Gravy

Ingredients

24/32 Spinach Leaves (large/medium)
4/8 blades Leeks/Spring Onion Greens
Salt

A pinch of *Meetha Soda*/Soda
Bicarbonate

The Filling

300g/11 oz *Paneer* (full fat)
60g/2 oz Mushrooms
1 *Laal Shimla Mirch*/Red Bell Peppers
1 *Peeli Shimla Mirch*/Yellow Bell Peppers
2 Tomatoes (large)
4 Green Chillies
5g/½" piece Ginger

0.5g/1 tsp *Zaafraan*/Saffron
25g/2 Tbs *Desi Ghee*/Clarified Butter
7.5g/1 Tbs *Shahi Jeera*/Black Cumin
  Seeds
6.25g/1 Tbs *Besan*/

15g/½ oz *Taaza Anaar*/Fresh
  Pomegranate

The Gravy

100g/½ cup *Moong Daal*
2 Tomates (medium)
1 Potato (medium)
30g/1 oz Pumpkim
1.5g/½ tsp *Haldee*/Turmeric Powder
Salt
1.5g/½ tsp *Kasoori Methi*/Dried
  Fenugreek Leaf Powder

1.5g/½ tsp *Chotti Elaichi*/Green
  Cardamom Powder
1.5g/½ tsp *Lavang*/Clove Powder
1.5g/½ *Daalcheeni*/Cinnamon Powder
0.75g/¼ *Jaiphal*/Nutmeg Powder
0.75g/¼ *Javitri* Mace Powder

Serves : 4
Preparation Times : 1 hour
Cooking Time : 45 minutes

Preparation

The Spinach : Clean and wash. Put enough water in a *handi*/pan, add salt and soda bicarbonate, bring to a boil, add spinach and blanch for 15 seconds. Drain, refresh in iced water, drain and pat dry.

The 'Strings': Clean leek or spring onion blades, wash, blanch in salted boiling water for 15 seconds, drain, refresh in iced water, drain, pat dry and cut each blade into half lengthwise.

The Filling : Grate *paneer* in a bowl. Slice off the lower bits of the earthy stalks of mushrooms, wash and dice. Remove stems, wash bell peppers, halve, seed and dice. Remove eyes, make a criss-cross incision at the opposite end, blanch tomatoes in slated boiling water for 15 seconds, drain, cool, remove the skin, halve, remove the pulp and dice. Wash green chillies, slit, seed, finely chop and discard stems. Scrape, wash and finely chop ginger. Crush saffron with pestle or back of spoon, reserve in 15ml/1 Tbs of lukewarm water for 5 minutes and then make a paste.

Heat *ghee* in a frying pan, add *shahi jeera*. Stir over medium heat for a few seconds, add gramflour, *bhunno*/stir-fry until it emits its unique aroma, add mushrooms and *bhunno*/stir-fry until the liquid evaporates. Then add *bhunno*/stir-fry for 30 seconds, add saffron and salt, and stir until fully incorporated. Remove, cool, add pomegranate, mix well, adjust the seasoning and divide into 8 equal portions.

The Potli : Arrange a set of 3 or 4 leaves (depending on the size) on a work surface, overlapping with the heads in a circular fashion so that they form a mesh. Place a portion of the filling in the middle of each set, bring together the loose ends to form a *potli* (pouch) and tie with leek/spring onion 'string'.

The Gravy : Pick, wash and soak *moong dal* for 30 minutes. Remove eyes, wash and roughly chop tomatoes. Peel, wash and roughly chop potato. Peel, wash and roughly chop pumpkin.

Cooking

Put *daal* and the chopped vegetables in a *handi*/pan, add turmeric and salt, cover with enough water, bring to a boil, reduce to low heat and simmer, stirring occasionally, until cooked. Remove to a blender and make a smooth purée. Remove to a saucepan, add 120ml/½ cup water, bring to a boil. Remove and pass through a fine mesh soup strainer into a saucepan. Return gravy to heat, add the remaining ingredients, stir, bring to a boil, reduce to low heat and simmer until of sauce consistency. Remove and adjust the seasoning. Transfer to a bowl.

Sunehri Khurchan

Stir-fried Chicken and Bitter Gourd Pies

Ingredients

4 Breasts of Chicken (90g/3 oz each)

The Bitter Gourd

150g/5 oz *Karela*/Bitter Gourd   45ml/3 Tsb Cooking Oil

The Marination

30ml/2 Tsb Lemon Juice
10ml/2 tsp Ginger Juice
3g/1 tsp Black Pepper (freshly roasted
   & coarsely ground)
1.5g/½ tsp *Chotti Elaichi*/Green
   Cardamom Powder

0.75g/¼ tsp *Chotti Elaichi*/Green
0.75g/¼ *Lavang*/Clove Powder
0.75g/¼ tsp *Daalcheeni*/Cinnamon
   Powder

The Dough

210g/1½ cups Flour
150ml/10 Tbs Milk
7.5g/1½ tsp Sugar
90g/7 Tbs *Desi Ghee*/Clarified Butter

0.75g/¼ tsp *Chotti Elaichi*/Green
   Cardamom Powder
Flour to Dust

The *Khurchan Masala*

60ml/¼cup Cooking Oil
120g/1 cup Onions
3g/1 tsp *Dhania*/Coriander Powder
1.5g/½ tsp Red Chilli Powder
1.5g/½ tsp *Haldee*/Turmeric Powder
2 Tomatoes (medium)
4.5g/1½ tsp *Amchoor*/Mango Powder
1.5 g/½ tsp *Jeera*/Cumin Powder
0.75g/¼ tsp *Chotti Elaichi*/Green
   Cardamom Powder
0.75g/¼ tsp *Lavang*/Clove Powder

0.75g/¼ tsp *Daalcheeni*/Cinnamon
   Powder
0.75g/¼ tsp *Javitri*/Cinnamon Powder
Salt
2 Green Chillies
10g/1" piece Ginger
6.5g/2 Tbs *Taaza Dhania*/Coriander
15ml/1 Tbs Lemon Juice

185

The Gravy

4 Apples (medium)
2 Pears (medium)
2 Carrots (medium)
4 *Lavang*/Cloves
2 sticks *Daalcheeni*/Cinnamon (1")

2 *Tej Patta*/Bay Leaf
12 Black Peppercorns
30g/2 Tbs Sugar
Salt
24 *Pudhina*/Mint

Serves: 4
Preparation Time: 2:45 hour
Cooking Time: 25-30 minutes

Preparation

The Chicken : Clean, bone, wash, pat dry and cut into 1/8" thick strips lengthwise.

The Marination : Mix all the ingredients, evenly rub the chicken strips with this marinade and reserve for 30 minutes.

The Bitter Gourd : Remove stems, scrape, halve lengthwise, seed and finely slice into half moon shapes. Arrange in a steel tray, sprinkle just enough salt, mix well and place the tray at a tilt for at least 2 hours to allow some of the bitterness to ooze out. Then put the slices in muslin, squeeze to drain the excess moisture and keep aside.

Heat oil in a *kadhai*/wok, add the bitter gourd and *bhunno*/stir-fry over medium heat until cooked (approx. 10 minutes). Remove to absorbent paper to drain excess fat.

The Dough : Boil milk in a *handi*/pan, add sugar, stir until dissolved, remove and cool. Melt *ghee* in a bowl, add cardamom powder, stir to mix well. Sift flour and salt in a *paraat*/tray or on a work surface, make a bay, pour in the milk and start mixing gradually. When fully incorporated, knead to make soft dough, cover with moist cloth and reserve for 10 minutes. Then add half the melted *ghee* and incorporate deftly with the fingers, cover with moist cloth and refrigerate for 30 minutes. Remove and incorporate the remaining melted *ghee*. Divide into four equal portions, make balls, cover with moist cloth and refrigerate until ready to bake.

The *Khurchan Masala* : Peel, wash and finely chop onions. Remove eyes, wash and finely chop tomatoes. Wash green chillies, slit, seed, finely chop and discard stems. Scrape, wash and finely chop ginger. Clean, wash and finely chop coriander.

The *Khurchan* : Heat oil (60ml/¼ cup) in a *kadhai*/wok, add onions, sauté over medium heat until translucent and glossy, add coriander, red chilli and turmeric powders (dissolved in 30ml/2 Tbs of water) and *bhunno*/stir-fry until the moisture evaporates. Then add tomatoes, *bhunno*/stir-fry until the fat leaves the sides, add the marinated chicken, and *bhunno*/stir-fry for a minute. Now add *amchoor*, cumin, *kasoori methi*, green cardamom, clove, cinnamon and mace powders, stir, add salt and stir. Remove, add green chillies, ginger and coriander, stir, add the cooked bitter gourd, mix well, stir in lemon juice, adjust the seasoning and divide into 4 equal portions.

The Oven : Pre-heat to 375°F.

The Pipes : Remove the dough from the refrigerator, dust the work surface with flour, roll out dough with a light rolling pin, constantly dusting with flour, into discs of 7" diameter. Prick the surface lightly with a fork. Line greased moulds with the rolled dough, arrange on a greased roasting tray, pack a portion of the filling in the mould and cover with the overlapping dough.

The Gravy : To make *bouquet garni*, put all the spices in a mortar and pound with a pestle to break the spices, fold in a piece of muslin and secure with enough string for it to hang over the rim of the *handi*/pan. Peel, core and roughly chop apples and pears, put in a *handi*/pan, cover with enough water, add *bouquet garni* and sugar, bring to a boil, reduce to low heat and simmer until the fruits are soft and squishy. Remove and discard *bouquet garni*. Transfer the fruits to a blender and make a purée. Peel carrots, wash, finely chop, blanch in boiling water for 3-4 minutes, drain, remove to a blender and make a purée. Clean and wash mint.

Cooking

Put the tray in the pre-heated oven and bake for 25-30 minutes or until the dough is golden.

To prepare the gravy, heat *ghee* in a saucepan, add *deghi mirch*, stir for a few seconds, add carrot purée, cook for a minute, add fruit purée and cook for another minute. Then add 120ml/½ cup of water, bring to a boil, remove, and pass through a fine mesh soup strainer into a separate saucepan. Return gravy to heat, add mint and salt, stir and simmer until of sauce consistency. Remove and adjust the seasoning. Serve the pies on a bed of gravy.

EPISODE 022

with Chef Sudhir Sibbal,
ITDC

Uttar Dakshin Murghbandi sought to pay tribute to the support of national integration in the realm of good taste. Sudhir Sibbal fiddled with his ladle. The delicious duet is reminiscent of the musical *jugalbandi* of Pt. Ravishankar and Lalgudi Jayaram Iyer!

Uttar-Dakshin Murghbandi

Stuffed Chicken Breast in North-South Fusion Gravy

Ingredients

8 Breasts of Chicken
Flour to dust

Cooking oil to shallow fry

The Marination

30ml Lemon Juice
10g/1¾ tsp Garlic Paste (strain)
10g/1¾ tsp Ginger Paste (strain)
1.5g/½ tsp *Dhania*/Coriander Powder

1.5g/½ tsp Red Chilli Powder
1.5g/½ tsp *Haldee*/Turmeric Powder
Salt

The Filling

250g/9 oz Chicken Mince
45g/3 Tbs Cooking Oil
1.25g/½ tsp *Sarsondaana*/Black
16 *Kaari Patta*/Curry Leaf
A small pinch of *Heeng*/Asafoetida
30g/1 oz Shallots/Madras Onions
30g/1 oz Coconut

60g/2 oz Cheese (processed/cheddar)
1.5g/½ tsp Black Pepper (freshly
    roasted) & Mustard Seeds (coarsely
    ground)
Salt
2 drops *Ittar*

The Gravy

50g/¼ cup *Desi Ghee*/Clarified Butter
5 *Chotti Elaichi*/Green Cardamom
3 *Lavang*/Cloves
2 *Motti Elaichi*/Black Cardamom
2 sticks *Daalcheeni*/Cinnamon (1″)
1 *Tej Patta*/Bay Leaf
60g/2 oz Shallots/Madras Onions
10g/1¾ tsp Garlic Paste (strain)
10g/1¾ tsp Ginger Paste (strain)

1.5g/½ tsp *Dhania*/Coriander Powder
1.5g/½ tsp Red Chilli Powder
1.5g/½ tsp *Haldee*/Turmeric Powder
Salt
30g/1 oz *Khus-khus*/Poppy Seed Paste
180ml/¾ cup Coconut Cream
0.5g/1 tsp *Zaafraan*/Saffron
15ml/1 Tbs Milk

The Garnish

A few Green Peppercorns   4 sprigs *Taaza Dhania*/Coriander
1 Tomato

Serves: 4
Preparation Time: 1:15 hours
Cooking Time: 1 hour

Preparation

The Chicken : Clean, remove the skin, bone but retain the winglet bones, wash and pat dry. With a sharp knife make a deep slit along the thick edge of each breast to make a pocket, taking care not to penetrate the flesh on the other side.

The Marination : Mix all the ingredients, evenly rub the breasts with this marinade and reserve for 15 minutes.

The Filling : Reserve asafoetida in 15ml/1 Tbs of water. Clean and wash curry leaf. Peel, wash and chop onions. Remove the brown skins and grate coconut. Grate cheese.

Heat oil in a frying pan, add mustard, stir over medium heat until it begins to pop, add curry leaf, stir until they stop spluttering, add asafoetida and stir. Then add onions and sauté until translucent and glossy. Now add the chicken mince and salt, and *bhunno*/stir-fry until the moisture evaporates. Remove, cool, add coconut, cheese and pepper, and mix well. Divide into 8 equal portions.

The Gravy : Peel, wash and chop onions. Crush saffron with pestle or back of spoon, reserve in lukewarm milk for 10 minutes and then make a paste.

The Stuffing : Pack a portion of the filling in the pockets of the marinated chicken breasts and then seal each with the tip of the knife ensuring that the meat is not pierced. Dust the breasts with flour and keep aside.

The Garnish : Remove stems, clean, wash and pat dry green peppercorns. (If using canned peppercorns, drain the brine and pat dry.) Remove eye, wash tomato, halve, seed and cut into small dices. Clean and wash coriander.

192

Cooking

Heat oil in a frying pan, add the stuffed breasts, two at a time, and sauté over low heat, turning a couple of times, until evenly golden (approx 2-3 minutes). Then cover and cook, turning at regular intervals, for 1-1½ minutes.

To prepare the gravy, heat *ghee* in a *handi*/pan, add green cardamom, cloves, black cardamom, cinnamon and bay leaf, and stir over medium heat until the green cardamom begins to change colour. Add onions, sauté over medium heat until translucent and glossy, add the garlic and ginger pastes, and *bhunno*/stir-fry until the moisture evaporates. Then add coriander, red chilli and turmeric (dissolved in 30ml/2 Tbs of water), *bhunno*/stir-fry until the moisture evaporates, add the poppy seed paste, and *bhunno*/stir-fry until the fat begins to leave the sides. Now add 420ml/1¾ cups of water, bring to a boil, reduce to low heat and simmer until liquor is reduced by half. Pass the liquor through a fine mesh soup strainer into a separate *handi*/pan, return gravy to heat, add the stuffed breasts, bring to a boil, reduce to low heat, stir-in coconut cream and bring to just under a boil. Add saffron, stir, remove and adjust the seasoning.

Chillah

Gramflour Pancakes

Ingredients

The Batter

300g/2¾ cups *Besan*/Gramflour
Salt
4g/2 tsp *Jeera*/Cumin Seeds

3g/1 tsp Red Chilli Powder
A generous pinch of *Heeng*/Asafoetida
Desi Ghee/Clarified Butter to shallow fry

The Topping

150g/5 oz *Paneer*
90g/3 oz Onions
75g/2½ oz ½ cup Tomatoes

12.5g/4 Tbs *Taaza Dhania*/Coriander
2 Green Chillies

Serves: 4
Preparation Time: 25 minutes
Cooking Time: 2 minutes per *Chillah*

Preparation

The Gramflour : Sift alongwith salt into a bowl, add cumin seeds and red chillies, mix well.

The Asafoetida : Reserve in 45 ml/3 Tbs of water.

The Batter : Mix the dissolved asafoetida and 540ml/2¼ cups of water with the gramflour mixture and make a batter of pouring consistency. Divide into 16 equal portions and keep aside.

The *Paneer* : Grate and divide into 16 equal portions.

The Vegetables : Peel onions, wash and make small dices. Remove eyes, wash tomatoes, quarter, seed and make small dices. Clean, wash and finely chop coriander. Remove stems, wash, slit, seed and finely chop green chillies. Mix all the ingredients in a bowl and divide into 16 equal portions.

Cooking

Melt just enough *ghee* in a small frying pan, spread a portion of the batter to make a pancake with a 4" diameter and shallow fry over low heat for a few seconds. Then sprinkle a portion each of the paneer and vegetables over the surface of the pancake, sprinkle a little *ghee* along the periphery and cook. Lift the pancake and, if perforations are visible and the *Chillah* is lightly coloured, flip it over. Sprinkle another small quantity of *ghee* and cook for 45 seconds. Fold and remove to absorbent paper to drain off the excess fat. Repeat the process with the remaining portions.

Battani Masala

Peppery Green Peas tempered with Cumin and Curry Leaf

Ingredients

400g/14 oz Green Peas (shelled)
45ml/3 Tbs Cooking Oil
1.25g/½ tsp *Sarsondaana*/Black
  Mustard Seeds
2g/1 tsp *Jeera*/Cumin Seeds
24 *Kaari Patta*/Curry Leaf
150g/5 oz Onions
25g/4 tsp Garlic Paste (strain)
25g/4 tsp Ginger Paste (strain)
4.5g/1½ tsp *Dhania*/Coriander Powder
3g/1 tsp Red Chilli Powder

0.75g/¼ tsp *Haldee*/Turmeric Powder
150ml/5 oz Fresh Tomato Purée
Salt
60ml/¼ cups Coconut Cream
0.75g/¼ tsp *Chotti Elaichi*/Green
  Cardamom Powder
0.375g/⅛ tsp *Lavang*/Clove Powder
2.25g/¾ tsp Black Pepper (freshly
  roasted & coarsely ground)
3.25g/1 Tbs *Taaza Dhania*/Coriander

Serves: 4
Preparation Time: 30 minutes
Cooking Time: 15 minutes

Preparation

The Green Peas : Blanch in salted boiling water for 3-4 minutes, drain, refresh in iced water, drain and pat dry.

The Remaining Vegetables : Wash curry leaf. Peel, wash and finely chop onions. Clean, wash and finely chop coriander.

Cooking

Heat oil in a *kadhai*/wok, add mustard and cumin, stir over medium heat until they begin to pop, add curry leaf, stir until it stops spluttering, add onions and sauté until translucent and glossy. Then add the garlic and ginger pastes, *bhunno*/stir-fry until onions are light golden, add coriander, red chilli and turmeric powders (dissolved in 30ml/2 Tbs of water), and stir until the moisture evaporates. Add tomato purée and salt, *bhunno*/stir-fry until fat leaves the sides. Now add peas, *bhunno*/stir-fry until the liquid evaporates, add coconut cream and bring to just under a boil and the masala coats the peas. Sprinkle cardamom and clove powder, stir, remove and adjust the seasoning. Sprinkle pepper and garnish with coriander.

EPISODE 023

with Chef Ashok Sharma,
THE HYATT

Aloo Dum Banarasi is as integral a part of a three thousand years old city as its waterfront, Siva shrine, music and paan. The denizens of Banaras, *alias* Varanasi and Kashi, are renowned for their love of food. They claim that their recipe for the *dum aloo* is superior to the Kashmiri or the Bengali variants.

Taar Qorma is a gourmet's dream come true and a cholesterol watcher's nightmare. Rich beyond imagination, the dish justifies its name by its fat content measured in finger-sticking one-string consistency.

Chura Mattar

Rose Water-soaked and pounded Rice Flakes, and Green Peas stir-fried with Mango Powder and Orange Juice

Ingredients

800g/1 lb 13 oz Green Peas
Salt
A pinch of Sugar
150g/5 oz *Chivra*/Pounded Rice Flakes
60ml/¼ cup Orange Juice
75g/6 Tbs *Desi Ghee*/Clarified Butter
4g/2 tsp *Jeera*/Cumin Seeds
2 Green Chillies
30g/3″ piece Ginger

A generous pinch of *Heeng*/Asafoetida
6g/2 tsp *Amchoor*/Mango Powder
15g/1 Tbs Sugar
30g/1 oz Raisins
30ml/2 Tbs *Gulaabjal*/Rose Water
0.5g/1 tsp *Zaafraan*/Saffron
15ml/1 Tbs Milk
60g/2 oz *Malaai*/Clotted Cream
30ml/2 Tbs Lemon Juice

The *Chura* Masala

4 *Lavang*/Cloves
4 sticks *Daalcheeni*/Cinnamon (1″)
5 *Motti Elaichi*/Black Cardamom

2 petals *Javitri*/Mace
4 *Tej Patta*/Bay Leaf

Serves: 4
Preparation Time: 30 minutes
Cooking Time: 3-4 minutes

Preparation

The Peas : Put enough water in a *handi*/pan, add salt and sugar, bring to a boil, add peas and boil until *al dente*. Drain and refresh in iced water. Drain at the time of cooking.

The *Chivra* : Clean, wash and reserve in orange juice for 15 minutes.

The Green Chillies : Wash, slit, seed, finely chop and discard the stems.

The Ginger : Scrape, wash and finely chop.

The Asafoetida : Reserve in 15ml/1 Tbs of water.

The Raisins : Remove stems, clean, soak in water for a few minutes, drain and reserve in rose water.

The Saffron : Crush the saffron threads with a pestle, reserve in lukewarm milk and then make a paste with the back of a spoon. Mix with *malaai* just before serving.

The *Chura* Masala : Sun-dry the spices, put in a mortar and pound with a pestle to make a coarse powder. Alternatively, put all the ingredients in a grinder and, employing short pulses, grind to a coarse powder. Remove and store in a sterilised, dry and airtight container.

Cooking

Heat *ghee* in a *kadhai*/wok, add cumin, stir over medium heat until it begins to pop, add chillies, ginger and asafoetida, stir for 30 seconds. Then add the green peas, *bhunno*/stir-fry until peas are devoid of moisture, sprinkle *chura* masala, salt, *amchoor* and sugar, stir until incorporated. Now add *chivra* along with orange juice, stir gently until mixed, reduce to low heat and simmer, stirring occasionally and carefully, for 1-1½ minutes. Remove, adjust the seasoning, add the raisins, the saffron-*malaai* mixture and lemon juice, stir carefully.

Aloo Dum Banarasi

New Potatoes in Coriander and Tamarind Gravy

Ingredients

600g/1 lb 5 oz Baby Potatoes

Desi Ghee/Clarified Butter to deep fry potatoes

The Ginger Paste Mixture

30g/5¼ tsp Ginger Paste (strain)
1g/¼ tsp *Methidaana*/Fenugreek Seeds
0.75g/¼ tsp *Sarsondaana*/Mustard Seeds

A pinch of *Ajwain*/Carom
A pinch of *Kalonji*/Black Onion Seeds
A pinch of *Heeng*/Asafoetida

The Coriander Mixture

13g/¼ cup *Taaza Dhania*/Coriander
9g/1 Tbs *Dhania*/Coriander Powder
3g/1 tsp Red Chilli Powder

3g/1 tsp *Haldee*/Turmeric Powder
0.375/1/8 tsp *Jaiphal*/Nutmeg Powder
1g/½ tsp *Jeera*/Cumin Seeds

The Gravy

50g/¼ cup *Desi Ghee*/Clarified Butter
2 Green Chillies
A pinch of *Kaala Namak*/Black Rock
Salt Powder
150g/5 oz Yoghurt
15g/½ oz *Imlee*/Tamarind Pulp

Salt
10g/2 tsp Sugar
1.5g/½ tsp Black Pepper (freshly
roasted & coarsely ground)
3.25g/1 Tbs *Taaza Dhania*/Coriander

Serves: 4
Preparation Time: 50 minutes
Cooking Time: 25 minutes

Preparation

The Potatoes : Wash and peel. Heat *ghee* in a *kadhai*/wok, add potatoes and deep fry over medium heat until light golden. Remove to absorbent paper to drain excess fat.

The Ginger Paste Mixture : Put the ginger paste in a bowl, add fenugreek, mustard, *ajwain*, *kalonji* and asafoetida, mix well.

201

The Coriander Mixture : Clean, wash and finely chop coriander. Put 300ml/1¼ cup of water in a bowl, add the chopped coriander, coriander powder, red chilli, turmeric, nutmeg and cumin, mix well and reserve for 30 minutes.

The Gravy : Wash green chillies, slit, seed, finely chop and discard the stems. Whisk yoghurt in a bowl. Put tamarind pulp in a *handi*/pan, add 120ml/½ cup of water, bring to a boil, reduce to low heat and simmer until reduced by half. Clean, wash and chop coriander.

Cooking

Heat *ghee* in a *handi*/pan, add the ginger paste mixture, *bhunno*/stir-fry over medium heat until the fat leaves the sides, add green chillies and stir for a minute. Then add the coriander mixture (with the water), salt and rock salt, bring to a boil, reduce to low heat and simmer, stirring occasionally, until the liquid is evaporated and specks of fat begin to appear on the surface. Now add the fried potatoes and stir. Remove *handi*/pan from heat, stir-in yoghurt, return *handi*/pan to heat, bring to a boil, stirring constantly. Once the gravy comes to a boil, reduce to low heat, cover and simmer, stirring occasionally, until the potatoes are cooked and napped, add the tamarind pulp, stir, add sugar, stir until it dissolves, add the pepper, stir, remove and adjust the seasoning. Garnish with coriander.

Bharra Murgh Khumbi Ki Tarri

Stuffed Chicken Breast in spicy Mushroom Gravy

Ingredients

8 Breasts of Chicken
Flour to dust

Cooking oil to shallow fry

The Marination

30m/½ Tbs Lemon Juice
15ml/1 Tbs Ginger Juice
4.5g/1½ tsp *Saunf*/Fennel Powder

1.5g/½ tsp Black Pepper
   (freshly roasted & coarsely ground)
Salt

The Filling

250g/9 oz Chicken Mince
60g/2 oz Cheese (processed/cheddar)
10g/1 Tbs Green Peppercorns

3.25g/1 Tbs *Taaza Dhania*/Coriander
60ml/¼ cup Cream
Salt

The Cashewnut Paste

30g/1 oz Cashewnuts
Cooking oil to deep fry cashewnuts
100g/3 oz Onions

15g/½ oz Garlic
2 Green Chillies

The Gravy

400g/1 lb Button Mushrooms
25g/2 Tbs Butter
15ml/1 Tbs Cooking Oil
120g/½ cup Yoghurt
5g/¾ tsp *Besan*/Gramflour
3g/1 tsp *Dhania*/Coriander Powder

60ml/¼ cup Cream
1.5g/½ tsp *Chotti Elaichi*/Green
   Cardamom Powder
0.75g/¼ tsp *Javitri*/Mace Powder
A pinch of *Saunth*/Dried Ginger Powder

Serves: 4
Preparation Time: 1:45 hours
Cooking Time: 1 hour

Preparation

The Chicken : Clean, remove the skin, bone but retain the winglet bones, wash and pat dry. With a sharp knife make a deep slit along the thick edge of each breast to make a pocket, taking care not to penetrate the flesh on the other side.

The Marination : Mix all the ingredients, evenly smear the breasts with this marinade and reserve for 30 minutes.

The Filling : Grate cheese. Remove stems, wash and pat dry green peppercorns. (If using canned peppercorns, drain the brine and pat dry.) Clean, wash and chop coriander. Mix these with the remaining ingredients and divide into 8 equal portions.

The Stuffing : Pack a portion of the filling in the pockets of the marinated chicken breasts and then seal each with the tip of the knife ensuring that the meat is not pierced. **Dust the breasts with flour just prior to cooking.**

The Cashewnut Paste : Heat oil in a *kadhai*/wok, add cashewnuts and deep fry over medium heat until golden brown. Remove to absorbent paper to drain the excess fat. Peel, wash and chop onions. Peel and chop garlic. Wash green chillies, slit, seed, chop and discard the stems. Put these ingredients in a blender, add 60ml/¼ cup of water and make a smooth paste.

The Gravy : Remove the earthy base of the stalks, wash in running water to remove grit, drain and slice mushrooms just prior to cooking. Whisk yoghurt in a bowl, add *besan* and coriander powder, mix well.

Cooking

Heat oil (to shallow fry) in a frying pan, add the dusted breasts, two at a time, and grill over low heat, turning a couple of times, until evenly golden (approx. 4-5 minutes). Then cover and cook, turning at regular intervals, for 2-3 minutes. Pierce a cooking needle into the breasts and if a white liquid oozes out, remove and keep aside. If not, cook a little longer. Reserve the *jus* (drippings) for the gravy.

To prepare the gravy, heat butter and oil in a *handi*/pan, add the cashewnut paste, *bhunno*/ stir-fry over medium heat until the fat begins to appear on the surface, add mushrooms and *bhunno*/stir-fry for 3-4 minutes. Remove *handi*/pan from heat, stir-in the yoghurt mixture, return *handi*/pan to heat, bring to a boil, reduce to low heat, add the *jus* and simmer, stirring continuously for 1½-2 minutes. Then add the grilled chicken, cover and simmer for 1-1½ minutes. Stir-in cream, sprinkle cardamom, mace and ginger powders, stir, remove and adjust the seasoning.

Taar Qorma

Kid/Lamb in Almond and Yoghurt Gravy

Ingredients

1.2 Kg/2¼ lb *Dasti*/Shoulder of Kid/Lamb
200g/1 cup *Desi Ghee*/Clarified Butter
8 *Chotti Elaichi*/Green Cardamom
5 *Lavang*/Cloves
4 sticks *Daalcheeni*/Cinnamon (1")
2 *Tej Patta*/Bay Leaf
30g/5¼ tsp Garlic Paste (strain)
20g/3½ tsp Ginger Paste (strain)
Salt
120g/½ cup Yoghurt
75g/2½ oz Fried Onion Paste
45g/1½ oz Fried Garlic Paste
30g/1 oz Almond Paste
4.5g/1½ tsp Red Chilli Powder

1.5 litres/6¼ cups Clear Kid/Lamb Stock
3g/1 tsp Black Pepper (freshly roasted & coarsely groud)
0.5g/1 tsp *Zaafraan*/Saffron
0.75g/¼ tsp *Chotti Elaichi*/Green Cardamom Powder
0.75g/¼ tsp *Daalcheeni*/Cinnamon Powder
0.75g/¼ tsp *Lavang*/Clove Powder
A pinch of *Javitri*/Mace Powder
A pinch of *Jaiphal*/Nutmeg Powder
2 drops *Ittar*

Serves: 4
Preparation Time: 45 minutes (plus time taken to make stock)
Cooking Time: 1:30 hours

Preparation

The Kid/Lamb : Clean, wash, pat dry, bone and cut into 1½".

The Yoghurt : Whisk in a bowl.

The Saffron : Crush with pestle or back of spoon, reserve in 15ml/1 Tbs of lukewarm water for 5 minutes and then make a paste.

The Oven : Pre-heat to 275°F.

Cooking

Heat *ghee* in a *handi*/pan, add cardamom, cloves, cinnamon and bay leaves, stir over medium heat until the cardamom begins to change colour, add meat, increase to high heat and sear for 1½-2 minutes. Reduce to low heat, add garlic paste, ginger paste and salt, stir for a minute, cover and cook, stirring occasionally, for 20 minutes, adding a little water if required. Uncover, increase to medium heat and *bhunno*/stir-fry until the liquid evaporates. Remove *handi*/pan from heat, stir-in yoghurt, return *handi*/pan to heat and *bhunno*/stir-fry until the fat leaves the sides. Then add the fried pastes, *bhunno*/stir-fry for 1½-2 minutes, add red chillies (dissolved in 30ml/1 Tbs of water), stir until the moisture evaporates, add the stock, bring to a boil, reduce to low heat and simmer until meat is cooked. Remove the meat and pass the gravy through a fine-mesh soup strainer into a separate *handi*/pan, add the cooked meat and remaining ingredients, seal with *atta* dough and cook on *dum* in the pre-heated oven for 15-20 minutes.

206

EPISODE 024

with Chef Manu Mehta,
WELCOMGROUP

It is easy to imagine that *Phaldari Murgh* was the favourite dish of Babur, the founder of the Moghul dynasty. The Central Asian prince came from an orchard land and has recorded his fondness for fruit, particularly pomegranate and grapes, in his autobiography. In fact, this dish was created for the viewers of our food show.

Murgh Jheenga Gucchiwali Tarri illustrates another interesting experiment in fusion. This time the striving was to span the distance from Kashmir to Kanyakumari when we introduced delicate morels gathered under the shadow of snow crested mountains to the succulent prawns from the Indian Ocean.

Phaldari Murgh

Stuffed Chicken Breast in Grape and Pomegranate Gravy

Ingredients

8 Breasts of Chicken   Cooking oil to shallow fry

The Marination

30ml/2 Tbs Pomegranate Juice   1.5g/½ tsp Red Chilli Powder
30ml/2 Tbs Ginger Juice   Salt

The Filling

150g/5 oz *Paneer*/Cottage Cheese   4 Green Chillies
60g/2 oz Cheese (processed/cheddar)   1.25g/½ tsp *Shahi Jeera*/Black
16 Black Grapes (seedless)   Cumin Seeds
30g/1 oz Pomegranate   Salt
30g/1 oz Spring Onions

The Gravy

50g/¼ cup *Desi Ghee*/Clarified Butter   1.5g/½ tsp Red Chilli Powder
5 *Chotti Elaichi*/Green Cardamom   30g/1 oz *Kharbooja*/Melon Seed Paste
2 *Lavang*/Cloves   240ml/1 cup Grape Purée
1 *Motti Elaichi*/Black Cardamom   120ml/½ cup Pomegranate Juice
1 stick *Daalcheeni*/Cinnamon (1″)   480ml/2 cups Clear Chicken Stock
1 ·*Tej Patta*/Bay Leaf   Salt
7.5g/1¼ tsp Ginger Paste (strain)

Serves: 4
Preparation Time: 1:45 hours
Cooking Time: 45 minutes

Preparation

The Chicken : Clean, remove the skin, bone but retain the winglet bones, wash and pat dry. With a sharp knife make a deep slit along the thick edge of each breast to make a pocket, taking care not to penetrate the flesh on the other side.

The Marination : Mix all the ingredients, evenly rub the breasts with this marinade and reserve for 30 minutes.

The Filling : Grate *paneer* and cheese in a bowl. Wash, pat dry and quarter grapes. Wash and pat dry pomegranate. Peel, wash and chop spring onion bulbs and greens. Wash green chillies, slit, seed, finely chop and discard stems. Mix these and the remaining ingredients with the *paneer* and cheese and divide into 8 equal portions.

The Stuffing : Pack a portion of the filling in the pockets of the marinated chicken breasts and then seal each with the tip of the knife ensuring that the meat is not pierced.

Cooking

Heat oil in a frying pan, add the stuffed breasts, two at a time, and sauté over low heat, turning once, until evenly golden (approx 2-3 minutes). Then cover and cook, turning at regular intervals, for 2-3 minutes.

To prepare the gravy, melt *ghee* in a *handi*/pan, add green cardamom, cloves, black cardamom, cinnamon and bay leaf, stir over medium heat until the green cardamom begins to change colour, add red chillies dissolved in ginger juice, and *bhunno*/stir-fry until the moisture evaporates. Then add melon seed paste, *bhunno*/stir-fry until the fat leaves the sides, add the grape purée and pomegranate juice, and bring to a boil. Now add stock, bring to a boil, reduce to low heat and simmer, stirring occasionally, until the liquor is reduced by a third. Pass the gravy through a fine mesh soup strainer into a separate *handi*/pan. Return gravy to heat, add the stuffed chicken breasts and salt, and simmer until gravy is of medium thin sauce consistency. Remove and adjust the seasoning.

210

Murgh-Jheenga Guchchiwali Tarri

Stuffed Chicken Breast in Morel and Pernod Gravy

Ingredients

8 Breasts of Chicken
12.5g/1 Tbs

10ml/½ tsp Cooking Oil
Unsalted Butter

The Marination

10g/1¾ tsp Garlic Paste (strain)
10g/1¾ tsp Ginger Paste (strain)
Salt

1.5g/½ tsp *Peeli Mirch*/Yellow Chilli
  Powder

The Filling

250g/9 oz Prawns (medium)
30g/1 oz Spring Onion Greens
2.5g/2 tsp *Sua/Soya*/Dill
45ml/3 Tbs Cream

1.5g/½ tsp *Peeli Mirch*/Yellow Chilli
  Powder
Salt
3g/1 tsp *Saunf*/Fennel Powder

The Gravy

12 Morels (small)
12.5g/1 Tbs
15ml/1 Tbs Pernod
15ml/1 Tbs Cooking Oil
15g/2½ tsp Almond Paste
45g/1½ oz Spring Onion Bulbs
60ml/¼ cup Yoghurt

360ml/1½ cups Clear Chicken Stock
4 flakes Garlics
1.5g/½ tsp Black Pepper (freshly
roasted & coarsely ground)
Unsalted Butter
Salt
45ml/3 Tbs Cream

Serves: 4
Preparation Time: 1:15 hours
Cooking Time: 50 minutes

Preparation

The Chicken : Clean, remove the skin, bone but retain the winglet bones of only 4 of the breasts, trim, wash and pat dry. Place the breasts, one at a time, between two polythene sheets and flatten with a bat ensuring that the meat is not ruptured and at the same time the shape is retained.

The Marination : Mix all the ingredients, evenly rub the breasts with this marinade and reserve for 30 minutes.

The Filling : Shell prawns, vein, wash, pat dry and mince coarsely. Clean, wash and chop spring onion greens and dill. Put these and the remaining ingredients in a bowl and mix well. Divide into 4 equal portions.

The Gravy : Soak morels in lukewarm water for 15 minutes, drain, remove stems, wash in running water to remove grit, drain, pat dry and cut into thick roundels. Peel and crush garlic. Peel, wash and finely chop onions. Whisk yoghurt in a bowl.

The Stuffing : Place breasts with winglet bones on a flat surface, spread a portion of the filling evenly on each, leaving ½" on all but the winglet bone side, cover with the boneless breasts and, using the blunt edge of a knife, beat gently to seal the edges. Tuck the edges and beat to seal again. Repeat the tucking and beating process until the overlapping meat touches the mince. Finally, continue to beat and seal to shape the breasts either into their original shape or into heart shapes. Keep aside.

Cooking

Heat butter and oil in a frying pan, add the stuffed breasts, two at a time, and sauté over low heat, turning once, until evenly golden (approx. 2-3 minutes). Then cover and cook, turning at regular intervals, for 2-3 minutes. Pierce a cooking needle into the breasts. If white liquid oozes out, it indicates that the filling is cooked. Remove and keep aside, reserve the *jus* (drippings) for the gravy.

To prepare the gravy, heat butter and oil along with the *jus* in a *handi*/pan, add garlic and onions, and sauté over medium heat until onions are translucent and glossy. Remove *handi*/pan from heat, stir-in yoghurt, return *handi*/pan to heat and *bhunno*/stir-fry until specks of fat begin to appear on the surface (ensure that the masala does not get coloured). Then add the almond paste and *bhunno*/stir-fry until the fat begins to leave the sides (ensure that the masala does not get coloured). Add morels, stir for a minute, add Pernod, stir for a minute, add stock, pepper and salt, bring to a boil, reduce to low heat and simmer, stirring occasionally, for 3-4 minutes. Now add chicken, bring gravy to a boil, reduce to low heat and simmer for a couple of minutes. Remove, stir-in cream, return gravy to heat and bring to just under a boil. Remove and adjust the seasoning.

EPISODE 025

with Chef Chingli,
THE HYATT

Working on *Daawat* we realised that no one can have enough of stuffed fare. In this genre there are no limits to curb the chef's imagination.

Bharwaan Murgh Seib ki Tarri presents a celebratory centre-piece for a special occasion.

Bharwaan Murgh Seib Ki Tarri

Stuffed Chicken Breast in Apple and Cinnamon Gravy

Ingredients

4 Breasts of Chicken
10g/2½ tsp Unsalted Butter

10ml/2 tsp Cooking Oil
Flour to dust

The Marination

20g/3½ tsp Garlic Paste (strain)
15g/2½ tsp Ginger Paste (strain)
15ml/1 Tbs Lemon

1.5g/½ tsp *Peeli Mirch*/Yellow Chilli
  Powder
Salt

The Filling

250g/9 oz Smoked Chicken
30g/1 oz Spring Onion Greens
1 Fresh Red Chilli
16 Pistachio
45g/1½ oz Cheese (Processed/
  Cheddar)

2g/1½ tsp Rosemary (dried)
1.5g/½ tsp *Daalcheeni*/Cinnamon
  Powder
1.5g/½ tsp *Peeli Mirch*/Yellow Chilli
  Powder
Salt

The Gravy

250g/9 oz Cooking Apples
15g/4 tsp Unsalted Butter
15ml/1 Tbs Cooking Oil
3 sticks *Daalcheeni*/Cinnamon (1")
2 *Motti Elaichi*/Black Cardamom
2 *Lavang*/Cloves
1 *Tej Patta*/Bay Leaf
4 flakes Garlic
3g/1 tsp *Haldee*/Turmeric Powder

60g/¼ cup Yoghurt
720 ml/3 cups Clear Chicken Stock
1.5g/½ tsp *Daalcheeni*/Cinnamon Powder
1.5g/½ tsp Black Pepper (freshly roasted
  & coarsely ground)
Salt
5g/1 tsp *Imlee*/Tamarind Pulp
30ml/2 Tbs Cream

Serves: 4
Preparation Time: 45 minutes
Cooking Time: 25 minutes

215

Preparation

The Chicken : Clean, remove the skin, bone but retain the winglet bone, trim, wash and pat dry. With a sharp knife, pressing at the thicker end gently, slit the breasts horizontally to make pockets ensuring that a third of the opposite side is left uncut.

The Marination : Mix all the ingredients, evenly smear the breasts with this marinade and reserve for 30 minutes.

The Filling : Chop the smoked chicken. Clean, wash and chop spring onion greens. Wash red chilli, slit, seed, finely chop and discard the stem. Blanch pistachios for 3-4 minutes, drain, remove to a cloth napkin, rub vigorously to peel, split into halves and keep aside. Grate cheese. Put these and the remaining ingredients in a bowl and mix well. Divide into 4 equal portions.

The Stuffing : Pack a portion of the filling in the pockets of the marinated chicken breasts and then seal each with the tip of the knife ensuring that the meat is not pierced. Dust the breasts with flour and keep aside.

The Gravy : Wash, peel, core and dice apples. Peel and crush garlic. Put yoghurt in a bowl, add turmeric and whisk to homogenize. Put tamarind pulp in a *handi*/pan, add 120ml/½ cup of water, bring to a boil, reduce to low heat and simmer to thick custard consistency.

Cooking

Heat butter and oil in a frying pan, add the stuffed breasts, two at a time, and sauté over low heat, turning a couple of times, until evenly golden (approx 2-3 minutes). Then cover and cook, turning at regular intervals, for 2-3 minutes. (Pierce a cooking needle into the breasts, if white liquid oozes out, it indicates that the filling is cooked). Remove breasts and reserve the *jus* (drippings) for the gravy.

To prepare the gravy, heat butter and oil alongwith the *jus* in a *handi*/pan, add cinnamon. black cardamom, cloves and bay leaf, stir over medium heat for 30 seconds, and garlic and sauté until light golden. Then add yoghurt mixture, *bhunno*/stir-fry until specks of fat appear on the surface, add apples and salt, sweat the fruit for 2-3 minutes. Now add stock, bring to a boil, reduce to low heat and simmer, stirring occasionally, until the apples are soft. Remove and force through a fine mesh soup strainer into a separate *handi*/pan, return gravy to heat, add tamarind, pepper and cinnamon, bring to a boil, reduce to low heat, add chicken breasts, cover and simmer until of sauce consistency. Remove, stir-in cream and adjust the seasoning.

Gosht-Palak-Kaleji Ka Roulade

Kid/Lamb, Spinach and Liver in Beetroot Gravy

Ingredients

24 *Pasanda*/Picatta of Kid/Lamb
(45g/1½ oz each; 3″ × 2″ × 1″)

50g/¼ cup Butter
Butter for basting and to grease roasting
    tray

The Filling

48 leaves Spinach
200g/7 oz *Kaleji*/Liver
240ml/1 cup Milk
30ml/2 Tbs Brandy (optional)
30g/1 oz Butter
20ml/4 tsp Cooking Oil
3g/1½ tsp *Jeera*/Cumin Seeds

150g/1½ cups Onions
20g/3½ tsp Garlic Paste (strain)
20g/3½ tsp Ginger Paste (strain)
2 Green Chillies
3.25g/1 Tbs *Taaza Dhania*/Coriander
    (chop)
Salt

The Marination

150g/5 oz *Chakka Dahi*/Yoghurt
    Cheese/Hung Yoghurt
100g/3 oz Fried Onion Paste
20g/3½ tsp Ginger Paste (strain)
20g/3½ tsp Garlic Paste (strain)

4.5g/1½ tsp *Lavang*/Clove Powder
3g/1½ tsp *Pudhina*/Dried Mint Leaf
    (crushed)
1.5g/½ tsp Red Chilli Powder
Salt

The Gravy

45ml/3 Tbs Cooking Oil
3 *Motti Elaichi*/Black Cardamom
2 sticks *Daalcheeni*/Cinnamom (1″)
2 *Tej Patta*/Bay Leaf
20g/3½ tsp Garlic Paste (strain)
150g/5 oz Boiled Onion Paste

175g/6 oz Beetroot
3g/1 tsp Red Chilli Powder
600 ml/2½ cups Kid Lamb Stock
Salt
30 ml/2 Tbs Lemon Juice

Serves: 4
Preparation Time: 1 hour
Cooking Time: 45 minutes

217

Preparation

The Picatta : Clean, wash, place each individually between 2 thick polythene sheets and gently flatten with a steak hammer or bat into 6″ × 4″ × ⅛″ rectangles, ensuring the flesh is not pierced.

The Filling : Clean, remove stems, wash and blanch spinach in salted boiling water for a minute, drain and refresh in iced water.

To prepare the liver, remove the sinews, clean, wash, pat dry, roughly chop and reserve in milk and brandy overnight in the refrigerator. Wash green chillies, slit, seed, finely chop and discard the stems. Clean, wash and finely chop coriander.

Heat butter and oil in a frying pan, add cumin seeds, stir over medium heat until they begin to crackle, add onions, sauté until light brown, add ginger, and garlic pastes and sauté until onions are golden brown. Drain and add liver, *bhunno*/stir-fry for 2-3 minutes, add green chillies, coriander and salt, *bhunno*/stir-fry for 2-3 minutes. Remove and keep aside.

The Roulade : Place the flattered picatta, in pairs, one slightly overlapping on the other, arrange 4 spinach leaves on top, leaving a quarter inch uncovered on all sides of the picatta pairs. Spread equal quantities of the cooked liver to cover the spinach leaves entirely. Now roll—like a Swiss Roll—to make roulade and then tie each roulade with a piece of string to ensure the filling does not spill out and the shape is maintained.

The Marination : Whisk yoghurt cheese in a bowl, add the remaining ingredients and mix well. Rub this marinade evenly on the roulade and reserve for 30 minutes.

The Oven : Pre-heat to 350°F.

The Gravy : Boil beetroot until cooked, drain, cool and chop.

Cooking

To prepare the roulade, heat oil in large pan, place the marinated roulade evenly spaced and grill over high heat until evenly—but lightly—coloured (approx 1½ minutes), remove and arrange on a greased roasting tray. Strain and reserve and drippings.

Put the baking tray in the pre-heated oven and roast for 4-5 minutes, basting with butter at regular intervals. Remove and keep warm.

To prepare the gravy, heat oil in a saucepan, add black cardamom. cinnamon and bay leaf, stir over medium heat for a few seconds, add garlic paste, sauté until lightly coloured, add boiled onion paste and *bhunno*/stir-fry until the fat begins to appear on the surface. Then add the strain drippings and red chillies, stir for 2-3 minutes, add stock, bring to a boil, reduce to low heat, cover and simmer, stirring occasionally, for 4-5 minutes. Now add beetroot, bring to a boil, reduce to low heat and simmer, stirring occasionally for 4-5 minutes. Remove to a blender, make a smooth purée and pass through a fine mesh sieve into a separate saucepan. Return gravy to heat and reduce over very low heat until of spoon coating consistency. Remove, add lemon juice, stir and adjust the seasoning.

Remove roulade, untie the strings, trim the edges, cut into halves diagonally and serve on a bed of sauce.

Bharwaan Gaajar Ka Timbale

Carrot Timbale in Coconut Coriander Gravy

Ingredients

The Mousse

350g/¾ lb Carrots
12.5g/1 Tbs Butter
15ml/1 Tbs Cooking Oil

Salt
3 Egg Yolks

The Filling

60g/2 oz Broccoli
1 Tomato (medium)
20g/⅔ oz Processed/Cheddar
  Cheese
20ml/4 tsp Cooking Oil

20g/4¾ tsp *Urad Daal* (husked)
3g/1½ tsp *Sarsondaana*/Black Mustard
  Seeds
16 *Kaari Patta*/Curry Leaf
Salt

The Gravy

30g/1 oz Coconut
15g/½ oz *Taaza Dhania*/Coriander
3 Green Chillies
25g/1 oz Spinach

240 ml/1 cup Clear Vegetable Stock
60 ml/¼ cup Cream
15ml/1 Tbs Lemon Juice

Serves: 4
Preparation Time: 1 hour
Cooking Time: 45 minutes

Preparation

The Carrot Mousse : Peel, wash and roughly chop carrots. Heat butter and oil in a frying pan, add carrots and sauté over medium heat for 7-8 minutes. Remove, cool, transfer to a blender, add the remaining ingredients and make a mousse. Remove and divide into 8 equal portions.

The Filling : Clean broccoli, wash, remove, stems, cut into small florets, blanch in salted boiling water for 30 seconds, drain, refresh in iced water, drain and pat dry. Remove the eye of the tomato, wash, quarter, remove the pulp and the skin and then cut into brunnoise. Cut cheese into brunnoise. Pick *daal*, wash in running water, drain and pat dry. Clean and wash curry leaf.

Heat oil in a frying pan, add *daal*, stir-fry over medium heat until golden brown, add mustard seeds, stir until they begin to crackle, add curry, leaves, stir for 30 seconds, remove and cool. Put these and the remaining ingredients in a bowl, toss to mix well and divide into 4 equal portions.

The Timbale : Spread a portion of the carrot mousse in each of 4 individual oven-proof earthenware or Pyrex bowls/moulds (3″ diameter), place—do not spread—a portion of the filling in the middle and spread another portion of the mousse on top. Cover securely with foil, pierce a couple of holes in the foil (to allow steam to escape), gently thump the bowls/moulds on the table to remove air pockets, if any, and arrange in a baking tray.

The Gravy : Remove the brown skin, wash and roughly chop coconut. Clean, wash and roughly chop coriander. Wash green chillies, slit, seed, roughly chop and discard the stems. Snip off the stems, wash and roughly chop spinach (the leaf is being use to provide good colouration). Put these ingredients in a blender, add 120ml/½ cup of vegetable stock and make a fine paste.

The Oven : Pre-heat to 225°F.

Cooking

Pour enough water in the baking tray to half cover the bowls/moulds, put in the pre-heated oven and bake for 30 minutes. (To check, pierce the mousse with a needle; if it comes out clean, it means the mousse is cooked. If not, bake for a few minutes more.) Keep warm.

To prepare the gravy, put the remaining vegetable stock in a saucepan, bring to a boil, reduce to low heat and simmer until reduced by half. Then add the paste, stir, add salt, stir and simmer, stirring constantly, for 3-4 minutes. Now add cream, simmer for 1-1½ minutes. Remove, add lemon juice, stir and adjust the seasoning. (The lemon juice should be added at the time of service).

To Serve : Make a bed of equal quantities of sauce on 4 individual plates, place a *timbale* in the middle and serve hot.

221

Bharwaan Mahi Kofta

Fish Quenelles in Coconut Coriander Gravy

Ingredients

The Mousse

250g/9 oz Fish Trimmings
10ml/2 tsp Lemon Juice
4 Egg Whites
1.5g/½ tsp *Jaiphal*/Nutmeg Powder
   (freshly ground)

Salt
240ml/1 cup Cream
Cooking Oil to moisten palms
Butter to baste

The Filling

2 Tomatoes (medium)
60g/2 oz Processed/Cheddar Cheese
10 Dried Plums
2.5g/1 tsp *Shahi Jeera*/Black Cumin
   Seeds

2.25g/¾ Black Pepper (fresh roasted
   & coarsely ground)
Salt

The Gravy

g/1 oz Coconut
5g/½ oz *Taaza Dhania*/Coriander
3 Green Chillies
25g/1 oz Spinach

240ml/1 cup Fish *Fumet*
60ml/¼ cup Cream
15ml/1 Tbs Lemon Juice

Serves: 4
Preparation Time: 1:15 hours
Cooking Time: 15 minutes

Preparation

The Mousse : Clean fish trimmings, wash, pat dry, put in a food processor/blender, add lemon juice, egg white, nutmeg and salt, process/blend into a mousse by adding cream in a steady trickle. Remove and divide into 20 equal portions.

The Filling : Remove eyes of the tomatoes, wash, quarter, remove the pulp and the skin and then cut into brunnoise. Cut cheese into brunnoise. Refresh dried plums in water for 10 minutes, drain, pat dry, remove the pits and cut into brunnoise. Mix all the ingredients in a bowl and divide into 20 equal portions.

The Gravy : Remove the brown skin, wash and roughly chop coconut. Clean, wash and roughly chop coriander. Wash green chillies, slit, seed, roughly chop and discard the stems. Snip off the stems, wash and roughly chop spinach (the leaf is being used to provide good colouration). Put these ingredients in a blender, add 120ml/½ cup of *fumet* and make a fine paste.

The Quenelles : Rub the left palm—assuming you are right-handed—with a little oil, place a portion of the mousse with a large (service) spoon on to the palm, flatten a bit with the spoon, place a portion of the filling in the middle, start rolling with the spoon and make a *quenelle* (which in a manner of speaking is an oval-shaped *kofta*) and poach immediately in salted boiling water for 2 minutes. Drain, transfer to a napkin, gently pat dry and keep aside. Repeat the process with the remaining portions.

The Oven : Pre-heat to 275°F.

Cooking

Baste the *quenelles* with butter, arrange on a roasting tray, put in the pre-heated oven and glaze under top heat, turning carefully, until very lightly coloured. Remove and keep aside.

To prepare the gravy, put the remaining *fumet* in a saucepan, bring to a boil, reduce to low heat and simmer until reduced by half. Then add the paste, stir, and salt, stir and simmer, stirring constantly, for 3-4 minutes. Now add cream and simmer for 1-1½ minutes. Remove, add lemon juice, stir and adjust the seasoning. (The lemon juice should be added at the time of service.). Serve quenelles on a bed of sauce.

EPISODE 026

with a Team of Chefs from
THE HYATT

Who says that too many cooks spoil the broth? For the X'mas special we had not less than three worthies sharing the chores and produce festive delights — traditional as well as innovative. Devinder Bungla, Raminder Malhotra and Stephen Magor joined hands to turn out a fabulous feast. Turkey was served *intact* — yes that is what musallam translates as — more impressive than the usual *murgh musallam*; *tandoori jheenga flan* was a fusion inspired improvisation, savoury pancake rivalled it to tickle the vegetarian palate and the rich X'mas pudding underlined the message 'more the merrier', be it the cooks or guests!

Turkey Mu sallam

Ingredients

1 Turkey
4 Onions (medium)
6 sticks *Daalcheeni*/Cinnamon (1")

1 litre/4¼ cups Clear Chicken Stock
Butter for basting

The Marination

60g/2 oz Garlic Paste (strain)
45g/1½ tsp Ginger Paste (strain)
4.5g/1½ tsp Red Chilli Powder

60ml/¼ cup *Sirka*/Malt Vinegar
Salt

The Filling

400g/14 oz Chicken Mince
60g/2 oz Spring Onions
15g/½ oz Garlic
20g/2" piece Ginger
2 Eggs
45g/1½ oz Almonds
45g/1½ oz Pistachio
30g/1 oz Raisins
15 ml/1 Tbs *Gulaabjal*/Rose Water
10g/3 Tbs *Taaza Dhania*/Coriander
6g/3 Tbs *Pudhina*/Mint (chop)
2 Green Chilli

3g/1 tsp Black Pepper (freshly
  roasted & coarsely ground)
1.25g/½ tsp *Shahi Jeera*/Black
  Cumin Seeds
0.75g/¼ tsp *Lavang*/Clove Powder
0.375/ ⅛ tsp *Gulaabpankhrhi*/Rose
  Petal Powder
0.375/ ⅛ tsp *Motti Elaichi*/Black
  Cardamom Powder
0.375/ ⅛ tsp *Saunf*/Fennel Powder
0.5g/1 tsp *Zaafraan*/Saffron
Salt

The Gravy

60g/5 Tbs *Desi Ghee*/Clarified Butter
30g/5¼ tsp Garlic Paste (strain)
20g/3½ tsp Ginger Paste (strain)
250g/1 cup Yoghurt
90g/3 oz *Narial ka Buraada/Kopra*/
  Desiccated Coconut Paste
45g/3 Tbs Almond Paste
15g/1 Tbs *Chironji* Paste

60g/2 oz Fried Onion Paste
1.5g/½ tsp Red Chilli Powder
Salt
1.5g/½ tsp *Chotti Elaichi*/Green
  Cardamom Powder
0.75g/¼ tsp *Javitri*/Mace Powder
0.5g/1 tsp *Zaafraan*/Saffron
15ml/1 Tbs *Gulaabjal*/Rose Water

Serves: 4
Preparation Time: 2:15 hours
Cooking Time: 1 hour

Preparation

The Turkey : Clean, remove the neck and the skin, prick the entire surface with a fork.

The Marination : Mix all the ingredients, evenly rub the turkey with this marinade and reserve for at least an hour (preferably overnight in the refrigerator).

The Filling : Peel, wash and finely chop the spring onion bulbs and greens. Peel and finely chop the garlic. Scrape, wash and finely chop $^2/_3$ of the ginger and cut the remaining $^1/_3$ into juliennes for the garnish. Hard-boil eggs, cool and shell. Blanch almonds and pistachio in boiling water for a minute, drain, cool, peel and cut into slivers, reserving $^1/_3$ of each for the garnish. Remove stems and soak raisins in water for a few minutes, drain and reserve in rose water. Clean, wash and finely chop the coriander and mint. Wash green chillies, slit, seed finely chop and discard the stems. Crush the saffron threads with a pestle or the back of spoon, soak in water and then make a paste. Mix these and the remaining ingredients with t chicken mince in a bowl.

The Stuffing : Stuff the abdominal cavity of the turkey with the filling from the tail end as follows: $^1/_3$ of the mince mixture, 1 hard-boiled egg, another $^1/_3$ of the mince mixture, the second hard-boiled egg and finally the remaining mince mixture. Then double up the legs, ensuring that drumsticks cover the opening through which the filling was stuffed and tie firmly with string. Gently twist the winglet bones to make the birds more stable when it is placed on the plate at the time of service.

The *Mirepoix*[1] : Peel, wash and cut onions into roundels.

The Gravy : Whisk yoghurt in a bowl. Crush the saffron threads with a pestle or the back of a spoon, soak in rosewater and then make a paste.

The Oven : Pre-heat to 325°F.

Cooking

Make a bed of the onion roundels in a large *handi*/pot, spread cinnamon sticks on the onions, arrange the stuffed turkey on top, place the *handi*/pot on the stove and start cooking over very low heat. Boil and pour the chicken stock over the turkey, cover, arrange charcoal embers on top and cook on *dum* for 15 minutes. Uncover and cook the turkey, basting at regular intervals

228

with the *jus* until cooked. To check if the filling is cooked, pierce with a cooking needle. If a white liquid oozes out, it means the filling is cooked. If not, cook longer. Remove and arrange the turkey on a greased roasting tray and reserve the cooking liquor for the gravy.

To prepare the gravy, heat *ghee* in a *handi*/pan, add the garlic and ginger pastes, *bhunno*/stir-fry until the moisture evaporates. Remove *handi*/pan from heat, stir in yoghurt, return *handi*/pan to heat, and *bhunno*/stir-fry until specks of fat begin to appear on the surface. Then add coconut, almond and *chironji* pastes, *bhunno*/stir-fry until the fat leaves the sides, add the fried onion paste, and *bhunno*/stir-fry until the fat leaves the sides. Add red chillies, stir for a minute, add the reserved cooking liquor and salt, bring to a boil, reduce to low heat and simmer until of sauce consistency. Remove and pass the gravy through a fine-mesh soup strainer into a separate *handi*/pan, return gravy to heat, add cardamom and mace powders, stir, add saffron, stir, remove and adjust the seasoning.

The Finishing

Pour the gravy over the turkey arranged in the roasting tray and cook in the pre-heated oven, basting with butter at regular intervals for 4-5 minutes or until the gravy becomes brown. Remove, untie the turkey, discard the string and reserve the gravy. Skim off the fat and pour the drippings on the turkey. Serve with a garnish of the reserved almonds, pistachio and ginger.

[1]A mixture of finely diced vegetables and ham or bacon which, when fried in butter, is used as a base for brown sauces and stews, or as a bed for braising meat.

Tandoori Jheenga Flan

Ingredients

450g/1 lb Prawns
120g/4 oz Spring Onions

200g/7 oz Cheese (processed/cheddar)

The First Marination

20g/3½ tsp Garlic Paste (strain)
15g/2½ tsp Ginger Paste (strain)

30ml/2 Tbs Lemon Juice
Salt

The Second Marination

120g/½ cup Yoghurt
4.5g/1½ tsp Red Chilli Powder
0.375g/¼ tsp Chotti Elaichi/Green
   Cardamom Powder
0.375g/¼ tsp Javitri/Mace Powder
0.375g/¼ tsp Lavang/Clove Powder

A small pinch of Ajwain/Bishops Weed
15g/1 Tbs Besan/Gramflour
30ml/2 Tbs Cream
30ml/2 Tbs Lemon Juice
Salt

The Dough

250g/9 oz Flour (all purpose)
1 Egg Yolk

20ml/4 tsp Cooking Oil
20g/4 tsp Salt

The Egg Mixture

4 Eggs (refrigerated)
240ml/1 cup Milk
160ml/5½ oz Cream
Salt

A pinch of Ajwain/Carom
A pinch Black Pepper Powder
A pinch Lawang/Clove Powder
A pinch Jaiphal/Nutmeg Powder

The Garnish

75g/2½ oz Caviar

75g/2½ oz Red Lump Fish Roe

Serves: 8
Preparation Time: 2 hours
Cooking Time: 25-30 minutes

Preparation

The Prawns : Shell, vein, wash and pat dry. Peel, wash and chop spring onions, both bulbs and greens, divide into 2 equal portions. Grate cheese in a bowl and divide into 2 equal portions.

The First Marination : Mix all the ingredients in a large bowl, evenly rub the prawns with this marinade and reserve in the same bowl for 15 minutes.

The Second Marination : Mix all the ingredients in a large bowl, evenly rub the prawns with this marinade and reserve in the refrigerator for 15 minutes.

The Dough : Beat the egg yolk in a bowl. Sift flour into a *paraat* or on to a worktable, make a bay, pour the egg yolk, oil, salt and 100ml/8 Tbs+2 tsp of water in it and start mixing gradually. When fully incorporated, knead to make soft dough, divide into 2 equal portions, make balls, put in a plastic bag and refrigerate. Remove, place the dough on a lightly floured surface and flatten with a rolling pin into 2 discs of 12″ diameter when ready to fill the moulds.

The Prawn Cooking : Skewer the prawns and grill either in a moderately hot *tandoor* or on a moderately hot charcoal grill for 2-3 minutes. Unskewer and cut the prawns into ½″ pieces.

The Filling : Put prawns and onions in a bowl, mix well and divide into two equal portions.

The Egg Mixture : Beat the eggs in a bowl, add the remaining ingredients and whisk until homogeneous. Divide into two equal portions.

The Oven : Pre-heat to 350°F.

The Moulds : Grease two 6″ savarin (or any other round) moulds and line each with a flattened disc, discarding the overlapping paste. Spread a portion of the filling on the dough, pour on a portion of the egg mixture in each, sprinkle a portion of the cheese on top and bake in the pre-heated oven for 25-30 minutes. To check if the flan is cooked, prick with a cooking needle. If it comes out dry, the flan is cooked. If not, bake for another few minutes more. Garnish each flan with equal quantities of caviar and lump fish roe or tuna and serve as an entrée.

Savoury Pancake

Ingredients

The Pancakes

120g/¼ lb Flour (all purpose)
300ml/1¼ cups Milk
30g/1 oz Butter
3 Eggs

225g/½ lb Sweet Corn
Salt
Cooking oil to make pancakes

The Filling

150g/5 oz Button Mushrooms
60g/2 oz Broccoli
60g/2 oz Carrots
60g/2 oz Cheese (processed/cheddar)
45g/1½ oz *Paneer*/Cottage Cheese
50g/¼ cup Butter
4g/2 tsp *Jeera*/Cumin Seeds

10g/1" piece Ginger
6 Green Chillies
3g/1 tsp Black Pepper (freshly roasted
 & coarsely ground)
Salt
A pinch of *Kasoori Methi*
15ml/1 Tbs Lemon Juice

The Crumbing

Eggs
Breadcrumbs to roll

Cooking oil to pan-grill

Serves: 4
Preparation Time: 1 hour
Cooking Time: 2 minutes per set

Preparation

The Batter : Melt butter (it shouldn't froth). Beat eggs. Sift the flour into a bowl, make a bay, add milk, whisk, add melted butter, whisk, add beaten eggs, whisk, add sweet corn, whisk, add salt and whisk to make a batter, mentally divide into 8 equal portions and keep aside. Heat 5ml/1 tsp of oil in a frying pan, add a portion of the batter, roll pan to evenly spread and cook until the underside is lightly coloured. Remove and stack. Repeat with the remaining portions.

The Filling : Remove the earthy base of the stalks, wash in running water to remove grit and cut into thin slices. Clean broccoli, wash, cut into tiny florets. Peel carrots, wash and cut into fine juliennes. Grate cheese and *paneer*. Scrape, wash and finely chop ginger. Wash green chillies, slit, seed, finely chop and discard stems.

The Filling : Melt butter in a frying pan, add cumin, stir over medium heat until it begins to pop, add ginger and green chillies, stir for a few seconds, add vegetables and mushrooms, and *bhunno*/stir-fry until the moisture evaporates. Then add pepper and salt, stir. Remove, cool, add cheese, *paneer*, *kasoori methi* and lemon juice, mix well and adjust the seasoning. Divide into 8 equal portions.

The Stuffing : Place a pancake on the worktable, spread a portion of the filling in the middle, fold the edges and roll. Dip in the beaten egg, dab evenly with crumbs and keep aside. Repeat with the remaining pancakes.

Cooking

Heat a little oil in a frying pan, place two pan rolls at a time in it and shallow fry over medium heat until golden and crisp. Remove to absorbent paper to drain excess fat.

X'Mas Pudding

Ingredients

The Pudding

200g/7 oz Candied Lemon Peel
100g/3 oz Black Currants
100g/3 oz Raisins
75g/2½ oz Almonds
60g/2 oz Candied Cherries
45g/1½ oz Candied Ginger
45g/1½ oz Dates
Zest of ½ Lemon
Zest of ½ Orange
60ml/¼ cup Rum
60ml/¼ cup Brandy
200g/7 oz Apples
60g/2 oz Sugar
150ml/10 Tbs Cream
3 Eggs

100ml/3 oz Malt/Liquid Molasses
100g/3 oz Fresh Breadcrumbs
60ml/¼ cup Fresh Orange Juice
30ml/2 Tbs Lemon Juice
3g/1 tsp *Daalcheeni*/Cinnamon Powder
3g/1 tsp *Saunth*/Dried Ginger Powder
1.5g/½ tsp *Chotti Elaichi*/Green
    Cardamom Powder
1.5g/½ tsp *Lavang*/Clove Powder
1.5g/½ tsp *Jaiphal*/Nutmeg Powder
Butter to grease moulds
Bread crumbs to line moulds
Flour to pack moulds
Butter Paper to cover mix

The Brandy Cream Sauce

480ml/2 cups Milk
100g/3 oz Sugar
5 Egg Yolks

40g/6½ Tbs *Arraroot*/Cornflour
45ml/3 Tbs Double Cream
180ml/¾ cup Brandy

Yield: 4 cakes
Preparation Time: 1:30 hours (plus time taken for soaking)
Cooking Time: 2:30 hours

Preparation

The Candied Ingredients & Dates : Cut into small dices.

The Black Currants & Raisins : Remove stems, clean, wash in running water, drain and pat dry.

The Almonds : Blanch for 5 minutes in boiling water, drain, remove to a cloth napkin, fold over, rub vigorously to remove the skin and then cut into juliennes.

The Zest : Grate.

The Fruit & Nut Mixture : Put the above ingredients in a ceramic bowl, add rum and brandy, mix well, cover with muslin and reserve for at least one week. (Ideally, the mix should be reserved for a month.)

The Apples : Wash, peel, core and finely chop.

The Oven : Pre-heat to 190°F.

The Pudding Mix : Transfer the soaked fruit & nut mix to a large stainless steel bowl, add apples and the remaining ingredients (except butter, breadcrumbs to line moulds and flour) and mix well. Divide into 4 equal portions.

The Brandy Cream Sauce : Dissolve cornflour in 90ml/6 Tbs of milk, add egg yolks, whisk until fully incorporated and keep aside.

The Butter Paper : Cut into discs larger than the rim to ensure that the flour does not come into contact with the pudding mix.

The Moulds : Grease 4 moulds of 500g/1 lb 2 oz each. Line each with breadcrumbs and pour a portion of the pudding mix in each. Place a butter paper disc on top of each, pack the moulds with flour ensuring that the butter paper is fully covered (this is done to ensure that the steam does not escape), seal with foil and arrange in a baking tray. Add just enough water (it should not spill out or boil over the tray) to create a double boiler.

Cooking

Put the tray in the oven and bake for 2:30 hours.

To prepare the Brandy Cream Sauce, boil the reserved milk, reduce to medium heat, add sugar and stir-in the cornflour-egg yolk mixture, cook until of pouring consistency, remove, strain into a sauceboat and cool. Then stir-in cream, add brandy, stir until fully incorporated and serve warm. It can also be served cold, in which case, refrigerate the sauce.

EPISODE 027

with Chef Manjit Singh Gill,
WELCOMGROUP

Daal is part of the staple diet of the Indian. *Daal-Roti, Daal-Bhaat* are the words used to describe a square meal — the basic food that sustains life, synonym for our 'daily bread'. At the same time *daal* is often treated with indifference if not contempt born of familiarity. When home cooked chicken is run down it is likened to *daal*. To give the *daal* its due we dedicated not one but two episodes to *daal* in *Daawat*.

The following recipes are from the episode that showcased lentils sans frills — time has not diminished the charm of these classics, *Sambhar, Cholar Daal, Daal Makhani* and *Kulthi ki Daal*. The quartet also 'represents' the four corners of Hindustan.

Sambhar

Drumsticks and Lentils

Ingredients

200g/1 cup *Arhar/Toor Daal*
3g/1 tsp *Haldee*/Turmeric Powder
3g/1 tsp Red Chilli Powder
Salt
200g/7 oz Drumsticks

4 Green Chillies
120g/¼ lb Madras Onions
300g/11 oz Tomatoes
30ml/1 oz *Imlee*/Tamarind Pulp
10g/3 Tbs *Taaza Dhania*/Coriander

The Sambhar Masala

30g/1 oz *Channa Daal*
30g/1 oz *Urad Daal* (husked)
30m½ Tbs Cooking Oil
5g/1 tsp *Heeng*/Asafoetida (coarsely
    broken)
4.5g/1½ tsp Garlic Powder
60g/2 oz *Dhania*/Coriander Seeds
45g/1½ oz *Jeera*/Cumin Seeds
30/1 oz Black Pepper

15g/½ oz *Sarsondaana*/Black Mustard
    Seeds
15/½ oz *Methidaana*/Fenugreek Seeds
8 Red Chillies
15g/5 tsp *Haldee*/Turmeric
    Powder
5ml/1 tsp Cooking Oil

The Tempering

30m/½ Tbs Cooking Oil
2g/1 tsp *Jeera*/Cumin Seeds
2g/1 tsp *Dhania*/Coriander Seeds
1.5/1 tsp *Kaaley Til*/ Black
    Sesame Seeds

1.25/1 tsp *Sarsondaana*/Black Mustard
    Seeds
5g/1 tsp *Urad Daal* (husked)
16 *Kaari Patta*/Curry Leaf
A generous pinch of *Heeng*/Asafoetida

Serves: 4
Preparation Time: 45 minutes
Cooking Time: 45 minutes

Preparation

The *Arhar/Toor Daal* : Pick, wash in running water, drain, soak in water for 30 minutes and drain.

The Vegetables : Peel, wash and cut drumsticks into 1″ pieces. Wash green chillies, slit, seed and discard stems. Peel, wash and slice onions. (If Madras onions are not available, use the other onions.) Remove eyes, wash and chop tomatoes. Clean, wash and chop coriander.

The Tamarind Pulp : Put the pulp in a *handi*/pan, add 180ml/¾ cup of water, bring to a boil, then simmer until reduced to one-fourth. Remove and keep aside.

The *Sambhar Masala* : Pick the *channa* and *urad daal*, wash in running water, drain and leave in the strainer for 5 minutes. Heat 20m/¼ tsp of oil in a frying pan, add both *daal*, fry over medium heat until light golden and remove to absorbent paper to drain excess fat.

Heat 10 ml tsp of oil in a frying pan, add asafoetida, fry over medium heat until it swells, remove and cool. Remove stems, wipe red chillies clean with a moist cloth, slit and seed. Sun-dry the spices, put in a mortar, alongwith asafoetida, red chillies and fried *daal* and pound with a pestle to make fine powder. Alternatively, put these same ingredients in a grinder and, employing short pulses, grind to a fine powder. Sift into a dry bowl, add the turmeric and garlic powders, mix well and transfer to a sterilised, dry and airtight container. Remember we will be using only 6g/2 Tsp of *sambhar* masala.

The Tempering : Pick *daal*, wash in running water and pat dry. Clean and wash curry leaves.

Cooking

Put the drained *arhar/toor daal* in a *handi*/pan, add water (approx 1 litre/4¼ cups), turmeric, red chilli powder, salt, drumsticks, green chillies, onions and tomatoes, boil until *daal* and drumsticks are cooked (approx 20 minutes). Then add 6g/2 tsp of *sambhar* masala, stir, add oil, stir, reduce to very low heat and simmer, stirring occasionally, for 5-6 minutes.

To prepare the tempering, heat oil in a frying pan, add cumin, coriander, black sesame and mustard seeds alongwith the *urad daal*, and stir over medium heat until the seeds begin to pop. Then add curry leaf and asafoetida, stir until the leaf stops spluttering and pour over the simmering *Sambhar*. Now add tamarind pulp, stir, reduce to low heat and simmer, stirring occasionally, for 10-12 minutes. Add chopped coriander, stir, remove and adjust the seasoning.

Cholar Daal

Lentils and Raisins tempered with Mustard Seeds

Ingredients

500g/2½ cups *Channa Daal*
1" piece *Haldee*/Turmeric (dried)
4 Green Chillies

10g/2 tsp
12.5g/1 Tbs *Desi Ghee*/Clarified Butter

The Paanch Phoron

60g/ 2 oz *Jeera*/Cumin Seeds
60g/ 2 oz *Saunf*/Fennel Seeds
30g/1oz *Methidaana*/Fenugreek Seeds

30g/1 oz *Ravi*/Yellow Mustard Seeds
30g/1 oz *Kalonji*/Onion Seeds

The Tempering

45ml/3 Tsb *Sarson*/Mustard Oil
1.5g/½ tsp *Sarsondaana*/Black Mustard Seeds
2 *Tej Patta*/Bay Leaf

30g/1 oz *Narial*/Coconut
4 Red Chillies
24 Raisins

Serves: 4
Preparation Time: 45 minutes
Cooking Time: 45 minutes

Preparation

The *Channa Daal* : Pick, wash in running water, drain, soak in water for 30 minutes and drain.

The Turmeric : Soak in water overnight and then grind into a paste on the stone (*sil-batta*). Alternatively, the grinding can be done in a blender.

The Green Chillies : Wash green chillies, slit into halves lengthways, seed and discard the stems.

The *Paanch Phoron* : Sun-dry the spices, put in a mortar, and pound with a pestle to make fine powder. Alternatively, put the spices in a grinder, make a fine powder, sift and store in a sterilised and airtight container. Remember we will be using 3g/1 tsp of *Paanch Phoron*.

The Tempering : Remove the brown skin and cut coconut into ¼″ long thin slices. Scrape, wash and finely chop ginger. Refresh red chillies in water, drain, pat dry, slit, seed and discard the stems. Remove stems and soak raisins in water.

Cooking

Put the drained *daal* in a *handi*/pan, add salt and 1.5 litres/6¼ cups of water, bring to a boil, reduce to low heat and remove the scum. Then add the turmeric paste and the green chillies, cover and simmer, stirring occasionally until the *daal* is cooked. Remove and keep aside.

To prepare the tempering, heat mustard oil to a smoking point in a *kadhai*/wok, remove and cool for 3-4 minutes. Reheat the oil, and mustard seeds and bay leaf, stir over medium heat until the seeds beings to pop, add *paanch phoron* and stir. Then add coconut, ginger and whole red chillies, stir over medium heat until coconut is light golden, add raisins and stir until coconut is golden brown. Now add the boiled *daal*, stir until the tempering is fully incorporated, add jaggery or sugar and simmer until the *daal* is thick. Remove and adjust the seasoning. Stir in *ghee* and serve.

Daal Makhani

Lentils enriched with Butter, Cream and Tomato Purée

Ingredients

400g/1 cups *Urad Daal* (whole)
Salt
30g/2 Tbs Cooking Oil
30g/5 tsp Garlic Paste (strain)
20g/3½ tsp Ginger Paste (strain)

9g/1 Tbs *Laal Mirch*/Red Chilli Powder
400g/14 oz Tomato Purée
180g/6 oz Butter (unsalted)
120ml/½ cup Cream

Serves: 4
Preparation Time: 30 minutes plus soaking time
Cooking Time: 6:15 hours

Preparation

The *Urad Daal*: Pick, wash in running water repeatedly until the water in which it is being washed is clear, soak overnight and drain. (The alternative method for this *daal's* treatment is to boil the lentils for a couple of minutes (after the repeated washing) and reserve them in the same water for an hour. Then drain the water and start as you usually would.

Cooking

Put the drained *daal* in a *handi*/pan, add 3 litres/12¾ cups of water and oil, bring to a boil, reduce to very low heat, cover and simmer until cooked (approx 4 hours). Then add garlic paste, ginger paste, red chillies and salt, and *ghooto*/continuously mash the lentils against the sides with a wooden spoon and, as you do that, scraps off the lentils that cling to the sides as the liquid diminishes and incorporate into the simmering *daal*, (approx 1 hour). Now add tomato purée and 150g/5 oz of butter, and continue to *ghooto*/continuously mash the lentils against the sides with a wooden spoon and, as you do that, scrape off the lentils that cling to the sides as the liquid diminishes and incorporate into the simmering *daal* (approx. 1 hours). Stir-in cream, remove and adjust the seasoning. Garnish with the remaining butter.

Preparation

The *Rice* : Pick, wash in running water, drain reserve in water for an hour and drain. Crush saffron threads with a pestle, reserve in lukewarm milk and then make a paste.

The *Bouquet Garni* : Put all the ingredients in a mortar and pound with a pestle to break the spices, fold in a piece of muslin and secure with enough string for it to hang over the rim of the *handi*/pan.

The *Kid/Lamb* : Clean, wash and cut into 1½ " chunks. Peel garlic and cut into juliennes. Whisk yoghurt in a bowl. Crush saffron threads with a pestle, reserve in lukewarm milk and them make a paste.

The *Syrup* : Boil sugar with 250ml of water over medium heat for 7-8 minutes, stirring constantly, to make thick syrup.

Cooking

Heat *ghee* in a *handi*/pan, add garlic, sauté over medium heat until light brown, add meat, salt and water (approx 240 ml/1 cup), bring to a boil, reduce to low heat, add green cardamom, cloves and cinnamon, cover and simmer, stirring occasionally, for 20 minutes. Remove *handi*/pan for heat, stir-in yoghurt, cover and simmer, stirring occasionally, until the liquid is reduced to one-third, add water (approx 540ml/2¼ cups), bring to a boil, reduce to low heat, cover and simmer, stirring occasionally, until the meat is almost cooked. Remove, add *kewra* mace, cardamom powder, saffron and lemon juice, stir and keep aside.

Put water (approx 2 litres/8 ⅓ cups), the *bouquet garni* and salt in a separate *handi*/pan, bring to a boil, add the drained rice, bring to a boil, reduce to medium heat and boil until rice is nine-tenths cooked. (To test, remove a few grains and squeeze between the thumb and forefinger- the rice will be slightly hard, will get mashed but a few white specks will show. The specks are a sign of uncooked rice.) Drain, spread three-fourths over the cooked meat, sprinkle saffron and spread the remaining rice on top. Seal the *handi*/pan with *atta* dough and cook over low heat for 12-14 minutes. Break seal, pour on the Syrup along the 'wall' of the *handi*/pan and seal again with *atta* dough.

Heat a *tawa*/griddle, reduce to medium heat, place *handi*/pan on the *tawa*/griddle and cook until the steam starts to escape through the dough. Reduce to low heat and cook for 20 minutes. Break the seal, stir, remove to a shallow silver dish and garnish with *varq*.

Kulthi Ki Daal

Wild Kidney Beans tempered with Himalayan Chives

Ingredients

200g/1 cups *Kulthi Daal*
3g/1 tsp *Haldee*/Turmeric Power
15g/2½ tsp Ginger Paste (strained)

15g/2½ tsp Garlic Paste (strain)
30g/2 Tbs Rice Flour

Ingredients

20g/4 tsp *Desi Ghee*/Clarified Butter
2g/1tsp *Jeera*/Cumin seeds

6 flakes Garlic
8 Green Chillies

Serves: 4
Preparation Time: 45 minutes
Cooking Time: 1:45 hours

Preparation

The Kulthi Daal : Pick, wash in running water, drain, soak in water for 30 minutes and drain.

The Rice Paste : Put the rice flour in a 60ml/¼ cup of water, stir and reserve for 15 minutes.

The Tempering : Peel and thinly slice garlic. Wash green chillies, slit, seed, cut into juliennes and discard the stems.

Cooking

Put the drained *daal* in a *handi*/pan, add turmeric, salt, ginger paste, garlic paste and 1 litre/4¼ cups of water, bring to a boil, reduce to low heat, simmer until the *daal* splits and is tender. Reduce to very low heat and continue to simmer.

Stir the rice paste until fully homogenous, add to the simmering *daal*, stirring simultaneously, until fully incorporated and simmer, stirring continuously, for 5-6 minutes. Remove and adjust the seasoning. (The continuous stirring is important to prevent lumps from forming).

To prepare the tempering, melt *ghee* in a frying pan, add cumin and stir over medium heat until it begins to pop. Then add garlic, *bhunno*/stir-fry until golden, add green chillies, *bhunno*/stir-fry until the garlic is golden brown and pour over the cooked *daal*.

EPISODE 028

with Chef Davinder Bungla,
THE HYATT

Daal Plus sought to play around with the 'pulses' by adding something to them. In many parts of the country such additions are common and not only fulfill the requirements of a balanced meal but also enhance the aesthetic appeal of the dish. *Kaddu ka Daalcha* is a traditional Hyderabadi speciality and *Keerai Kootu* is relished in the south. *Kheema Chholey* and *Soney Chandi ke Moong* are 'originals'– delicacies designed for *Daawat*.

Kaddu Ka Daalcha

Bottle Gourd with Lentils

Ingredients

300g/1½ cups *Channa Daal*
600g/1lb 5 oz *Kaddu*/Bottle Gourd
3g/½ tsp *Haldee*/Turmeric Powder
Salt
45 ml/3 Tbs Cooking Oil
2g/1 tsp *Jeera*/Cumin Seeds

20g/3½ tsp Ginger Paste (strain)
15g/2½ tsp Garlic Paste (strain)
3g/1 tsp Red Chilli Powder
3g/1 tsp *Dhania*/Coriander Powder
150g/5 oz *Imlee*/Tamarind Pulp

The Tempering

15ml/2 tsp Groundnut Oil
1g/½ tsp *Sarsondaana*/Black
  Mustard Seeds

24 *Kaari Patta*/Curry Leaf
4 Whole Dried Red Chillies

Serves: 4
Preparation Time: 55 minutes
Cooking Time: 1:25 hours

Preparation

The *Daal* : Pick, wash in running water, soak for 30 minutes, drain, transfer to a *handi*/pan, add 1 litre/4¼ cups of water, turmeric and salt, bring to a boil, reduce to low heat and simmer until the liquid is absorbed. Remove to a blender and make a paste. Remove to a *handi*/pan and keep aside.

The *Kaddu* : Peel, seed, cut into 2″ x 1″ diamonds, put in a pan of salted boiling water and blanch for 2-3 minutes, drain, refresh in iced water and drain again when ready to cook.

Cooking

Heat oil in a *handi*/pan, add cumin seeds, stir over medium heat until they begin to pop, add the ginger and garlic pastes, and *bhunno*/stir-fry until the moisture evaporates. Add red chilli and coriander (dissolved in 30ml/2 Tbs of water), *bhunno*/stir-fry until the moisture evaporates, add tamarind pulp and *bhunno*/stir-fry for 2 minutes. Then add *daal* paste and water (approx. 720ml/3 cups), bring to a boil, reduce to low heat and simmer, stirring occasionally, for

20 minutes. Now add blanched *kaddu* and simmer, stirring occasionally, for 6-7 minutes. Remove and adjust the seasoning.

To prepare the tempering, heat oil in a frying pan, add mustard seeds, stir over medium heat until they begin to pop, add curry leaf, stir until they stop spluttering, add red chillies and stir until they change colour. Pour this tempering over the *daalcha* and stir.

Keerai Kootu

Spinach with Lentils

Ingredients

400g/14 oz Spinach
45ml/3 Tbs Groundnut Oil
2 Whole Red Chillies
2.25g/½ tsp *Sarsondaana*/Black
   Mustard Seeds
2g/1 tsp *Jeera*/Cumin Seeds
16 flakes Garlic

200g/7 oz Onions
1.5g/½ tsp *Haldee*/Turmeric Powder
130g/¾ cup Tomatoes
4 Green Chillies
Salt
12 *Kari Patta*/Curry Leaf

The Lentil

125g/¼ lb *Moong Daal* (husked)
A pinch of *Heeng*/Asafoetida

A pinch of *Haldee*/Turmeric Powder

Serves: 4
Preparation Time: 1:10 hours
Cooking Time: 10-12 minutes

Preparation

The Spinach : Clean and wash in running water to remove grit. Do not remove the stalks.

The Remaining Vegetables : Peel and crush garlic. Peel, wash and chop onions. Remove eyes, wash and quarter tomatoes. Wash green chillies, wash, slit, seed and discard the stems. Clean and wash curry leaf.

The Red Chillies : Wipe with moist cloth.

The Lentils : Pick, wash in running water, drain, soak in water for 30 minutes and drain again.

Put the drained lentil in a *handi*/pan, add water (approx. 600ml/2½ cups) and turmeric, boil over medium heat until ¾ths cooked. Then add asafoetida, stir, reduce to low heat and simmer, mashing the lentil against the sides with a ladle until cooked. Remove and keep aside.

Cooking

Heat oil in a *handi*/pan, add red chillies, stir over medium heat until they begin to change colour, add mustard and cumin, stir until they begin to pop, add garlic, sauté until light golden, add onions and *bhunno*/stir-fry a minute. Then add spinach and salt, stir, increase to high heat, *bhunno*/stir-fry until the juices of the spinach are released, reduce to low heat, cover and simmer, stirring occasionally, until the spinach stalks are soft. Now add the mashed lentils, stir, add water (approx. 240ml/1 cup), bring to a boil, add curry leaf, stir and then simmer, stirring occasionally, for 2-3 minutes. Remove and adjust the seasoning.

Kheema Chholey

Chick Peas and Kid/Lamb Mince Timbale

Ingredients

The *Chholey*

100g/½ cup *Chholey*/Chickpeas
A pinch of *Meetha Soda*/Soda Bicarbonate
25g/2 Tbs *Desi Ghee*/Clarified Butter
10g/1¾ tsp Ginger Paste (strain)
10g/1¾ tsp Garlic Paste (strain)
Salt
1.5g/½ tsp *Amchoor*/Mango Powder
1.5g/½ tsp Black Pepper (freshly roasted Leaf Powder & coarsely ground)

0.375g/¼ tsp *Jeera*/Cumin Powder
0.375g/¼ tsp *Daalcheeni*/Cinnamon Powder
0.375g/¼ tsp *Motti Elaichi*/Black Cardamom Powder
0.375g/¼ tsp *Jaiphal*/Nutmeg Powder
A pinch of *Kaala Namak*/Black Rock Salt Powder
A pinch of *Kasoori Methi*/Fenugreek

The *Potli/Bouquet Garni*

4 *Motti Elaichi*/Black Cardamom
4 *Chotti Elaichi*/Green Cardamom

2 sticks *Daalcheeni*/Cinnamon (1″)
2 *Tej Patta*/Bay Leaf

The Mince

600g/1 lb 5 oz *Kheema*/Kid/Lamb Mince
75g/6 Tbs *Desi Ghee*/Clarified Butter
85g/¾ cup Onions
30g/5¼ tsp Garlic Paste (strain)
20g/3½ tsp Ginger Paste (strain)
200g/7 oz Fresh Tomato Purée
3g/1 tsp *Kashmiri Deghi Mirch* Powder
1.5g/½ tsp Black Pepper (freshly roasted & coarsely ground)

A pinch of *Lavang*/Clove Powder
A pinch *Motti Elaichi*/Black Cardamom Powder
A pinch of *Chotti Elaichi*/Green Cardamom Powder
A pinch of *Daalcheeni*/Cinnamon Powder
A pinch of *Javitri*/Mace Powder
30g/1 oz Processed Cheese

The Filling

8 Almonds
8 Pistachio
16 Raisins

2 Green Chillies
16 *Taaza Pudhina*/Mint Leaf
30g/1 oz Processed Cheddar Cheese

Serves: 4
Preparation Time: 3 hours
Cooking Time: 45 minutes

Preparation

The *Potli/Bouquet Garni* : Put all the ingredients in a mortar and pound with a pestle to break the spices, fold in a piece of muslin and secure with enough string for it to hang over the rim of the *handi*/pan.

The *Chholey* : Pick, wash, put in a *handi*/pan, add 1 litre/4¼ cups of water, bring to a boil, continue to boil for 2 minutes, remove and reserve in the same water overnight. Drain just prior to cooking. Put the drained *chholey* in a *handi*/pot, add soda bicarbonate, salt and 1 litre/4¼ cups of water, bring to a boil, reduce to low heat, add the *potli*, cover and simmer until *al dente* (cooked but not mushy). Drain, remove and discard the *potli*, keep aside.

The Mince : Peel, wash and finely chop onions. Grate cheese.

The Filling : Blanch almonds and pistachio separately, drain, cool, peel and cut into slivers. Refresh raisins in water, drain and pat dry. Wash green chillies, slit, seed, finely chop and discard the stem. Clean and wash mint. Grate cheese. Put all the ingredients in a bowl, mix well and divide into 4 equal portions.

Cooking

To prepare the *chholey*, melt *ghee* in a *kadhai*/wok, add ginger and garlic pastes, stir over medium heat until the moisture evaporates, add the drained *chholey*, stir gently for 4-5 minutes (ensuring that they do not break). Sprinkle *amchoor*, black pepper, cumin, cinnamon, black cardamom, nutmeg, black rock salt and *Kasoori Methi*, stir carefully to incorporate and divide into 4 equal portions.

To prepare the *kheema*, melt *ghee* in a *kadhai*/wok, add onions, sauté over medium heat until light golden, add garlic and ginger pastes, and sauté until onions are golden. Now add mince, *bhunno*/stir-fry for 2-3 minutes, add tomato purée, stir, add *deghi mirch* and salt, *bhunno*/stir-fry until the fat leaves the sides. Sprinkle black pepper, clove, black cardamom, green cardamom, cinnamon and mace, and mix well. When cool, add cheese, mix well and divide into 4 equal portions.

Finishing

Arrange 4 pie rings of 4½" diameter on a baking tray, spread a portion of the mince in each, spread a portion of the filling and, finally, top with a portion of the *chholey*. Cook in the pre-heated oven (to 275°F) for 8-10 minutes.

Soney Chaandi Ke Moong

Green Moong Lentil garnished with Gold and Silver "Marbles"

Ingredients

300g/1½ cups *Moong Sabut*/Green
    Moong (whole)
4.5g/1½ tsp Red Chilli Powder
3g/1 tsp *Haldee*/Turmeric Powder
Salt
150g/¾ cup Butter (unsalted)
20g/2″ piece Ginger
4 Green Chillies
6.5/1½ *Taaza Dhania*/ Coriander
45g/1½ oz Golden Fried Onions
    (sliced)

3g/1 tsp *Jeera*/Cumin Powder
1.5g/½ tsp Black Pepper (freshly roasted
    & coarsely ground)
1.5g/½ tsp *Chotti Elaichi*/Green
    Cardamom Powder
1.5g/½ tsp *Motti Elaichi*/Black Cardamom
    Powder
0.75g/¼ tsp *Daalcheeni*/Cinnamon Powder
25ml/5 tsp Lemon Juice
Cream

The Lentils

200g/7 oz *Khoya*/Milk Cake
30g/1 oz *Chhenna*/Casein
25g/2½ Tbs Flour

Desi Ghee/Clarified Butter to deep fry
8 *Soney ka Varq*/Gold Leaf
8 *Chandi ka Varq*/ Silver Leaf

The Dumpling Filling (optional)

3 pods *Chotti Elaichi*/Green Cardamom
12 Pistachio

0.5g/1 tsp *Zaafraan*/Saffron

The Tempering

25g/2 Tbs *Desi Ghee*/Clarified Butter

1g/1 tsp *Sua*/*Soya*/Dill

Serves: 4-6
Preparation Time: 1 hour
Cooking Time: 2 hours

Preparation

The *Moong Daal* : Pick, wash in running water, drain, soak in water for 30 minutes and drain
again just prior to cooking.

The Vegetables : Scrape, wash and finely chop ginger. Wash green chillies, slit, seed, finely chop and discard the stems. Clean, wash and chop coriander.

The Fried Onions : Crumble with the hands.

The Dumpling Mixture : Knead *khoya* and *chhenna* gently with the palm to mash any granules and mix. Sift and add flour to the mixture and then knead gently. Reserve 30g/1 oz for the filling, divide the remaining mixture into 16 equal portions, make balls and keep aside.

The Filling : Peel cardamom and discard the skin. Blanch pistachio, cool, remove the skin and cut into slivers. Crush saffron with pestle or back of spoon, to break the flakes, add the reserved mixture, cardamom seeds and pistachio slivers, mix well and divide into 16 equal portions.

The Stuffing : Flatten the balls, place a portion of the filling in the middle, seal and make smooth balls again.

The Dumplings : Melt *ghee* in a *kadhai*/wok, add the balls and deep fry over medium heat until golden brown. Swirl *ghee* with a *pooni*/perforated spoon constantly and without touching the balls until they come to the surface (this prevents sticking). Remove to absorbent paper to drain excess fat and cool. When cool, wrap 8 balls with gold leaf and the remaining 8 balls with silver leaf.

The Tempering : Clean, wash and chop dill.

Cooking

Put the drained *daal* in a *handi*/pan, add 1.5 litres/6½ cups of water, red chillies, turmeric and salt, bring to a boil, reduce to very low heat, cover and simmer, without stirring, until cooked (approx 1:30 hours). Then add the remaining ingredients, except lemon juice and cream increase to medium heat and *ghootto*/continuously mash the lentils against the sides with a wooden spoon and, as you do that, scrape off the lentils that cling to the sides as the liquid diminishes and incorporate into the simmering *daal*. Stir-in lemon juice, simmer for 2-3 minutes, stirring at regular intervals, stir-in cream, remove and adjust the seasoning.

To prepare the tempering, melt *ghee* in a frying pan, add dill, stir and pour the tempering over the *daal*. Garnish with gold leaf and silver leaf covered *khoya* balls.

EPISODE 029
with Chef Devinder Bungla,
THE HYATT

This episode addressed itself to tickling the sweet tooth. It had the classic Indian fudge – *Badam Burfi* – as well as many western desserts in their Indian *avatar*.

Anjheer-Akhrot-Rabarhi Mille Feuille

Fig and Walnut Mille Feuille

Ingredients

225g/8 oz Puff Pastry Dough[1]
120g/4 oz *Anjeer*/Figs
16 *Akhrot*/Walnut Halves

Flour for Dusting
Icing Sugar for Dusting

The *Rabarhi*

2 litres/8½ cups Milk

3g/1 tsp *Chotti Elaichi*/Green Cardamom Powder

The Sauce

225g/8 oz Plums
100g/ ½ cup Castor Sugar

5ml/1 tsp Lemon Juice
10ml/2 tsp *Khus Sherbet*

Serves: 4
Preparation Time: 3 hours
Cooking Time :

Preparation

The Oven : Pre-heat to 200°F.

The Puff Pastry : Divide dough into 2 equal portions, dust the work surface with flour, roll each with a light rolling pin into 10″ x 7″ x ⅛ ″ rectangles and arrange in baking trays. Then prick the surface with a fork and bake in a pre-heated oven for 25 minutes or until light golden. Remove, cool and cut into 4 equal sized strips to obtain 2½″ x 7″ x ⅛ ″ rectangles. Keep aside.

The Figs & Walnuts : Cut figs into small dices and walnuts into fine juliennes and divide each into 6 equal portions.

The *Rabarhi* : Put milk in a *handi*/pan, bring to a boil, reduce to low heat and cook, stirring constantly, until milk is reduced to 450g/1 lb and is granular and thick. Then pass through a fine mesh sieve into a bowl, add cardamom powder, mix well and refrigerate. Remove at the time of assembling and divide into 6 equal portions.

The Sauce : Wash plums, halve, remove the pits, put in a saucepan, add sugar, lemon juice and 100ml/7 Tbs of water, bring to a boil, reduce to medium heat and cook, stirring occasionally, for 5 minutes. Remove, pass through a fine mesh sieve into a separate saucepan, return sauce to heat and simmer until of spoon coating consistency (approx. 5 minutes). Remove, stir-in *khus sherbet*, cool and then refrigerate.

The Mille Feuille : Arrange a strip of baked puff paste on a work surface, spread a portion of the *Rabarhi*, sprinkle a portion each of the figs and walnuts, arrange a second rectangle and repeat the process twice (remember nothing goes on top of the fourth strip). Repeat the process with the remaining strips, *rabarhi*, figs and walnuts. Then press the tiers gently, dust with icing sugar and make a criss-cross design on the surface with a hot skewer. Cut each piece into half to obtain four 3½" x 2½" pastry.

The Puff Paste

Ingredients

205g/1½ cups Flour
190g/15 Tbs Butter

5ml/1 tsp Lemon Juice
Flour to dust

Preparation

Sift flour, (reserve 15g/5 tsp to mix with butter) in a *paraat*/tray or on a work surface, make a bay, add lemon juice and 95ml/6 Tbs + 1 tsp ice-cold water, and start mixing gradually. When fully incorporated knead to make hard dough (*illustration 1*), make a ball and a criss-cross from edge to edge (*illustration 2*), cover with moist cloth and refrigerate for at least 30 minutes.

In the meanwhile, soften the butter, add the reserved flour, make a 1" thick rectangular slab by pressing with a spatula or your hands (*illustration 3*) and refrigerate for 15 minutes. (The dimensions: 4½" x 3".)

Dust the work surface with flour, roll out the dough with a light rolling pin, constantly dusting with flour, into a ⅛" thick rectangular shape. Arrange the butter slab in the middle and fold to envelop the butter (*illustration 4*) in the same rectangular shape. Then roll carefully, constantly dusting whilst rolling to ensure that the butter doesn't ooze out of the sides (*illustration 5*), into 1½" thick rectangle. Fold the bottom third up, the top third down keeping the edges straight, seal the edges by pressing gently with the rolling pin (*illustration 6*) and refrigerate for 10 minutes. Remove, roll out into a 1″ thick rectangular shape, dusting constantly, and repeat the process of folding and refrigeration for 10 minutes. Repeat the process twice more, reducing the thickness by ½″ each time and then roll out into a ⅛″ inch thick rectangle.

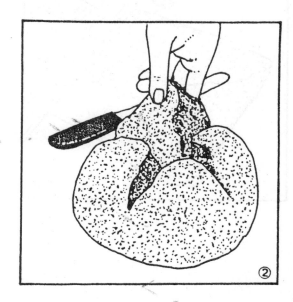

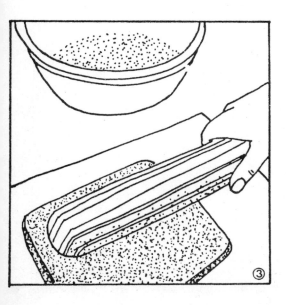

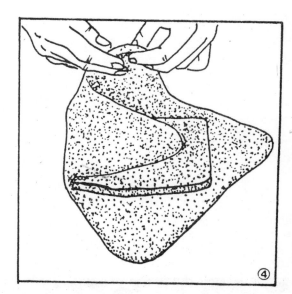

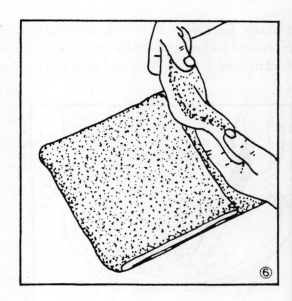

Shrikhand Strudel

Saffron-tinged Yoghurt Cheese Strudel

Ingredients

500g/1 lb 2 oz Mangoes

Butter Paper

The Dough

400g/3 cups Flour (all purpose)
7g/1 Tbs Salt
20m/¼ tsp Cooking Oil
1 Egg

50g/2 oz Butter (unsalted)
60g/½ cup Breadcrumbs
Icing Sugar to sprinkle

The *Shrikhand*

600g/2⅓ cups Yoghurt Cheese
120ml/½ cup Single Cream

30g/7 tsp Icing Sugar
0.5/1 tsp *Zaafraan*/Saffron

15ml/1 Tbs Milk
3g/1 tsp *Chotti Elaichi*/Green Cardamom
  Powder
100g/3 oz *Kishmish*/Raisins
Zest of 1 Lemon

The Vanilla Sauce

480m/½ cups Milk
100g/7 Tbs Sugar
4 Egg Yolks

35g/5 Tbs *Arraroot*/Cornflour
5ml/1 tsp Vanilla Essence

Serves: 8
Preparation Time: 1:30 hours
Cooking Time: 30 minutes

Preparation

The Mangoes : Peel and dice.

The Dough : Sift flour and salt into a *paraat*/tray and make a bay. Beat the egg and pour into the bay alongwith oil and 260ml/1 cup + 4 tsp of water, start mixing gradually. When fully mixed, knead to make medium soft and elastic dough. Cover with moist cloth and refrigerate for 30 minutes.

Melt butter at the time of *Assembling*.

The *Shrikhand* : Crush three quarters of the saffron threads with a pestle or the back of a spoon, soak in lukewarm milk and then make a paste. Reserve the remaining threads for garnish.

Put yoghurt cheese in a bowl, fold-in cream, add sugar and whisk until fluffy. Add the saffron paste and cardamom powder, mix well, divide into 3 equal portions and refrigerate. Clean raisins, reserve in water until ready to use, drain and pat dry. Divide in a **4** (for the *Shrikhand* mixture) : **1** (for garnish) ratio. Grate lemon zest and divide in a **2** (for the *Shrikhand* mixture) : **1** (for garnish) ratio.

The Vanilla Sauce : Dissolve cornflour in 90ml/6 Tbs of milk and keep aside. Beat egg yolks in a bowl.

Put the remaining milk in a *handi*/pan, bring to a boil, add sugar and the beaten egg yolks, stir-in the dissolved cornflour and cook over medium heat until of pouring consistency. Remove, strain into a sauceboat, cool, add vanilla essence, stir and keep aside.

The Butter Papper : Cut into 3 rectangles of 10″ x 6″.

The Oven : Pre-heat to 250°F.

Assembling

Remove the dough from the refrigerator, divide into 3 equal portions, place a portion on each sheet of butter paper and roll out into paper-thin rectangles to cover the butter paper. (Use your hands to press the dough, if necessary to make sure the butter paper is fully covered.) Brush the rolled out dough with melted butter and evenly sprinkle the breadcrumbs. Evenly spread a portion of *Shrikhand* on each rectangle of dough, sprinkle equal quantities of mangoes, raisins and lemon zest on the *Shrikhand* and roll each tightly along the length (like a Swiss Roll). Press to seal the edges, place on the baking tray and brush each roll with butter.

Cooking

Put the tray in the pre-heated oven and bake, brushing with butter at regular intervals, until crisp and golden (approx. 30 minutes). Remove and sprinkle icing sugar on top.

Slice off the sealed ends and cut the Strudel into 8 equal slices and serve with Vanilla Sauce and garnish with the reserved saffron threads, raisins and lemon zest. Serve hot or cold.

Malpua "Omelette"

Fruit Salsa in Semolina Pancakes

Ingredients

100g/3 oz *Sooji*/Semolina
250g/9 oz *Khoya*/
100g/3 oz Flour

7.5g/1 Tbs *Saunf*/Fennel Seeds
Desi Ghee to shallow fry *Malpua*
Whipped Cream to fill the "omelette"

The Fruits

4 Pears
4 Apples
4 *Cheekoo*/Mud Apples
8 Plums

48 Grapes
Fruit of 1 Pomegranate
100g/3 oz Sugar
Juice of 1 Lemon

The Sauce

750g/1 lb 11 oz *Khubaani*/Dried Apricots
350g/13 oz Sugar

15ml/1 Tbs Lemon Juice

Serves: 12
Preparation Time: 1 hour
Cooking Time: 30 minutes

Preparation

The Semolina : Pick, wash in running water, drain and reserve in water for 35-40 minutes.

The *Khoya* : Cover in enough lukewarm water and reserve until ready to make the batter.

The Batter : Drain the semolina and *khoya*. Sift flour. Mash the *khoya* on the work surface with the base of the palm to remove granules. Mix semolina with *khoya* in a *paraat*, add flour and fennel seeds, mix well to make a batter and divide into 12 equal portions.

The Fruits : Peel pears, apples and mud apples. Halve, core and cut into ½" cubes and refrigerate. Wash plums and grapes. Halve the plums, remove the pits and cut into slices. Cut grapes into roundels. Reserve both in chilled water. Refrigerate the pomegranate. Divide all the fruits into 12 equal portions.

Put sugar in a pan, add 180ml/¾ cup of water and the juice of 1 lemon, bring to a boil, add the pear and apple cubes and stew until soft but not mushy. Drain and refrigerate.

Cooking

To prepare the sauce, put apricot purée in a saucepan, add sugar, lemon juice and 420ml/1¾ cups of water, bring to a boil, reduce to low heat and simmer, stirring constantly, for 5 minutes. Remove, pass through a fine mesh soup strainer into a separate saucepan, return sauce to heat and simmer until of spoon coating consistency (approx. 5 minutes). Remove and keep aside.

To make the "omelette", spread a portion of the batter into a pancake of 5½" diameter in a non-stick frying pan, as it begins to cook, spread a little *ghee* around the periphery and shallow fry, turning once, until light golden. Remove to absorbent paper to drain any excess fat. Repeat the process with the remaining portions of the batter.

To Serve

Pipe whipped cream down the middle of each pancake and fold over. Fill as much of a portion of the assorted fruits in the omelette, and serve on a bed of sauce. Sprinkle the left over assorted fruits on the sauce and serve.

Badam Burfi

Almond Fudge

Ingredients

1kg/2¼ lb Almonds   1kg/5 cups Sugar
1g/2 tsp *Zaafraan*/Saffron   25g/1 oz Pistachio
60ml/¼ cup *Gulaabjal*/Rose Water   *Chandi Ka Varq*/Silver Leaf

Yield: 36 pieces
Preparation Time: 1:45 hours (plus time taken to soak almonds)

Preparation

The Almonds : Soak overnight in a *handi*/pan, drain, add water and boil for 5 minutes. Remove a few almonds at a time from the boiling water, peel and grate with an almond grater. Spread the grated almonds on a table to dry. Then dry the grated almonds on a double boiler. It is important to dry them by indirect heat to ensure that the almonds do not get coloured. This cannot be done in the sun, oven or under a salamander. (An almond grater is easily available in the market and costs approximately Rs 25.)

The Saffron Mixture : Crush saffron with pestle or back of spoon, reserve in *gulaabjal* for 10 minutes and then make a paste. Reserve one-fourth for garnish.

The Syrup : Boil sugar with water (approx 1 litre/4¼ cups) in a *handi*, skim the scum completely, reduce to low heat and simmer until of one-string consistency. Then add the saffron mixture and simmer until of slightly thicker than two-string consistency, Ensure that it does not achieve soft-crack or else the *burfi* will not set.

The Pistachio : Blanch, cool, peel and cut into slivers.

Assembling

Put the dried, grated almonds in the hot syrup and mix well. Spread out the mixture on a clean, inverted metal tray and shape into a square or a rectangle of 1″ thickness. Then gently press the *burfi* with a moistened palm at regular intervals to remove the excess almond oil and syrup, using a kitchen towel to soak up the oozing liquid. (Cleanliness of the tray is of utmost importance to give the *burfi* a shelf life.) Once the oil and syrup stops oozing, keep aside to set in a cool place.

With the tip of a knife, cut the set *burfi* into 1½ inch squares (or diamonds). Remove carefully (with a flexible spatula) to a silver platter, cover with *varq*, garnish with pistachio, sprinkle the remaining saffron mixture and serve.

EPISODE 030

with Chef Manjit Singh Gill,
WELCOMGROUP

Mushq-e-Tanjan is the name of the exotic dish that is popularly referred to as *muthanjan*. Few are familiar with this sweet meat *pulav*. The name translates as a 'treasure trove of aromas' and the mystique of this delicacy has long bewitched epicures. Making available the rare recipe to hundreds of thousands of viewers of *Daawat* was a particularly satisfying moment.

Neither a flower, nor a fruit, but both, at the same time equally enjoyable hot or cold, asks the riddler tantalizingly. Not easy to answer if the mouth is full of a juice dripping *Gulaab Jaamun*, arguably the most popular *mithai* in India. Manjit cooked this for our viewers on *Daawat* and also demonstrated how to prepare the *Khoya* and *Rabarhi* at home. The dessert special included the *shrikhand* for those who like it less sweet and also explained *chhenna* making.

Mushq-E-Tanjan

Rare Sweet Rice and Savoury Lamb Dessert

Ingredients

The Rice

500g/2½ cups Basmati Rice
5 *Chotti Elaichi*/Green Cardamom
3 *Lavang*/Cloves
2 sticks *Daalcheeni*/Cinnamon (1")

Salt
0.5g/1 tsp *Zaafraan*/Saffron
15ml/1 Tbs Milk

The Kid/Lamb

750g/1 lb 11 oz *Dasti*/Shoulder of Kid/Lamb
100g/½ cup *Desi Ghee*/Clarified Butter
8 flakes Garlic
Salt
3 *Chotti Elaichi*/Green Cardamom
3 *Lavang*/Cloves
2 sticks *Daalcheeni*/Cinnamon (1")
125g/½ cup Yoghurt

2 drops *Kewra*
1.5g/½ tsp *Javitri*/Mace Powder
1.5g/½ tsp *Chotti Elaichi*/Green
   Cardamom Powder
0.5g/1 tsp *Zaafraan*/Saffron
10m½ tsp Lemon Juice

The Syrup

500g/2½ cups Sugar

The Garnish

Chandi ka Varq/Silver Leaf

Serves: 8
Preparation Time: 1:15 hours
Cooking Time: 2:30 hours

Preparation

The Rice : Pick, wash in running water, drain, reserve in water for an hour and drain. Crush saffron threads with a pestle, reserve in lukewarm milk and then make a paste.

271

The *Bouquet Garni* : Put all the ingredients in a mortar and pound with a pestle to break the spices, fold in a piece of muslin and secure with enough string for it to hang over the rim of the *handi*/pan.

The Kid/Lamb : Clean, wash and cut into 1½" chunks. Peel garlic and cut into juliennes. Whisk yoghurt in a bowl. Crush saffron threads with a pestle, reserve in lukewarm milk and then make a paste.

The Syrup : Boil sugar with 250ml of water over medium heat for 7-8 minutes, stirring constantly, to make thick syrup.

Cooking

Heat *ghee* in a *handi*/pan, add garlic, sauté over medium heat until light brown, add meat, salt and water (approx 240ml/1 cup), bring to a boil, reduce to low heat, add green cardamom, cloves and cinnamon, cover and simmer, stirring occasionally, for 20 minutes. Remove *handi*/pan from heat, stir-in yoghurt, cover and simmer, stirring occasionally, until the liquid is reduced to one-third, add water (approx 540ml/2¼ cups), bring to a boil, reduce to low heat, cover and simmer, stirring occasionally, until the meat is almost cooked. Remove, add *kewra*, mace, cardamom powder, saffron and lemon juice, stir and keep aside.

Put water (approx 2 litres/8⅓ cups), the *bouquet garni* and salt in a separate *handi*/pan, bring to a boil, add the drained rice, bring to a boil, reduce to medium heat and boil until rice is nine-tenths cooked. (To test, remove a few grains and squeeze between the thumb and forefinger—the rice will be slightly hard, will get mashed but a few white specks will show. The specks are a sign of uncooked rice.) Drain, spread three-fourths over the cooked meat, sprinkle saffron and spread the remaining rice on top. Seal the *handi*/pan with *atta* dough and cook over low heat for 12-14 minutes. Break seal, pour on the syrup along the 'wall' of the *handi*/pan and seal again with *atta* dough.

Heat a *tawa*/griddle, reduce to medium heat, place *handi*/pan on the *tawa*/griddle and cook until the steam starts to escape through the dough. Reduce to low heat and cook for 20 minutes.

To Serve

Break the seal, stir, remove to a shallow silver dish and garnish with *varq*.

Gulaab Jaamun

Saffron-tinged Yoghurt Cheese Strudel

Ingredients

300g/11oz *Khoya/*
50g/2 oz *Chhenna/*
40g/4 Tbs Flour
A pinch of *Meetha Soda/*Soda
  Bicarbonate

900g/4 cups Sugar
Cooking Oil to deep fry

The Filling

6 pods *Chotti Elaichi/*Green Cardamom
24 Pistachio

1g/2 tsp *Zaafraan/*Saffron
2 drops *Ittar*

Yield: 20 *Gulaab Jaamun*
Preparation Time: 40 minutes
Cooking Time: 10-12 minutes for each set

Preparation

The *Khoya* : Knead gently with the palm to mash any granules.

The *Chhenna* : Crumble and knead gently with the palm to mash any granules.

The Syrup : Boil the sugar with 540ml/2¼ cups of water, removing the scum at regular intervals, to obtain syrup of one-string consistency. Remove and keep warm.

The *Gulaab Jaamun* Mixture : Sift flour and soda bi-carb. Mix *chhenna* with *khoya*, add flour and soda bi-carb, knead gently. Reserve 50g/2 oz for the filling, divide the remaining mixture into 20 equal portions, make balls and keep aside.

The Filling : Peel cardamom and discard the skin. Blanch pistachio, cool, remove the skin and cut into slivers. Pound saffron with a pestle or the back of a spoon to break the flakes, add the reserved *Gulaab Jaamun* mixture, cardamom seeds, pistachio slivers and *ittar*, mix well and divide into 20 equal portions.

The Stuffing : Flatten the balls, place a portion of the filling in the middle, seal and make smooth balls again.

Cooking

Heat oil in a *kadhai*/wok, add the balls and deep fry over medium heat until golden brown. Swirl oil with a *pooni*/perforated spoon constantly and without touching the *Gulaab Jaamun* until they come to the surface (this prevents sticking). Remove and immerse immediately in the warm syrup.

Shrikhand

Fruit Salsa in Semolina Pancakes

Ingredients

1.35 Kg/3 lb Yoghurt
100g/½ cup Castor Sugar
1g/2 tsp *Zaafraan*/Saffron
15ml/1 Tbs Milk

3g/1 tsp *Chotti Elaichi*/Green
  Cardamom Powder
12 Pistachio

Yield: 900g/2 lb
Preparation Time: 8:30 hours

Preparation

The Yoghurt : Hang in muslin in a cool place (refrigerator in the summer with a large bowl underneath to collect the whey) for 4 hours or until completely drained of whey.

The Saffron : Crush saffron with pestle or back of spoon, reserve in 15ml/1 Tbs of lukewarm milk and then make a paste.

The Pistachio : Blanch, cool, remove the skin and cut into slivers.

The *Shrikhand* : Transfer the yoghurt cheese to a bowl, add sugar and whisk until fluffy. Then add saffron and cardamom, whisk again, level with a spatula, garnish with pistachio and refrigerate.

Rabarhi & Khoya

Reduced Milk

Ingredients

2 litres/8⅓ cups Milk (fresh & full fat)   100g/3 oz Sugar

Yield: The *Rabarhi*—Approx 650g/1 lb 7 oz
The *Khoya*—Approx 400g/14 oz
Preparation Time: 1:30 hours

Preparation

The *Rabarhi* **:** Put milk in a *kadhai*/wok, bring to a boil, reduce to between medium and high heat and stir constantly until reduced by half. Reduce to medium heat and stir constantly and simultaneously scrape to incorporate the milk that sticks to sides of the *kadhai*/wok — this will ensure that the milk does not acquire a 'burnt' flavour — until reduced to a third. Remove and pass through a fine mesh soup strainer into a bowl. Now add sugar and stir until it dissolves. To serve *Rabarhi* as a dessert, sprinkle slivers of pistachio and almonds and garnish with *chandi ka varq*.

The *Khoya* **:** For *Khoya* reduce milk to a mashed potato consistency. Remove to a bowl, cool and refrigerate.

Shelf life: 48 hours in the refrigerator.

Note: A Teflon-coated wok or pan is an ideal alternative to the *kadhai*.

Chhenna

Cassein

Ingredients

2 litres/8⅓ cups Milk (fresh & full fat)   15ml/1 Tbs White Vinegar

Yield: Approx 400g/14 oz
Preparation Time: 1 hour

Preparation

The *Chhenna* : Put milk in a *handi*/pan, bring to a boil, remove and cool to 120°F, add vinegar in a steady stream over the entire surface and stir until the milk curdles. This takes approximately 3 minutes. Put a large enough piece of muslin over a separate *handi*/pan and pour on the curdled milk to drain the whey. Bring together the four corners of muslin and squeeze gently until whey starts to ooze out. Transfer residue while it is still warm onto a flat tray, knead firmly with the palm to mash the granules, cool, wrap in silver foil and refrigerate.

EPISODE 031

with Chef Manjit Singh Gill,
WELCOMGROUP

There are many who believe that the greatest delight is to steal the smallest bite when on a diet. Without going this far, we are quite prepared to admit that snacks are an independent genre and one can indeed snack around most joyously. The *Daawat* episode that focused on snacks aroused great interest. Frying the *samosa* for our viewers we went back in time to trace its origins and were pleasantly surprised to find its ancestor samushak on the imperial dastarkhwan of Delhi.

Goolar Kebab is shaped like the fig — that is what *goolar* translates as. We filled it up with raisins in *Daawat*; you can try chopped figs if you like. Manjit cooked the snacks that kept disappearing for explicable reasons before the shooting was over.

Samosa

Spicy Potatoes and Green Peas Pastry

Ingredients

300g/11 oz Flour
Salt
60ml/¼ cup Cooking Oil

Flour to dust
Desi Ghee/Clarified Butter or Cooking
  Oil to deep fry

The Filling

750g/5 cups Potatoes
250g/9 oz Green Peas
60ml/¼ cup *Desi Ghee*/Clarified Butter or
  Cooking Oil
3.5g/1¾ tsp *Jeera*/Cumin Seeds
30g/3" piece Ginger
3g/1 tsp Red Chilli Powder

Salt
4 Green Chillies
15g/5 tsp *Anaardana*/Pomegranate Seed
  Powder
30g/1 oz Cheese (Processed/Cheddar)
10g/3 Tbs *Taaza Dhania*/Coriander

Yield: 18
Preparation Time: 1:30 hours
Cooking Time: 12-15 minutes/set

Preparation

The Dough : Sift flour and salt together in a *paraat* or on a work surface, make a bay, pour oil in it and start mixing gradually. When the oil is fully mixed, add water (approx. 90ml/6 Tbs) knead gently to make semi-hard dough (the dough should be harder than that for *Poori* and softer than that for *Matthi*), cover with moist cloth and reserve for 15 minutes. Divide into 9 equal portions and make balls. Cover with moist cloth.

The Filling : Peel, wash, cut potatoes into ⅛" dices and reserve in water. Boil peas until *al dente*, drain and refresh in iced water. Scrape, wash and finely chop ginger. Wash green chillies, slit, seed, finely chop and discard stems. Grate cheese. Clean, wash and finely chop coriander.

    Heat oil in a *kadhai*/wok, add cumin, stir over medium heat until it begins to pop, add ginger and stir for a minute. Then add potatoes, red chillies and salt, *bhunno*/stir-fry until potatoes are cooked — firm and not soft and squishy. Now add the boiled peas and green chillies, stir until the mixture is completely dry. Remove, cool, add cheese and coriander, mix well and divide into 18 equal portions.

The Stuffing : Place the balls on a lightly floured surface, flatten each ball with a rolling pin into a round disc (approx 6″ diameter) and cut into half. Stuff as follows: place a half on the palm with the straight edge along the forefinger, dip the other forefinger in water, line the edges, make a cone, stuff a portion of the filling in it and seal the open end by pressing firmly. Sprinkle flour on a tray, arrange the stuffed Samosa on it and reserve until ready to fry.

Cooking

Heat oil in a *kadhai*/wok and deep fry *Samosa* over between low and medium heat until golden and crisp. Remove to absorbent paper to drain the excess fat.

Goolar Kebab

Fig and Orange Rind Stuffed Kid/Lamb Meatballs

Ingredients

600g/1 lb 5 oz Kid/Lamb Mince
75g/2½ oz *Channa Daal*
4 *Chotti Elaichi*/Green Cardamom
3 *Motti Elaichi*/Black Cardamom
3 *Lavang*/Cloves
2 sticks *Daalcheeni*/Cinnamon (1")

2 *Tej Patta*/Bay Leaf
Salt
15ml/1 Tbs Cooking Oil
1 Egg
Cooking Oil to deep fry

The Chutney

20g/½ cup *Pudhina*/Mint
40g/¾ cup *Taaza Dhania*/Coriander
4 Green Chillies
10g/4 tsp Orange Rind

30g/1 oz Raisins
Salt
3g/1 tsp *Amchoor*/Mango Powder

Serves: 4
Preparation Time: 1:35 hours
Cooking Time: 4-5 minutes for each set

Preparation

The Lentils : Pick and wash in running water.

The Mince : Put mince and *daal* in a *handi*/pan, add the whole spices, salt and water (approx. 720ml/3 cups), bring to a boil, reduce to low heat, cover and simmer, stirring occasionally, until the lentils are cooked. Remove and keep aside.

Heat oil in a *kadhai*/wok, add the cooked mince and *bhunno*/stir-fry over medium heat until the liquid has evaporated and the mixture is completely dry. Remove, discard the whole spices, mince again and remove to a bowl. Beat egg and knead into the mince. Divide into 24 equal portions, make balls and keep aside.

The Chutney : Clean and wash mint and coriander. Wash green chillies, slit, seed, finely chop and discard stems. Remove the white coating on the inside and finely chop orange rind. Put mint, coriander and green chillies in a blender, add raisins and salt, and pulse to make a chutney. Remove, add mango powder and orange rind, and mix well. Divide into 24 equal portions.

The Stuffing : Flatten the mince balls between the palms, place a portion of the chutney in the middle of each and make balls again. Refrigerate for 15 minutes.

Cooking

Heat oil in a *kadhai*/wok and deep fry the stuffed balls over medium heat until golden brown. Remove to absorbent paper to drain the excess fat.

Note: To make cocktail snack-size *Goolar*, make 48 mince balls and divide the filling into 48 equal portions.

EPISODE 032

with Chef Manjit Singh Gill,
WELCOMGROUP

No meal can be considered complete without the accompaniments—pickles and preserves. It is the *achaar* and *murabba* that not only adorn the main dishes but also make possible the enjoyment of out of season produce. For *Daawat* we chose to be adventurous and offer mouthwatering exotica from all over the land. This episode had *Nariyal ka Murabba*, *Papite ka Murabba*, *Murgh ka Achaar* and *Prawn Balchao* from Goa.

Narial Ka Murabba

Coconut Preserve

Ingredients

1 kg/2¼ lb Coconut
3 litres/12¾ cups Milk

960m½ lb Honey
960m¼ cups *Gulaabjal*/Rose Water

Yield : 2.75 Kg/6¼ lb
Preparation Time : 30 minutes
Cooking Time : 25 minutes
Shelf Life : 45 days

Preparation

The Coconut : Remove the brown skin and cut into 1″ long pieces. Wash and soak in 1 litre/4¼ cups of milk for a day. Drain and repeat the process the following two days. Then drain and blanch in boiling water for 10 seconds, drain and keep aside.

Cooking

Put honey and rosewater in a *handi*/pan, cook over medium heat for 2-3 minutes, add the blanched coconut, bring to a boil thrice, remove and cool.

Transfer to a sterilized glass jar, secure muslin around the opening and leave it to mature for a day. Remove the muslin and cover with a lid.

Murgh Ka Achaar

Chicken Pickle

Ingredients

48 *Tangrhi*/Chicken Drumsticks
White Vinegar to cover drumsticks
1.5 litre/6½ cups Cooking Oil

60g/2 oz Garlic
45g/1½ oz Ginger

The Masala

10g/5 tsp *Jeera*/Cumin Seeds
18 *Chotti Elaichi*/Green Cardamom
12 *Lavang*/Cloves
3 flowers *Javitri*/Mace

½ *Jaiphal*/Nutmeg
15g/5 tsp Red Chilli Powder
Salt

The Garnish

24 Cashewnuts
24 Almonds

48 Raisins
Cooking Oil to deep fry

Preparation Time : 30 minutes (plus time taken to pickle drumsticks)
Cooking Time : 25 minutes
Shelf Life : 45 days

Preparation

The Chicken : Remove the skin, trim, wash and pat dry. Put in a large pan, add just enough white vinegar to cover the drumsticks and reserve overnight—not less than 10 hours, but not exceeding 12—in the refrigerator.

The Masala : Sun-dry cumin seeds, cloves, green cardamom, mace and nutmeg, put in a mortar and pound with a pestle to make fine powder. Alternatively, put the spices in a grinder and, employing short pulses, grind to a fine powder. Sift, add red chillies and salt, and mix well.

The Garlic : Peel and finely chop.

The Ginger : Scrape, wash and finely chop.

The Garnish : Blanch almonds in boiling water for 2 minutes, remove to a cloth napkin, rub vigourously to peel, remove and keep aside. Clean raisins, remove stems, wash and pat dry.

Heat enough oil in a frying pan, add cashewnuts, deep fry over medium heat until light golden, drain and remove to absorbent paper to drain excess fat. In the same oil, add the almonds, deep fry over medium heat until light golden, drain and remove to absorbent paper to drain excess fat. In the same oil, add raisins, deep fry over medium heat until they swell (approx 30-40 seconds), drain and remove to absorbent paper to drain excess fat.

Cooking

Heat oil in a *kadhai*/wok to a smoking point (be sure you do not burn the oil), reduce to low heat, add the garlic and ginger, *bhunno*/stir-fry until golden brown. Then add chicken, along with the vinegar marinade, stir, add the *masala* and cook, stirring occasionally, until chicken is *al dente*–nine-tenth cooked. Now add the cashewnut, almonds and raisins, stir, remove, adjust the seasoning and cool.

Transfer to a sterilized glass jar, secure muslin around the opening and leave it to mature for 2 days. Remove the muslin and cover with a lid.

Kachche Papite ka Murabba

Raw Papaya Preserve

Ingredients

1 Kg/2½ lb Raw Papaya	675g/1½ lb Sugar
120ml/½ cupVinegar	Salt
5g/2 tsp *Saunf*/Fennel Seeds	120/¼ lb Walnut Quarters
3g/1 tsp *Kalonji*/Onion Seeds	30g/1 oz *Kishmish*/Raisins
8 Whole Red Chillies	

Yield : 1.5 Kg/3 lb 5 oz
Preparation Time : 25 minutes
Cooking Time : 30 minutes
Shelf Life : 45 days

Preparation

The Papaya : Peel, quarter, seed and cut into ⅛" thick slices.

The Red Chillies : Wipe clean with moist cloth, slit and seed.

The Kishmish/Raisins : Clean and remove stems

Cooking

Put the papaya slices in a *handi*/pan, add vinegar and 400ml/1²/₃ cups of water, bring to a boil, reduce to low heat, add fennel, *kalonji* and chillies, stir and simmer, stirring occasionally, until the papaya is three-fourths cooked. Then add sugar, stir until the sugar dissolves. Continue to simmer, stirring occasionally, until the papaya is tender. Remove, add salt and stir to mix well. Adjust the seasoning. Now add the walnut quarters and raisins, mix well and cool.

Transfer to a sterilized glass jar, secure muslin around the opening and leave it to mature for a day. Remove the muslin and cover with a lid.

Prawn Balchao

Goan Prawn Pickle

Ingredients

2 Kg/4½ oz Prawns (30-40/Kg)

The Red Masala

48 Kashmiri Deghi Mirch
150g/5 oz Garlic
90g/3 oz Ginger
240ml/1 cup Toddy Vinegar
60ml/2 oz *Imlee*/Tamarind Pulp

9g/1 Tbs *Haldee*/Turmeric Powder
12 *Lavang*/Cloves
12 *Chotti Elaichi*/Green Cardamom
4 sticks *Daalcheeni*/Cinnamon (1″)

The Balchao Paste

1 litre/4¼ cups Cooking Oil
400g/14 oz Onions
60g/2 oz Garlic
400g/14 oz Tomatoes
8 Green Chillies

Salt
100g/3 oz Sugar
60g/2 oz *Golmo* (tiny dry prawns)
90ml/6 Tbs Coconut Feni

Serves : 4
Preparation Time : 40 minutes
Cooking Time : 30 minutes
Shelf Life : 45 days

Preparation

The Prawn : Shell, vein, wash and pat dry.

The Red Masala : Peel garlic. Scrape, wash and roughly cut ginger. Put these and remaining ingredients in a blender, add water (approx. 45ml) and make a smooth paste.

The Balchao Paste : Peel, wash and roughly chop onions. Peel garlic. Remove eyes, wash and roughly chop tomatoes. Wash green chillies, slit, seed, roughly chop and discard stems. Crush golmo into a fine powder.

291

Cooking

Heat oil in a *handi*/pan, add onions, sauté over medium heat until transparent, add garlic, saute until light golden, add tomatoes and green chillies, *bhunno*/stir-fry until the fat leaves the sides. Reduce to very low heat, add the red masala paste and salt, *bhunno*/stir-fry until the fat leaves the sides. Now add sugar and *golmo*, stir, add prawns, cook for 2-3 minutes, add *feni*, stir carefully, remove, adjust the seasoning and cool.

Transfer to a sterilized glass jar, secure muslin around the opening and leave it to mature for a day. Remove the muslin and cover with a lid.

APPENDICES

Masalas

GARAM MASALA

If spices are the basis of Indian cooking, the blending of these spices to make a *garam masala* or 'hot spices' is the essence of it. The use of a solitary spice or herb is all that the rest of the world, particularly the West, can cope with. There seems to be a fear of using more than one spice. Which is why Westerners find the use of a melange of spices in Indian cookery incomprehensible. To us, each spice in the melange has a specific purpose to perform. To go into the details of each spice is beyond the scope of this book, leave alone this chapter. Suffice it to say it is important to be a good *masalchi* before one can become a good chef. It is advisable to try out various combinations of spices fearlessly. Before that, however, a clear understanding of each and every spice is imperative. Accordingly, the proportions of spices can be changed as the seasons change. For example, in the hot summer months, reduce the quantity of mace and nutmeg — they can give a nosebleed.

There are as many versions of the garam masala as there are chefs. However, in general, some garam masala are chilli hot (those with cloves and pepper), while others use only aromatic spices (cinnamon, mace, nutmeg, cardamom, etc.). Garam masala is used sparingly or it will put the 'body on fire'. It is almost always introduced toward the end of cooking a delicacy. Often it is used as a garnish — sprinkled over cooked food to provide aromatic flavouring at the time of service.

The art of blending garam masala involves grinding or pounding a combination of dried spices. All the spices are roasted in the oven (or under the salamander) before they are ground into a fine powder. It is important that the spices be blended freshly.

If you are using a grinder, it is better to sun-dry the spices instead of roasting them. The reason is very simple. When pounded with a pestle, the heat dissipates. In the grinder, on the other hand, there is no 'outlet' for the heat emitted by the grinding. If the spices are broiled, it is likely that the garam masala will be 'over-done' and darker. The same holds true for the other masala.

293

Garam Masala I

Ingredients

200g/7 oz Cumin seeds
60g/2 oz Coriander seeds
45g/ 1½ oz Black Cardamom
35g/1¼ oz Black Peppercorns
30g/1 oz Green Cardamom
30g/1 oz Ginger powder

20 sticks Cinnamon (1-inch)
20g/ ¾ oz Cloves
20g/ ¾ oz Mace
15g/ ½ oz Bay leaves
2 Nutmeg

Preparation

Put all the ingredients in a mortar and pound with a pestle to make a fine powder. Sieve and store in a sterilised, dry and airtight container.

Yield : approx 450g/1 1b

Note : This blend is ideally suited for meat preparations.

Garam Masala II

Ingredients

90g/3 oz Cumin seeds
75g/2½ oz Black Cardamom seeds
75g/2½ oz Black Peppercorns
45g/1½ oz Green Cardamom
30g/1 oz Coriander seeds
30g/1 oz Fennel seeds
20g/¾ oz Cloves

20 sticks Cinnamon (1-inch)
20g/ ¾ oz Mace
20g/ ¾ oz Black Cumin seeds
15g/ ½ oz Bay leaves
15g/½ oz Dry Rose petals
15g/½ oz Ginger powder
3 Nutmeg

Preparation

Put all the ingredients, except ginger powder, in a mortar and pound with a pestle to make a fine powder. Transfer to a clean, dry bowl, add ginger powder and mix well. Sieve and store in a sterilised, dry and airtight container.

Aromatic Garam Masala

Ingredients

175g/6 oz Green Cardamom
125g/4½ oz Cumin seeds
125g/4½ oz Black Peppercorns

20 sticks Cinnamon (1-inch)
20g/ ¾ oz Cloves
2 Nutmeg

Preparation

Put all the ingredients in a mortar and pound with a pestle to make a fine powder. Sieve and store in a sterilised, dry and airtight container.

Yield : approx 450g/1 lb

Note : This blend is used in mildly-spiced gravies.

Chaat Masala

Ingredients

65g/ 2¼ oz Cumin seeds
65g/ 2¼ oz Black Peppercorns
60g/ 2 oz Black Salt (pound, if using a grinder)
30g/ 1 oz Dry Mint leaves
5g/ 2 tsp Ajwain
5g/ 1 tsp Asafoetida (pound, if using a grinder)

4g/ ¾ tsp Tartric (pound, if using a grinder)
150g/ 5¼ oz Mango powder
60g/ 2 oz Salt
20g/ ¾ oz Ginger powder
20g/ ¾ oz Yellow Chilli powder

Preparation

Put all the ingredients, except mango powder, salt, ginger powder and yellow chilli powder, in a mortar and pound with a pestle to make a fine powder. Transfer to a clean, dry bowl, add the remaining ingredients and mix well. Sieve and store in a sterilised, dry and airtight container.

Yield : approx 450g/1 lb

Note : Like *Chaat Masala*, the *Tandoori Chaat Masala* must be used in small quantities and not indiscriminately.

Tandoori Chaat Masala

Ingredients

50g/ 1¾ oz Cumin seeds
50g/ 1¾ oz Black Peppercorns
50g/ 1¾ oz Black Salt (pound, is using a grinder)
30g/1 oz Dry Mint leaves
20g/¾ oz Fenugreek (*Kasoori Methi)*
30g/Green Cardamom
15 Cloves
5 sticks Cinnamom (1-inch)
5g/2 tsp *Ajwain*

5g/1 tsp Asafoetida (pound, is using a grinder)
4g/¾ tsp Tartric (pound, if using a grinder
2g/½ tsp Mace
125g/4½ oz Mango powder
50g/1¾ oz Salt
20g/¾ oz Ginger powder
20g/¾ oz Yellow Chilli powder

Preparation

Put all the ingredients, except mango powder, salt, ginger powder and yellow chilli powder, in a mortar and pound with a pestle to make a fine powder. Transfer to a clean, dry bowl, add the remaining ingredients and mix well Sieve and store in a sterilised, dry and airtight container.

Yield : approx 450g/1 lb

Note : Like *Chaat Masala*, the *Tandoori Chaat Masala* must be used in small quantities and not indiscriminately.

Dum Ka Masala

Ingredients

45g/ 1½ oz Fennel seeds
45g/ 1½ oz Ginger powder

20g/ ¾ oz Green Cardamom
20g/ ¾ oz Black Cardamom

Preparation

Put all the ingredients in a mortar and pound with a pestle to make a fine powder. Sieve and store in a sterilised, dry and airtight container.

Yield : approx 125g/¼ lb

Note : This masala is used in very small quantities – usually a pinch – after the dish has been cooked and before it is put on *dum*. That is, before you seal *handi* with a lid. It adds to the aroma.

Dhansak Masala

Ingredients

45g/ 1½ oz Fenugreek (*Kasoori Methi*)   45g/ 1½ oz Black Cardamom
45g/ 1½ oz Cloves

Preparation

Put all the ingredients in a mortar and pound with a pestle to make a fine powder. Sieve and store in a sterilised, dry and airtight container.

Yield : approx 125g/¼ lb.

Sambhar Masala

Ingredients

120g/ 4¼ oz Coriander seeds   30g/1 oz Turmeric powder
80g/2¾ oz Cumin seeds   10g/2 tsp Garlic powder
30g/1 oz Black Peppercorns   60g/2 oz *Channa daal*
30g/1 oz Mustard seeds   60g/2 oz *Urad Dal*
30g/1 oz Fenugreek seeds   10g/2 tsp Asafoetida
20 Whole Red Chillies   Groundnut Oil to fry

Preparation

The Lentils : Pick, wash the *daal* together in running water and pat dry. Heat oil in a *kadhai* and fry the lentils over medium heat until light golden. Transfer the *daals* to an absorbent paper napkin to remove excess fat. Cool.

The Asafoetida : Reheat the oil in which the lentils were fried and fry asafoetida over medium heat until it swells up. Transfer to an absorbent paper napkin to remove excess fat. Cool and then break it up into little pieces.

The Masala : Put all the ingredients, except turmeric and garlic powder, in a mortar and pound with a pestle to make a fine powder. Transfer to a clean, dry bowl, add the remaining ingredients and mix well. Sieve and store in a sterilised, dry and airtight container.

Yield : approx 450g/1 lb.

Mulagapodi

Ingredients

20 Whole Red Chillies
5g/ 1 tsp Asafoetida
100g/ ½ cup *Channa daal*
100g/ ½ cup *Urad daal*

10g/ 2 tsp Sesame seeds
Sesame seed oil to fry
Salt

Preparation

The Lentils : Pick, wash in running water and pat dry.

Cooking

Heat oil in a *kadhai*, and asafoetida and stir over low heat until it swells. Remove the asafoetida, add the *daals* and stir until golden brown. Remove the *daals*, and red chillies and stir until crisp, remove. Broil the sesame seeds on a *tawa* until they stop popping.

Put the fried lentils in a grinder and make a coarse powder, remove. Put the fried red chillies, asafoetida and salt in the grinder and make a coarse powder, remove. Put the broiled sesame seeds in the grinder and make a coarse powder. Mix all the powder. Store in a sterilised, dry and airtight container.

Yield : approx 250g/9 oz

Note : Add a spoon of clarified butter or sesame seed oil with every spoon of *Mulagapodi* to reduce its pungency.

Gravies

The success of an Indian banquet lies in the extensive variety of gravies served. Only a hack would allow the dishes – vegetarian and non-vegetarian – to taste the same. It reflects a lack of interest and imagination. Even simple fare can be made tasty and interesting with a slight variation of spices and herbs in the gravies. The hallmark of a good chef is his ability to create different aromas, hues and flavours.

The purpose of this appendix is not to make you reliant on these basic gravies. It is to enable you to first strengthen the base and then let your artistic talent come to the fore. Let your imagination run riot and create gravies that will make the epicure want to chew his fingers. I repeat: *Do not* follow the recipes blindly and cook *everything* in these basic gravies.

Basic Gravy I

Ingredients

150g/ ¾ cup Ghee
Whole Garam masala
   5 Green Cardamom
   1 Black Cardamom
   5 Cloves
   1 Stick Cinnamom (1–inch)
250g/ 1 cup Boiled Onion paste*
30/ 5 tsp Ginger paste
30g/ 5 tsp Garlic paste
10g/ 2 tsp Red Chilli powder

5g/ 1 tsp Coriander powde
3g/ ½ tsp Turmeric
Salt
225g/ 1 cup Yoghurt
50g/3 Tbs Fried Onion paste*
30g/5 tsp Cashewnut paste
100ml/7 Tbs Cream
5g/1 tsp Garam Masala
3g/ ½ tsp Green Cardamom
   and Mace powder

Preparation

The Yoghurt : Whisk in a bowl.

Yield : approx 700ml/1½ lb

Preparation : 5 minutes

Cooking time : 15-18 minutes

Note : This is a yoghurt–based gravy, mainly for *kofta*, *korma* and *pasanda* delicacies.

*See section on Onions.

Basic Gravy II

Ingredients

150g/ ¾ cup Ghee
Whole Garam masala
    5 Green Cardamom
    1 Black Cardamom
    5 Cloves
    1 Stick Cinnamom (1–inch)
    1 Bay Leaf
    A pinch Mace
125g/ ½ cup Boiled Onion paste*
10g/ 1¾ tsp Ginger paste
10g/ 1¾ tsp Garlic paste

10g/ 1 tsp Red Chilli powder
5g/ 1 tsp Coriander powder
3g/ ½ tsp Turmeric
Salt
1 kg/2¼ lb Tomatoes
30g/ 5 tsp Fried Onion paste*
30g/ 5 tsp Cashewnut paste
100ml/7 Tbs Cream
5g/ 1 tsp Garam Masala
2g/ ¹/₃ tsp Green Cardamom
    and Mace powder

Preparation

The Tomatoes : Wash and chop.

Cooking

Heat ghee in a *handi*, and whole garam masala and sauté over medium heat until it begins to crackle. Add boiled onion paste, sauté for 2 minutes, add ginger and garlic pastes and sauté for 30 seconds. Then add red chillies, coriander powder, turmeric and salt, *bhunno* for 2 minutes. Add tomatoes, stir constantly until the fat comes to the surface, add water (approx 200 ml/ ¾ cup + 4 tsp), bring to a boil and then simmer until once again the fat comes to the surface.

Now add fried onion paste, cashewnut paste and cream, bring to a boil. Correct the consistency by adding water. Add garam masala, cardamom and mace powder, stir.

Yield : approx 800ml/1¾ lb

Preparation : 10 minutes

Cooking time : 35 minutes

Note : This is a tomato–based gravy, used for basic lamb and chicken curries.

*See section on Onions.

Makhani Gravy

Ingredients

1 kg/2¼ lb Tomatoes
10g/1¾ tsp Ginger paste
10g/1¾ tsp Garlic paste
6 Green Chillies
10g/ 2 tsp Red Chilli powder
10 Cloves
8 Green Cardamom

Salt
150g/ ²⁄₃ cup Butter
150ml/ ²⁄₃ cup Cream
15ml/ 4½ tsp Honey (option)
10g/ 2½ tsp Fenugreek
(*Kasoori Methi*)
10g/ 1 Tbs Ginger

Preparation

The Vegetables : Wash and chop tomatoes. Remove stems, wash, slit, dessed and chop green chillies. Scrape, wash and cut ginger into juliennes.

Cooking

Put the tomatoes in a *handi*, add water (approx 1 litre/4 cups), add the ginger and garlic pastes, green chillies, red chillies, cloves, cardamom and salt, reduce to a sauce consistency over low heat. Force through a strainer into a separate *handi*, bring to a boil, add butter and cream, stir. If the gravy is excessively sour, add honey. Then add fenugreek and ginger juliennes, stir.

Yield : 550ml/1¼ lb

Preparation : 20 minutes

Cooking time : 20–25 minutes.

Kadhai Gravy

Ingredients

75g/6 Tbs Ghee
30g/5 tsp Garlic paste
15g/ 7½ tsp Coriander seeds
10 Whole Red Chillies
4 Green Chillies

45g/ ¼ cup Ginger
675g/ 3 cups Tomatoes
5g/ 1 Tbs Fenugreek (*Kasoori Methi*)
Salt
5g/ 1 tsp Garam Masala

Preparation

The Spices : Pound the coriander seeds and whole red chillies with a pestle.

The Vegetables : Remove stems, wash, slit, dessed and chop green chillies. Scrape, wash and chop ginger. Wash and chop tomatoes.

Cooking

Heat ghee in a *kadhai*, and garlic paste and sauté over medium heat until light brown. Add the pounded spices, sauté for 30 seconds, and green chillies and ginger, sauté for 30 seconds. Then add tomatoes and *bhunno* until the fat comes to the surface. Now add fenugreek and salt, stir. Sprinkle garam masala and stir.

Yield : approx 550ml/1¼ lb.

Preparation time : 25 minutes.

Cooking time : 18–20 minutes.

Pastes

The Onion Pastes

In a cuisine renowned for its exotic gravies – each surface different from the other – one of the most important ingredients is the humble onion. It is chopped, sliced, grated or quartered before being fried or boiled to make a paste, which is the basis of most gravies. Different gravies require the onions to be processed differently. The gravy that goes with *kofta* for example, requires a boiled onion paste. A *Rogan Josh* gravy, on the other hand, will require a fried onion paste.

Frying of Onions

When we talk of sautéeing onions in Indian cooking, we are actually describing the process of browning them. Contrary to how easy it sounds, the process requires great skill and concentration. There are many hues and shades of brown and each imparts its colour to the final product.

Boiled Onion Paste

Ingredients

1 kg/ 2¼ lb Onions

3 Bay leaves

3 Black Cardamom

Preparation

Peel, wash and roughly cut onions. Put in a *handi*, add bay leaves, cardamom and 200ml/¾ cup + 4 tsp of water, bring to a boil, simmer until onions are transparent and the liquid has evaporated. Transfer to a blender and make a fine purée.

Yield : approx 1 kg/2¼ lb

Note : The onion-water ratio is crucial to this preparation. Excess water will make a thin purée and if the water is not enough, the onions will remain uncooked and in all likelihood the lower layer will stick. The correct ratio is 5:1.

Fried Onion Paste

Ingredients

1 kg/ 2¼ lb Onions

Groundnut Oil to fry

100g/ 3½ oz Yoghurt

Preparation

Peel, wash and slice onions. Heat oil in a *kadhai*, add onions and sauté over medium heat until brown. Remove onions, spread over any absorbent material and cool. Transfer to a blender, add yoghurt and make a fine paste.

Yield : approx 300/ ²⁄₃ lb

Note : The paste can be stored in sterilised, airtight containers for up to 15 days in a refrigerator.

Other Pastes

Ginger Paste

Ingredients

170g/1 cup Ginger

Preparation

The Ginger : Scrape, wash and roughly chop.

The Paste : Put the chopped ginger in a blender, add 45ml/3 Tbs of water and make a fine paste. Remove and refrigerate. Shelf life : 72 hours in the refrigerator.

Yield : approx 210/ 7½ oz.

Note : The containers in which these pastes are kept must be covered with foil or plastic wrap before refrigeration. The alternatives are ziplock bags or freezer bags.

Garlic Paste

Ingredients

170g/1 cup Garlic

Preparation

The Ginger : Peel and roughly chop.

The Paste : Put the chopped garlic in a blender, add 45ml/3 Tbs of water and make a fine paste. Remove and refrigerate. Shelf life : 72 hours in the refrigerator.

Yield : approx 210/ 7½ oz.

Cashewnut Paste

Ingredients

160g/1 cup Cashewnuts (broken)

Preparation

The Cashewnuts : Soak in water for 30 minutes and drain.

The Paste : Put the drained cashewnuts in a blender, add 10ml/7 Tbs of water and make a fine paste. Remove and refrigerate. Shelf life: 24 hours in the refrigerator.

Yield : approx 250/ 9 oz.

Coconut Paste

Ingredients

100g/1¼ cup Coconut

Preparation

The Coconut : Remove the brown skin and grate.

The Paste : Put the grated coconut in a blender, add 75ml/5 Tbs of water (preferably coconut water) and make a fine paste. Remove and refrigerate. Shelf life : 12 hours in the refrigerator.

Yield : approx 160/ 5½ oz.

Poppy Seed Paste

Ingredients

150g/1 cup Poppy seeds

Preparation

The Poppy Seeds : Soak in warm water for 30 minutes and drain.

The Paste : Put the drained seeds in a blender, add 100ml/ 7 Tbs of water and make a fine paste. Remove and refrigerate. Shelf life : 24 hours in the refrigerator.

Yield : approx 330/ 11 oz.

Tamarind Pulp

Ingredients

50g/2 oz Tamarind

Preparation

Soak tamarind in 50ml/10 tsp of lukewarm water for 30 minutes and force through a strainer. Discard the residue.

Yield : approx 75ml/ 3 oz.

Tamarind grows on tropical trees, is shaped like a bean (except that it is longer and wider) and the main 'fruit' is the pulp inside the brittle shell. *Imli* is dried before it is sold and, before use it is soaked in lukewarm water until soft – usually 25 to 30 minutes. It is squeezed until it dissolves in the water at which stage the seeds and fibres are strained out.

Dahi (Yoghurt)

An Indian meal in inconceivable without *dahi* or yoghurt. It is omnipresent, so to speak. Either a part of the food is cooked in it or it is partaken in its natural from – unflavoured. Derivatives are consumed as *raita*, *lassi*, or *chaas* (buttermilk). Remember, in Indian cooking, yoghurt is always unflavoured.

Setting yoghurt is not as easy as it looks. It requires an understanding of the role enzymes play in the process. This is how it done :

Boil the milk and allow it to cool. The temperature of milk at which the ferment is to be added has a direct co-relation with the atmospheric temperature. If the weather is cold, the milk should be warm and, after introducing the ferment, the vessel in use must be placed in warm surroundings (well-wrapped in a blanket at home and in the warmest place, not the oven, in a commercial kitchen). In summer months, the milk should be allowed to cool to room temperature and the vessel must be kept in a cool place.

If the milk is too hot, the *dahi* is likely to become sour. It will leave water and will not set firmly. On the other hand, if the milk is not warm enough (approx 80-90°F) it will not set properly. Once the milk is kept for setting, do not move or shake the container. If you do, the yoghurt will not set.

Traditionally, yoghurt is set in clay bowls. It sets just as well in other vessels.

It takes between four to six hours to set. Once it is set, the utensil *must* be placed in the refrigerator to prevent any further souring.

The most commonly used ferment to set *dahi* is *dahi* itself. Lemon juice and vinegar make excellent substitutes. In ideal conditions, a tablespoon of the ferment is sufficient to make approx 1kg/4½ cups of yoghurt. One litre/4 cups of milk give you 1 kg/ 4½ cups of yoghurt.

The recipes below are from my mother's collection.

Paneer

There is no Western or Oriental equivalent of *Paneer*, which is often called cottage cheese in India. The cottage cheese available on the shelves of supermarkets elsewhere is quite different. Riccotta cheese is the nearest in terms of taste but not in terms of texture. In fact, Riccotta cheese cannot be converted into a block like *paneer*. Besides, Riccotta cheese becomes sticky and 'leathery' when heated. *Paneer* is an extraordinary source of protein in a largely vegetarian sub-continental diet. It is no exaggeration to say that what meat is to the non-vegetarian, *Paneer* is to the vegetarian. The spin-off in terms of the number of delicacies that can be conceived with our *desi* cheese matches that of the meats. Strangely, it is the easiest cheese to make and requires no curing time or expertise.

Ingredients

3 litres/ 12½ cups Milk   90ml/6 Tbs Lemon juice or White Vinegar

Preparation

Boil milk in a *handi*, stirring occasionally to ensure that a skin does not form on the surface. When the milk begins to rise, add lemon juice or vinegar. The milk will curdle and the whey will separate. Strain the curdled milk through fine muslin allowing the whey to drain out. Hang the muslin for at least an hour to ensure that any remaining moisture is drained out. What is left behind is *Paneer*. It can be used as it is for a number of dishes. Or it can be converted into a block. To convert the *Paneer* into a block, keep it wrapped in the muslin and place a weight on top for 2-3 hours. The block facilitates the cutting of *Paneer* into cubes, slices and batons.

Shelf life : 48 hours in the refrigerator.

Yield : approx 600/ 1 ¹/₃ lb

Preparation time : 8:30 hours.

Coconut

While coastal cooking is inconceivable without it, the coconut is an important ingredient in the kitchens of the North as well. The only difference is that whereas in the coastal areas, fresh coconut is used, north of the Vindhyas it is the dry coconut that is in greater use.

While fresh, grated coconut is used mainly as a garnish or as an ingredient for wet masala, when it comes to cooking, it is 'coconut milk' that lends its unique flavour. Coconut milk is not to be confused with the liquid inside the coconut – that is just coconut water and is a delicious and cool soft drink sold at street corners and even in restaurants. Coconut milk is extracted by squeezing the freshly ground white meat of a mature coconut. Here is how to do it: Remove the brown skin, grate 100g/ 1¼ cups of the white meat, put in a blender, add lukewarm water (approx 100 ml/7 Tbs) and liquidise. Then force the liquid through a fine strainer. The strained liquid is called the **First Milk** or **First Extract**.

To obtain the **Second Milk** or **Second Extract**, put the residue in the blender, add lukewarm water (approx 100ml/ 7 Tbs) and liquidise. Force the liquid through a fine strainer. The 'Second Milk' is thinner and has less flavour.

How to Make Desi Ghee from Butter

Heat and fully melt unsalted butter over low heat in a heavy–bottomed *handi* without letting it brown. Now increase the heat and bring the butter to a boil. When the butter starts foaming, stir once and reduce to very low heat. Simmer gently for about 45 minutes until the milk solids settle on the bottom of the pan and the transparent butter is afloat.

Drain the transparent butter, *i.e. desi ghee*, through muslin into another container without disturbing the sediment. Once cold, it will solidify. Store at room temperature.

Index

Rice, 59, 61, 64, 101, 102, 103, 199, 271
  see also Pongal

S

Saffron, 13, 33, 35, 87, 169, 263, 273
  see also zaafraan
Sambhar, 237
Sambhar masala, 237
Samosa, 281
Sasam
  avanasa, 127
Scallops, 71
Seekh-e-Dum Pukht, 75
Sesame seeds, see Til
Semolina, 265, 275
Shahjehani paste, 3
Shanks see Meat
Shrikhand, 263, 273
Soney Chandi ke Moong, 255
Spinach, 9, 11, 23, 111, 181, 183, 217, 251
Squid, 71
Sunehri Khurchan, 185
Strudel, 263, 273
Surmai, 45, 111
  tarlleli, 111

T

Taar Qorma, 205
Tarlleli Surmai, 111
Tarri
  akhrot ki, 161-162
  guchchiwali
  Murg-seib, 213
  khumbi ki, 201
Thaeer saadam, 5
Thalna
  coondapur koli, 131

Thengenkai kori, 91
Tikka
  paneer, 29
Tikki,
  til ki, 147
Tandoori Jheenga Flan, 230
Turkey musallam, 227

U

Undhiya, 115
Uttar-Dakshin Murghbandi, 191

V

Vadai
  masala, 106

W

Walnut, 85
  see Akhrot ki tarri
Wheat
  cakes, 66

X

X'mas Pudding, 234

Y

Yam, 131, 149
Yoghurt, 5, 19, 45, 71, 77, 81, 91, 151, 205, 273, 307
  see also Dahi

Z

Zaafraani kofta, 3

314

curry leaf

cloves

garlic

cardamom

nutmeg

coriander

cinnamon

bay leaf

saffron

cumin

pepper

ginger